THE JOHN RYLANDS LIBRARY
UNIVERSITY LIBRARY

DA01J

D0411447

UNDERSTANDING
─── AGEING ───
IMAGES, ATTITUDES AND PROFESSIONAL PRACTICE

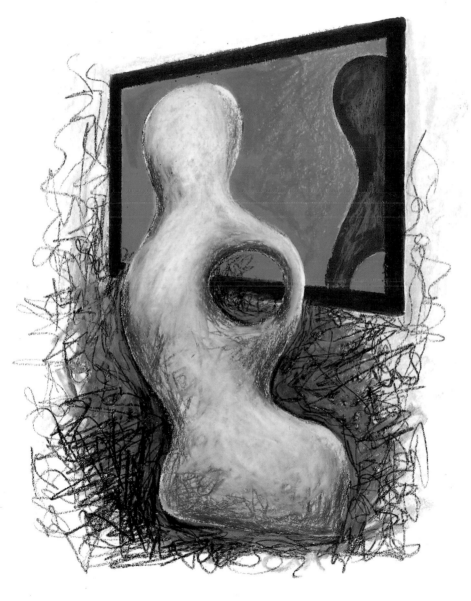

SIMON BIGGS

M S406

Understanding ageing

Understanding ageing

IMAGES, ATTITUDES AND
PROFESSIONAL PRACTICE

SIMON BIGGS

Open University Press
BUCKINGHAM • PHILADELPHIA

PS-18

(DA01J)

UML WITHDRAWN

Open University Press
Celtic Court
22 Ballmoor
Buckingham
MK18 1XW

and
1900 Frost Road, Suite 101
Bristol, PA 19007, USA

First Published 1993

Copyright © Simon Biggs 1993

All rights reserved. Except for the quotation of short passages for the
purposes of criticism and review, no part of this publication may be
reproduced, stored in a retrieval system, or transmitted, in any form or
by any means, electronic, mechanical, photocopying, recording or otherwise,
without the prior written permission of the publisher or a licence from
the Copyright Licensing Agency Limited. Details of such licences (for
reprographic reproduction) may be obtained from the Copyright Licensing
Agency Ltd of 90 Tottenham Court Road, London, W1P 9HE.

A catalogue record of this book is available from the British Library

ISBN 0 335 15724 6 (pb)   0 335 15725 4 (hb)

Library of Congress Cataloging-in-Publication Data
Biggs, Simon, 1955–
    Understanding ageing: images, attitudes & professional practice /
    Simon Biggs.
       p. cm.
    Includes bibliographical references and index.
    ISBN 0–335–15725–4 (hard). — ISBN 0–335–15724–6 (pbk.)
    1. Old age. 2. Aging — Social aspects. 3. Aging — Psychological
aspects. I. Title. II. Title: Understanding aging.
HQ1061.B53   1993
305.26—dc20   92–46227
                                                              CIP

B6.53
B22

JOHN RYLANDS
UNIVERSITY
LIBRARY

Typeset by Graphicraft Typesetters Ltd, Hong Kong
Printed in Great Britain by Biddles Ltd, Guildford and King's Lynn

Contents

Preface

An urgency has been given to the question of understanding older age by an emphasis on choice in social policy. Older people use health and welfare services in large numbers, a fact that makes questions of how generations interact and the social climate in which such interactions take place, centrally important to professional practice.

However, the study of ageing has tended either toward the broad brush of social attitude surveys, or is concerned with deficits in individual functioning, leaving the 'how' of interpersonal behaviour to fall through the middle. This book constitutes an attempt to address that gap, by suggesting an appreciation, both theoretical and practical of how elders and workers understand each other and why this so often results in devaluation of the former. The central thesis of the book is that age confers different priorities, existential projects that may or may not be allowed voice. The reasons why are complex and reciprocal. They reflect the way that individuals deal with unwelcome news, such as awareness that they might one day be old; the way in which groups and institutions protect themselves from chaos by limiting the boundaries of legitimate experience and the way that common and often inaccurate stereotypes suffuse everyday thinking about older age.

The book begins by examining and attempting a fusion between psychodynamic insights into how old age is imagined, located and defended against and how social reality, as evidenced by social policy and institutional practice, constructs a common-sense view of elders. Three limiting factors – body, time and media imagery – are then discussed in greater detail, to focus on specific elements of the human condition that contribute to the experience of ageing. Research on self-perception, intergenerational communication and power relations is then reviewed to give an insight into the ground on which practice figures.

The three longest chapters are reserved for a concentrated understanding of the role of professional discourse in defining access to services, how new initiatives in community care have reconstructed relations between elders, carers and practitioners and the role of residential care in providing a socially acceptable space in which to be old. In conclusion, it becomes clear, at least to the present author, how interactions between the psychic and social worlds have much to offer as key determinants of freedom and participation in health and welfare. Greater understanding can avoid the pitfalls that often frustrate the best of intentions.

Weaving its way through each chapter is an argument consisting of the following points: (i) existential priorities, that is to say the tasks of personal renewal and the creation of meaning, differ with age. This is most notable between earlier and later periods of adult life; (ii) the legitimacy afforded these priorities, or projects, is given differential value, with those of relative youth eclipsing those of later life; (iii) relationships between practitioners and service-users are influenced by this inequality in ways that reflect the institutional base and context in which they take place.

Acknowledgements

I would like to thank Naina Patel, Chris Phillipson and Patrick Pietroni for support and a supply of readings that have considerably enhanced this book. To this must be added the forbearance of Jilly Crosbie and Helen Moneypenny, at the Centre for Policy on Ageing, whose library proved a valuable mine of information. Simon Catlin generously read the text, whilst Mary Odigbo's help was most welcome in typing some of the early draft chapters.

Finally, I would like to thank Clare Allen for her continued encouragement, and our two children Eve and Guy for entertainment and reminding me that there is more to life than sitting at a desk. It is to them that I dedicate this book.

Section 1
Theory

1

Outward understanding: creating social realities

INTRODUCTION

This chapter examines ideas that can be used to understand how older age is experienced by elders and the not-yet-old in the context of an advanced industrial society. It does this by elaborating the implications of theoretical positions for how ageing is perceived, but always from the viewpoint that social and psychological understanding are intimately related. These understandings reflect and perpetuate each other, and this process is seen as an important starting point from which to consider how older age is defined and evaluated, and its influences on inter-personal discourse.

Some useful concepts are explored before drawing out their significance for the study of ageing itself. First, the predicament of modern living is outlined briefly as it affects the ground on which all social relationships must develop. Two perspectives – outward and inward understanding – are then examined in more detail. This chapter addresses outward understanding, arising from the ways in which social reality is created and construed. Inward understanding, or how the psyche interprets self and others under these circumstances, is examined in Chapter 2. The conclusions that are reached are threaded through subsequent chapters. Both perspectives emphasize the often hidden means by which an image of older age is maintained and its implications for younger and older people.

THE PROBLEMS OF MODERN LIVING

Any consideration of images, attitudes and self-perceptions of older age in Western society needs to examine the context in which these exist, and the social ground on which they figure. Social existence in present-day society has been characterized by both modernist and post-modernist thinkers as fragmented and confusing, consisting of a multiplicity of viewpoints that make personal meaning either difficult to achieve or illusory. However, whereas post-modernists embrace this indeterminateness, others, such as social constructionists and some psycho-dynamic thinkers, see it as problematic. The former emphasize the liberating effects of roles and positions that are essentially interchangeable; the latter see indeterminateness as a symptom of life's lack of meaning and the ability of late capitalism to obscure structured inequality for its own ends.

Post-modernism, as exemplified in the writings of Leyotard (1984), Foucault (1979) and Lacan (1977), begins by noting the importance of language in defining experience. This leads to the possibility of continuous reinterpretation, whereby reality, if it has any viability as a concept, only exists inside the limited boundaries of any one discourse. Step outside that discourse, and you enter a different reality. Social roles would more accurately be described as 'discursive formations' (Foucault, 1979) or 'language-games' (Leyotard, 1984) rather than defining the characteristics of social actors. This analysis would suggest that an older person inhabits a certain linguistic domain that restricts some potentials and enhances others. To understand this state of affairs, the post-modern actor must enter into that stream of discourse, rather than attempting to adopt the role of that other (Pardeck *et al.*, 1992). They must therefore attempt to 'read' rather than 'be' that other person. The experience of existing in a world of discourses means that people are not enslaved by any particular conception of self, rather they can step in and out of different definitions. So, whilst recognizing the fragility of modern realities, post-modernism sees the advantages of the relativism that is thereby created.

A positive value of post-modernism is that it focuses attention on the fictional nature of social relationships. An older person may interact with others by playing at being old, whilst others play at talking to or helping them. To take this further, by playing, as Sartre (1958) has pointed out, actors simultaneously distance themselves from each other. The definition of successful interaction becomes how well each plays their part, and not direct and meaningful contact with either the other person or the self. This raises the question of what informs the play, how, if older and younger people are encouraged to act their age-specified parts, do those roles find content, when this is unlikely to be based on personal conviction? Game (1991) notes that post-modernist thought emphasizes the subversive opportunity that then arises to unravel the dominant narrative and subject it to critical analysis.

It is, of course, arguable whether anyone chooses to be old any further than being able to take a position regarding the physical and temporal limits that increased age make more pressing. At some point, linguistic interpretation must meet external constraint and, however much elders may wish it were possible to step out of older age, this possibility does not arise. The insubstantiality occasioned by linguistic reality must then come to terms with the fragility of existence itself.

Social reality is not constructed evenly (Berger and Luckman, 1971), indeed it has evolved in such a way as to constrain actively the choices that any one individual can make, or even perceive as being realistic options. Old age is, for example, defined partly by exclusion from working life (Phillipson, 1982), a constuct over which individual elders have little control. Critics of post-modernism, such as Jameson (1984), have noted that its very relativism obscures power and conflict to such a degree that it is no more than an apologist for 'the cultural logic of late capitalism'. Thinking of oneself as infinitely flexible in an eternal present of alternative discourses fits in well with demands for a malleable workforce that feels superficially free and is at the same time relatively affluent, but fails to address the position of groups that have been marginalized from these circumstances.

The debate over post-modern experience has provoked a number of valuable reflections on the state of contemporary existence, which can be used to examine the state of ageing and intergenerational understanding. Frosh (1989: 8) states that we all live in '...an environment in which personal integrity means something as a potentiality, but is always in danger of being fragmented by forces beyond our control.'

In other words, the modern world holds out the prospect of variety and choice, but these combine inextricably with the danger of personal disintegration. It is rather like riding a wave of dissolving realities and boundaries, tacking and weaving to maintain a continuing sense of self, which is continually threatened by being overturned. The temptation, according to Frosh (1989: 16), is to maintain distance from others and '...take refuge in superficial and narcissistic relationships precisely because they are superficial, so that their inevitable loss will cause no pain.'

Holding identity together

The task for successful existence is, then, the ability to hold an identity together without it being eclipsed by the surrounding chaos. It is here that any means of simplifying the world are of central personal importance. Finding an artificial yet commonsensually maintained space (which is contributed to because it holds that personal reality and sustains its shape and boundaries), lends some certainty to existence. Inconvenient parts of the whole self may be suppressed in order to create an illusion of wholeness, depending upon the reality currently being maintained.

The limitations of old age, and contact with older people, thereby become an unwelcome reminder that the wheel must stop. Older people embody, to the observer, an ultimate inability to exchange one identity for another, not only in terms of constraints on the human enterprise, but also in terms of active engagement in making sense of life. Biggs (1989a) has suggested that younger people's conceptions of older age have much to do with maintaining a positive self-image by contrasting it to that of the elder, this being related to a fear of future personal disintegration. The dominant discourse on older age that then results may have little in common with the lived experience of elders. As social policy, relations with caring agencies and images of later life largely depend upon decisions made by the not-yet-old, this has extensive implications for whether the requirements of elders are met.

Questions of understanding older age now become ones of exploring something that is essentially hidden from younger people. Moreover, it is hidden because of strategies that have been adopted to sustain an essentially fragile personal identity, which it would seem is intimately tied to the condition of contemporary existence. In exploring the nature of this hiddenness, a distinction will be drawn between looking inward, to psychological processes that operate to maintain self-images, and looking outward to the common understandings or common-sense realities that form the space in which discourse takes place. These two foci often merge and support each other in the service of a world made predictable, and have implications for the choices that can be safely made within that space. However, rather than seeing any sense of personal existence as depending entirely on the history and environment that is created, an attempt will be made to see how people struggle with that reality in order to become fuller human beings and exert genuine existential choice.

So, maintaining these predictable worlds has a particular meaning for relations between younger and older people, and the degree to which the latter can find a voice within the discourse created (if, as will be proposed, looking both inward and outward is a gerontized process). That is to say, how far and in what way intergenerational activity is determined by threats to the self-construals of younger people (which are resolved in terms of age difference) and how far this process contributes to the maintenance of social realities, will influence the degree to which younger and older people can achieve life goals and existential choice.

OUTWARD UNDERSTANDING

Action and the contribution of existential social construction

Outward understanding addresses the way that social discourse is constructed and reproduces itself. I have begun by examining individuals as active beings who, rightly or wrongly, experience themselves as having the potential to influence events around them. This perspective is seen as being true regardless of age, although the ground on which elders perform may be less hospitable. For example, the ability to actively create social projects is seen as crucial by existentialists such as de Beauvoir (1970) to maintaining a sense of 'freedom and clarity', to be 'busy and useful' and escape from 'boredom and decay'. In *La viellesse* (published in the UK as *Old age* and in the USA as *The coming of age*) de Beauvoir (1970) identifies major obstacles to personal action in old age in the unwillingness of society to ascribe a positive role for older people, plus an increasing difficulty in relating to the world brought on by physical and sensory disability.

As Giddens (1984) points out, action plus its limiting circumstances and structures are complementary to defining what it is possible to achieve. All action takes place in the context of duration, of passing time, which social institutions constrain and channel. These two themes – self-directed action and its limitations – are key to understanding ageing in this book. The analysis that follows explores the contribution of existentialism and social constructionism to this line of investigation.

As actors, we are all immersed in the world; we make sense of the world through our actions upon it. This state of affairs has been called 'being in the world' (Heidigger, 1962) and is an attempt to overcome the distinction between mind and body evident in Western thought since at least the time of Descartes (1637/1968). The extent of this dualism makes 'being in the world' initially quite difficult to grasp, but simply means that the world in which we act, hope and remember suffuses our entire existence and cannot be stepped out of. To illustrate this point it is only necessary to consider what happens when we meet another person for the first time. It is impossible to greet them without drawing on a whole number of preconceptions, which both shape our actions and are used by us to make guesses about how we will be received. The rules used to make contact, such as offering one's hand and saying 'Hello', pre-exist and are assumed to be shared. Even the fact that we are both wearing clothes implies an interconnectedness with those who made them. Our intentions and plans make a whole number of assumptions about people who dress in a particular way and about what their friends, associates and lovers might be like. It is simply not possible to treat the situation as if it were a blank sheet.

Of course, we are not necessarily concerned with this interconnected-ness. When meeting another person, one is focusing primarily upon an objective, of which the greeting is merely a means to an end; something that can be used by the active subject to communicate a message.

This concept of an active subject is essential to clarify the construction of meaning. Objects and people are only attributed meaning in so far as they are of some use and integrated into a project (Schutz, 1967; de Beauvoir, 1970; Sartre, 1976). Constructing meaning, therefore, depends largely upon the context and point in time at which a project takes place. Similarly, when remembering an event from the past, that act of remembrance will itself depend upon priorities in the here and now when a memory is evoked. People are continually acting upon the world in conformity, with intentions and objectives that are to a greater or lesser degree explicit and known only to them. However, there are ways in which the reasons for doing something are not necessarily obvious to the actor.

As both Schutz (1967) and Berger and Luckman (1971) have pointed out, activity exists in a 'natural attitude' or 'common-sense awareness' whereby much behaviour is taken for granted as a perfectly normal, unproblematic way of going about everyday business. Both the social and physical worlds exist prior to our actor coming along to influence them. Behaviour is structured and choice constrained by materials and acceptable ways of doing things that are already determined to a large degree and which channel action in certain directions. This has the useful quality of not making every encounter unpredictable and saves psychological space for concentrating on immediate objectives. Unfortu-nately, 'common sense' can lead to unthinking and habitual activity that is not at all critical until the actor comes across a situation impeding the smooth running of events. Such a situation then becomes a problem, as it does not fit expectations. At this point it becomes clear that immersion in the world in this sense is not an entirely good thing. It can reduce freedom, choice and creativity and closes people off from truly appre-hending their own and others' circumstances. Perhaps our new ac-quaintance refuses to respond to strangers, cannot speak English or interprets our raised hand as an attack. If we have no way of dealing with this situation in our established repertoire, the opportunity to make a professional intervention is lost and our understanding depleted.

Projects

The practical world, Schutz says, is ordered into projects. Projects are firstly sketched out in one's intentions, then brought to varying degrees of fulfilment by action. This process takes place in a 'meaning context' – a sort of route-map inside the actor's head that gives coherence to all of the intentions and activities taking place as a project is fulfilled. The length of projects is indeterminate, they both define meaning and are sustained by the meaning context. It is possible for a project to last as long as a conversation, or to encompass existential life-goals over a number of years.

According to this view, engaging in a project, which goes beyond wage labour to encompass all creative activity, allows actors to experience themselves as originators of action. For that instance the project can become the 'total self', as actors become immersed in activity. Schutz claims that a multiplicity of selves are created in different contexts; however, what he calls a sense of 'I', which is greater than these contextual 'me's', is available only through reflection. Unfortunately Schutz did not seem to be greatly interested in how the relationship between 'me' and 'I' changes over time or, for that, matter within a lifetime. What does become clear is the importance of the role of the active subject, creating and recreating itself from a particular point in experience, both for the construction of a meaningful world in older life and in building a personal life history. This perspective, at one point in time and space, has implications for memory and reflection. Memories are not simply stored from the point of view taken at the time, they are remembered in the service of present projects. This follows, once it is accepted that the world, physical and social, is always seen from the actors' point of view, as she or he moves toward a goal.

Projects and activity

The active subject, as portrayed here can be clarified by comparing it to a related but distinct conception of older age exemplified by 'activity theory', first proposed by Havinghurst (1963). According to Victor (1986), who draws on Lemon *et al.*'s (1972) assumption that high involvement in social networks and social integration are positively related to high morale and life satisfaction, the theory propounds the value judgement that activity in old age is 'a good thing'. As Estes (1979: 8) observes 'Activity is proposed as essential to successful ageing'. However, activity is not the same as being an active subject. One can engage in activity which has little to do with intentions, strategies and outcomes that are created and owned. To be an active subject, creative construction of personal projects is essential if the process is to be authentic, in other words, the expression of one's true self.

An everyday example of this contradiction can be found in paid work, which may or may not be self-directed or in the overall interests of the person engaged in it (Leonard, 1984). In a similar vein, Gubrium and Wallace (1990) ridicule 'activity schedules' in some old people's homes precisely because they have more to do with the need to be seen to be fulfilling management targets than engaging with the requirements of older residents themselves. It would follow that 'activity' is problematic because it says little about who defines and ultimately controls it. If this were not a problem, existential phenomenologists would not spend so much time agonizing on whether choices made and projects initiated stem genuinely from ourselves or from common sense and social conformity.

The active subject would have more in common with notions of continuity throughout the life course. However, whereas continuity includes a positive valuation of attempts to preserve habits and preferences acquired over a lifetime, the current position would question the value of actions that fail to construct new meaning in line with current circumstances. The concept of retaining a favoured lifestyle, for example of extending that of middle age into older age, is essentially a static attempt to protect previously acquired habits in the face of assault from the outside world. The primary value of the active subject, however, is that of continuous development, itself an inevitable consequence of being in a changing social environment.

Limits

All projects are subject to limits, a phenomenon which has been called 'facticity'. Limits are imposed by the fact that one's body cannot be exchanged for that of another; the historical and social world that one finds oneself thrown into; the constraints, both physical and social, of the immediate situation and the fact that one does not live forever. Actors find themselves caught up in events shaped by others and in situations with fairly narrow limits and with limited time available for the completion of their plans. These limiting factors circumscribe one's 'field of possibility', or what has been commonly described as the 'art of the possible'. Two forms of facticity of particular interest to the study of ageing are related to the body and time. These will be explored in Chapter 3. The current argument continues by examining how action takes place in the social world.

The social world

Social life is more complex than the relation to the physical world for many reasons. Objects can be used to satisfy ordinary human requirements. They are not reflexive and do not comment on, react to or have opinions about being used as social beings do. However, other people also have their own projects to fulfil, which may or may not fit well with those of the self. The world is already structured by rules for personal behaviour, group activity and finally the rule of law. Each of these factors leads to mutually created meaning by conformity, co-operation, competition and shared creative ventures, that are so familiar to most of us they are almost taken for granted until the tacit rules are transgressed.

This, of course does not stop our active subject from being active, although it does make the stance taken toward others problematic. Ideally, it would be wonderful if everybody adopted the position recommended by Martin Buber (1958), the judaic theologian. Buber claims that actors should not see others as a means nor as ends, rather, by becoming open to the other, an 'I–Thou' relationship should be the ultimate goal. 'Thou', here translated from the German, denotes the personal rather than the formal or plural use of 'you'. In order to relate genuinely to other people, projects should only be undertaken with a receptiveness stemming from 'the whole being', whilst allowing others to exist simultaneously in their own right. As such, Buber's exhortation chimes well with the expressed aims of the professional helper's ideology. Unfortunately, as Buber is the first to admit, people often 'mistake' others for objects and create what he calls 'I–it' relationships. Here, the other remains external to us as an instrument to be used in the fulfilment of a personal plan.

As living a personally meaningful life requires an active subject, some form of 'use' of others would seem to be inevitable. To some extent Schutz (1945) comes to the rescue, in proposing that meaning can be mutually constructed when projects overlap in pursuit of shared objectives. Whilst Cox (1965) proposes that in everyday life the best that can be hoped for is 'I–You', whereby others are treated with respect, but without the depth and intimacy implied by Buber's original formulation.

Buber's ideas have not gone without criticism. How, for example, does one know whether the 'whole-self' is engaged or not? The Jungian analyst Jacoby (1984) draws our attention to a point that is common to the whole debate thus far. The model is predominantly conscious and does not address the presence of unconscious motivations of which an actor may be unaware. Maquarrie (1973) questions the possibility of continuous encounters marked by such intense personal relating, whilst Brooke (1991), taking a more formal approach (that is, formal from the point of view of phenomenology) says that an ontologically separate other is a myth anyway, as experience and intention take place 'out there' and not inside two separate heads that happen, so to speak, to bump into each other. However, for the present purposes, as ontological separateness is the common experience for most people, I will maintain the distinction between a separate Self and other.

This critique is not intended to dismiss Buber's claims. It opens the possibility of viewing social relationships as partial and indicates a central problem for helping professionals in so far as their job involves understanding and helping other people. For Buber the problem is profoundly moral and centres on a dynamic between relation and distance because, in order to respect the other in their 'otherness', we need to leave each individual room to be themselves. Similarly, in order to relate authentically to another we have to know what we contribute. If the preceding analysis is correct in proposing that modern life provokes an unavailability to others arising from anxiety to maintain the self, the process of sharing projects in this way may be an exceedingly difficult one.

I–Thou and I–it also begs the question why we are encouraged to use others, and indeed be used within a pre-determined set of social relations. I–it also helps to personalize the Marxist understanding of commodity fetishism and alienation (Marx, 1884). Commodity fetishism, the dominant social construction in capitalist society (Leonard, 1984; Laing, 1961), describes the way in which people not only treat others as if they were objects, but also the way objects assume the characteristics of people. Alienation is the mirror image of this process, whereby relations between people come to take the form of relations between things. Rather than seeing oneself as an active subject, the experience becomes one of being acted upon, whilst projects accrue value in so far as their products can be seen as commodities. Other people are valued as a means of enhancing profit and other personal or collective qualities become marginalized. This process enhances a sense of personal fragmentation, as the pressures of daily life address only parts of the Self (Richards, 1989a). Individual and institutional control then take the form of defences against a fear of personal disintegration and social chaos.

However, any understanding should be wary of assuming a single logic to modern culture and the power dynamics within it. Game (1991), following Foucault, has argued that the state both totalizes and individualizes. 'Totalizing' is used here in a similar sense to Gramsci's (1971) concept of hegemony. That is to say, the state attempts to create a single dominant project for the whole of society, which defines and legitimizes only certain forms of action. Emphasis lies, here, on the way in which totalization homogenizes individuals without qualitative distinction. Individualization separates people one from another in an attempt to make them interchangeable, which is necessary if people are to be seen as commodities. However, 'Strategies of individualisation provoke demands for diversity, difference and particularity, a reversal of the totalisation of individualisation' (Game, 1991: 45), so, the '. . . target nowadays is not to discover what we are, but to refuse what we are' (Foucault, 1982: 216).

These observations have profound implications for the status of others and for projects themselves in older age, because elders are no longer part of this narrowly defined contribution to society. Their status as a burden on the system, as not having a valid perspective, legitimizes their use by others in pursuit of objectives that are not their own. We are thus given a bleak vision of action, where the active subject is valued primarily as the source of activity in the service of goals that are not 'owned' in a personal sense and is encouraged to treat others as objects. Sartre (1958) has pointed to a number of consequences of the state restricting which projects can legitimately emerge. Individuals, he says, exist largely in a state of self-deception that is both limited and limiting. Self-deception occurs either by an exclusive focus on the immediate significance that actions might have, without considering intent or history, or by attributing transcendent meaning. Transcendence refers to idealized images that actions suggest, again precluding critical thought. These observations lend themselves relatively easily to the construal of older people. For example, immediate significance would locate meaning only on bodily difficulty and its limitations without examining relations between able-bodied and disabled people. Transcendence might obscure an elder's intentions by seeing them as instances of 'wisdom'. The elder may then be safely perceived as engaging in idealized discourse, which somehow flies above their lived circumstances. Engagement in these grossly particularized or generalized forms of discourse ensure that elders are not seen as capable of active contribution or being subject to the will of others; issues of power evaporate.

Relations between generations, and in particular between the working helper and the older (retired) person requesting help, may therefore take specific forms. The analysis implies that each will have projects determined in part by their immediate circumstances, the pressures upon them and their relative power to influence an outcome. This will affect how they reach agreement about the reason for their mutual activity and how the result is received. Moreover, both will feel that they are not entirely in control of events and be tempted to see the other as an object in pursuit of an instrumental goal. Power is distributed unequally (one has, so both are encouraged to think, what the other seeks). The situation is defined in such a way that the helper's need simultaneously to modify the elder's life in a predefined direction according to whatever ideology of welfare is dominant dictates (in other words, treat them as an object), whilst the helper also becomes 'open' to the elder's needs, i.e. available as an object for that person's project. In the case of an older person in need of help, their status in society is likely to be predominantly negative, as they are no longer part of the process of producing commodities. The question of whose interests are being served and in what way is therefore complex and fraught with difficulty.

Schutz (1967), whilst being largely uncritical of the context of activity, notes that a common response to the daunting complexity of genuine co-operation is to see the other as an example of 'type'. Seeing another person as a representative example with preconceived associations attached, has certain advantages for the self. It simplifies the responses that need to be made and allows the repetition of habitual behaviour, thus leaving more thinking time for personal priorities. Walsh and Lehnert (1967) have even gone so far as to characterize Schutz's description of 'type' as typical of the way some social workers think of their clients. Unfortunately the 'type' solution depends heavily on previous experience of similar situations and people to make responding more flexible. Groups who the subject rarely encounters outside formal situations, have been marginalized, or are easily labelled, may find themselves being objectified as the worker takes more for granted the less information she or he has available or is open to. Such is often the case for a younger helper confronted by an older user. The helper may merely indulge in a process of 'self-elucidation'. Aspects of the other's behaviour, and questions asked of them can become a means of filling the gaps in a pre-existing thesis about 'one of them'. Whilst seeming to interact with the other, older, individual elders become an occasion for engaging in an essentially closed internal dialogue about the nature of a classifiable example.

COMMON-SENSE REALITY

The limited social relations described above reflect a simplification of attitudes and behaviour which is central to making sense of everyday life. Within the boundaries thus created, a relatively predictable environment allows a degree of manageable spontaneity. This is the life most of us lead as, by degree, we become attuned to daily routines, Schutz's (1945) natural attitude, or Berger and Luckman's (1971) common-sense reality. The term 'common sense' here draws on its colloquial meaning, but only in order to highlight a sense of something held in common and unquestioned by members of the same socially defined space. Reality in everyday life is, then, taken for granted as 'the reality' and as a consequence a tacit intersubjective agreement becomes experienced as objective. So long as this defined space is not interrupted, it lends itself to types of, and recipes for, behaviour so that eventually participants are unaware of the assumptions on which they are based. However, common sense can only be maintained if problems that cannot be solved within its boundaries are excluded. If the context changes so that 'the rules' no longer apply, or a person or group is encountered that cannot fit in with this assumptive reality, the common sense itself becomes questionable. Individual disconfirming examples concerning older life might include the following: (i) a diagnosis of dementia as permanent turns out to be confusion arising from the toxic effects of constipation – the irreversible becomes reversible; (ii) when one's own grandmother appears across the counter of the supplementary benefit office – the public becomes personal; (iii) if a person in a wheelchair replies directly to a question asked of their assistant – the passive becomes active. Each example disqualifies the simplifying assumption being imposed and requires an adjustment of common-sense habit.

As routines in work, family and personal life are an essential component in binding everyday discourse together, it is to some extent inevitable that serious disruption evokes an attempt to reassert the balance of established common sense. Berger and Luckman (1971) refer to processes of 'nihilation' that arise as dominant parties attempt to right their rocking boat. First, disruptive events or persons may be given a negative status, concerns may be marginalized and not taken seriously. The other is defined as 'not-me' or 'us'; so, 'She's only doing that because she's "too old"'. Second, attempts are made to translate or incorporate the newly disturbing project into a pre-existing commonsensical scheme, so, 'He hasn't been here before, he doesn't understand how the system works.' If these strategies fail, more radical solutions such as segregation may be tried. Pluralism is a particular form of nihilation found in liberal institutions (everyone's entitled to a point of view – the subtext being, so yours is no more valid than anybody else's). An example of how a dominant form of common sense can invalidate alternative voices can be found in what Goffman (1969) called 'collusive nets' or 'collusive alignments'. These may arise when actors with more in common, perhaps a doctor, social worker and a member of an older person's family, attempt to re-establish normality if that older person is in some way disrupting 'normal' family life. The definition of a problematic situation is secretly managed on behalf of whom Goffman calls the 'ex-colluded'. Those marginalized persons allow themselves to be put in hospitals or nursing homes against their better judgement, is in part explained by actual dependence (the reliance on goodwill if at least some of their own projects are to be achieved) but also that personal relationships that are felt to exist would be undercut if the collusive relationship were challenged. Whether the actions are seen as coercive or not may in Stokols' (1975) view, depend upon how far the actor feels in command, via the saliance of alternatives and the presence or absence of a perceived 'thwarting motive' on the part of others. If there seems to be no alternative and one feels manipulated against one's own interests, alienation sets in.

Solutions to problems raised by our examination of the conditions in which projects take shape relies on the degree to which the dominant assumptive reality allows the toleration of ambiguity. Both Berger and Luckman (1971) and Schutz (1945) refer to a psychical 'jolt' experienced via disconfirming events that may require significant restructuring of the social environment. If this is not possible, glimpsed alternatives may only acquire the status of 'fantasy reality', supplementary to everyday discourse, and sometimes finding outlets in private life.

Common sense is conceived, however, as tacit rather than unconscious, the taken for granted rather than the unknown. It describes the field of possibilities that is legitimated by a socially constructed space and therefore the limits to understanding within it. Other perspectives are thereby hidden to those immersed in that particular common-sense world. A second form of hiddenness arises from the psychological processes that accommodate such pressures and it is to this that we now turn.

CONCLUSIONS

Modern life has been conceptualized as both holding the promise of a multiplicity of identities and the danger of psychological disintegration. Under such circumstances, individual actors will attempt to find socially constructed spaces that lend some form of predictability to everyday relationships. However, issues concerning the dominance of one group over another, or to do with the way value is associated with being a productive member of capitalist society, mean that these spaces are often biased in terms of the choices that individuals can make once they have entered that discourse. Age is one factor that is used to attribute value to participants in the social worlds that have thereby been created, with elders often having their experience disqualified as a result. This may take the form of being simply seen as a means to an alien and imposed end or by having to enter a discourse that has its own common sense logic of which the projects of later life are rarely a part. As meaningful choice depends on an ability to construct one's own existential projects and contribute to the development of shared action, the ability to create meaning in later life may be significantly reduced.

2
Inward understanding: reflection and the role of analytical psychology

THE SELF AND CONSCIOUS AWARENESS

The previous chapter focused on the conscious world and the active construction of meaning within it. Although influences may not always have been overt, they were amenable to conscious scrutiny by experiment and the disconfirmation of assumptions through novel experience. This chapter examines the influence of unconscious motivation on intention and the construction of personal projects and the perception of others.

Here, active subjects might not be fully aware of influences on their behaviour because certain options have been suppressed, either for reasons of personal history or social constraint. If activity includes motivation that is unconscious, and if these unconscious elements mingle with conscious ones in the creation of meaning, then, so far as the actor is concerned, the world itself tacitly contains both. An important consequence of this position is that unconscious meaning is intimately related to intention and interaction.

Two lines of psychodynamic thought have examined lifespan development and older age. First, Erikson (1982) has proposed a number of stages that every person must go through in order to encounter a final crisis of integrity versus despair. Second, Jung (1967) has developed a system of adult psychology. Within this, images of different ages in archetypal form, and a distinction between priorities in the first and second halves of life, play an important part.

Erikson's position will be examined briefly, but is found to be too specifically located for extensive use. Jung's analytic psychology concentrates on the process of psychic transformation and mechanisms that inhibit this from happening and will be explored in greater detail.

ERIKSON'S LIFE STAGES

Psychological development in later life has been addressed by the ego psychologist, Erik Erikson (1982; Erikson *et al.*, 1986). Ego psychology arose in the US after the Second World War and, as the name suggests, is concerned with the dynamics of conscious psychic processes. Erikson's model arose from his initial work with children and adolescents and extended to eight stages, the last two of which, adulthood and old age concentrate on adult life. Each stage is seen to centre on the working through of polar opposites. In adulthood these would be generativity versus stagnation as alternative resolutions to the life-task of procreativity. Old age is seen to centre on resolving tensions between integrity and despair, the adaptive goal being the achievement of wisdom. Although it is difficult to pin stages down to particular ages, Erikson does note that the quality of each depends upon the way in which previous stages were resolved, and that each individual must go through the stages in succession. This has the advantage of putting older age in the context of development over a lifespan. However, this very approach has led to criticism that it is overly proscriptive in so far as it suggests (Woodward, 1991: 20–21) that there are tasks '. . . appropriate to that "stage" in life, tasks which must be completed properly.'

Erikson's stages closely follow, perhaps uncritically, what could be thought of as normal adaptation to presently existing social definitions of acceptable ageing, and thus are open to the charge of functionalism, the unreflective acceptance of conformity to ascribed age-related roles. Reading wisdom, defined as '. . . informed and detached concern with life itself in the face of death itself' and its antithesis, disdain 'A reaction to feeling (and seeing others) in an increasing state of being finished, confused, helpless' (Erikson, 1982: 61) in this way brings Erikson's formulations close to choices predetermined by withdrawal. It should be stated in Erikson's defence that he is aware of social restrictions in older age, for example (Erikson, 1982: 63), 'There can be little doubt that today the discontinuity of family life as a result of dislocation contributes greatly to the lack in old age of that minimum of vital involvement that is necessary for staying really alive.'

The problem with Erikson's position would seem to be that this state of affairs is more or less accepted rather than being analysed critically. A focus on age-appropriate stages thus drains older age of self-created meaning to which integrity, both in the sense of achieving self-worth and integrating experience over a lifetime, is an end in itself rather than a means to continuing development.

It was noted above that each stage depends on the resolutions achieved in preceding ones. Older age is seen as being particularly dependent on decisions made in 'adulthood':

Old age must be planned, which means that mature (and, one hopes well informed) middle-aged adults must become and remain aware of the long stages that lie ahead. The future of these long-lived generations will depend on the vital involvement made possible throughout life, if old people are somehow to crown the whole sequence of experience in the preceding life stages. (Erikson, *et al.*, 1986: 14)

As this preceding stage centres on procreation and care, the authors would seem to be advocating prudent anticipatory self-care as the means of ensuring the most hospitable environment for integration of one's life in the stage to come. In conceptual terms this would again seem to emphasize the arguable position that choice in older age is determined individually, rather than posing as problematic the relation between existential choice and the circumstances in which one finds oneself, and also that a focus on continuity across the lifespan has lead to the sacrifice of spontaneity in older age itself. Older age emerges as a sort of personal tidying up, the real business of life having already happened.

This is not to say that certain tasks fail to exist in older age. Kivnick (1988), following Erikson, describes these as 'post-maintenance generativity' or 'grand-generativity', which in her understanding are closely related to grandparenthood. Being a grandparent thereby:

Is understood to incorporate all five dimensions of meaning as follows: (i) centrality – grandparenthood as central to a grandparent's current daily life; (ii) valued elder – passing on tradition, history and advice; (iii) immortality through clan – patriarchal or matriarchal responsibility, identification with grandchildren, and family immortality; (iv) reinvolvement with personal past – grandparent's re-experiencing their own pasts and identifying with their own grandparents; and (v) indulgence – grandparental attitudes to leniency, permissiveness and gratification. (Kivnick, 1988: 68)

Although the joy and involvement that grandparenthood can bring should not be doubted (see for example Thompson, 1992), this view says little about the lot of elders who do not, either by choice or circumstance, have grandchildren. This focus also makes the projects of older age noticeably second-hand. First, as a surrogate form of experience through the lives of grandchildren and, second, as an extension, at once removed, of the life-tasks of the preceding age-stage. Rather than being an attempt at genuine confrontation with the issues of personal ageing, it seeks either to replace these with the concerns of an earlier phase or ignore them in favour of the needs of and associations with the requirements of others. Alexander *et al.* (1992) indicate that whilst non-grandparents do engage in personal generativity in later life, this is closely related to questions of the self, death and immortality. However, this constellation of concerns, which has been defined by Kotre (1984: 10) as 'A desire to invest one's substance in forms of life and work that will outlive the self', is, according to Alexander *et al.* (1992) specifically a Western cultural phenomenon arising from an individualistic definition of continuity. Unfortunately neither Erikson nor Kivnick dwell on the negative implications of this formula. If one of the goals of older age is to ensure immortality through others, the related desire to control them to ensure that things continue in ways that the elder wants would be likely to have a negative effect on intergenerational relations and would ultimately undermine the original project.

It seems, from this review of Erikson's view of older age, that it generates a discourse that is somewhat rigidly and uncritically located. The issues it proposes are perhaps most useful as a description of old-aged goals arising from the current circumstances of many older adults, rather than being existential priorities that are confronted by those circumstances. It does, however, draw attention to the question of continuity versus discontinuity in assessing progress in life and the need to have this experience validated through other generations.

JUNGIAN OR ANALYTIC PSYCHOLOGY

The developed adult psyche has been the primary focus for Jungian, or analytic, psychology and some key concepts are explored below. Analytic psychology holds a particular relevance to a study of ageing because of its conceptualization of changing priorities across the adult lifespan, which influence the balance between conscious awareness and unconscious influence.

The Self

A central concept in Jungian psychology is that of the Self, always spelt with a capital S to distinguish it from self as used in everyday language. Self refers to the whole personality and potential contained within an individual, parts of which can become conscious at any one point in time. The conscious elements, those that one is aware of in daily life and are open to direct reflection, Jung refers to as the ego. The ego acts as a bridge between the outside world and the rest of the personality. This relationship between the ego and Self becomes modified as certain potentials are called into consciousness in response to 'outside' events. Constraints inspired by expectations and values in the social world also require acceptable self-presentation, which again influences the balance between conscious and unconscious parts of the Self.

According to Jung, then, the Self is unitary. It contains all of the facets of an individual, although only parts of the Self are allowed to operate in any one set of circumstances or period of development. Adaptation to the social world means that parts of this whole Self are hidden. They may be hidden as artefacts, discrete memories that can be recalled by a process of psychic archeology, or hidden as potential, as seeds for self-development that, given the right environment, can come to fruition. Analytic psychology refers to the location of these hidden elements as the shadow personality.

Adaptation to the social world thereby forces the personality to become polarized into dominant areas and ones that are suppressed. Perhaps one of the most commonly known examples of this process, identified by Jung himself, is the artificial split between 'masculine' and 'feminine' or, as Jung called them, animus and amina. Men would characteristically allow the animus freer play whilst for women, the opposite would happen. Social behaviour and attitudes become gendered in the individual to fit in with socially acceptable forms of expression. This is not only true of gender, but for any potential in the psyche that is subject to social sanction. Roles are 'gerontized' as much as they are gendered. Indeed there is some evidence (Schlossberg, 1984; Guttman, 1988) to indicate that gender and age-related potential might be closely entwined and to some extent reversed over a lifetime.

This relationship between acceptable and unacceptable parts of the self results in a continuing tension between those parts that find expression via the ego and parts that are pushed out of consciousness and into the shadow. The degree to which suppression takes place will influence the amount of this internal tension as the ego attempts to control the impression it creates. These hidden parts can, however, bob up again in an ongoing contest for expression and are then likely to be experienced as awkward, primitive or simply an embarrassment by those parts that are already in conscious awareness.

The shadow self

The shadow is, in Jung's (1967, 16: 470) words, '... the thing a person has no wish to be':

> It is a moral problem that challenges the whole ego personality, for no one can become conscious of the shadow without considerable moral effort. To become conscious of it involves recognising the dark aspects of the personality as present and real. This act is the essential condition for any self-knowledge, and it therefore, as a rule, meets with considerable resistance. (Jung, 1967, 9: 13)

However, Jung did not greatly extend the concept, having Freud's formulation of the unconscious and preconscious close to hand. Perhaps because of its appeal as an accessible metaphor, shadow has been elaborated by Jung's followers (Hillman, 1983; Samuels, 1985a; Shelburne, 1988; Henderson, 1990). Although the conscious ego perceives the shadow as unacceptable traits that must be suppressed, the shadow itself may appear to the active subject in an externalized and seemingly alien form, as a concrete image, a scapegoat or enemy. Such images can provoke strong emotional reactions in subjects who are tied to them by unconscious bonds, yet experience them as separate and external. The stronger the conscious ego is in promoting an idealized image of itself, the more strongly is the shadow activated in this oppositional way. The ego becomes increasingly rigid and the harder it gets, the more brittle and the more punitive toward perceived sources of attack.

It would, however, be wrong to assume that shadow parts of the self are universally negative and unchanging. The shadow contains potential that for some reason cannot currently find fulfilment, which itself depends upon the circumstances that active subjects find themselves in. It follows that if projects change in priority across the lifespan, so does the relationship between the ego and shadow, and what is unacceptable at one age may be acceptable at other times.

Older age holds an image of Self in future time, of potential that may be fulfilled as subjects themselves age, with older people as carriers of this message. If contact is characterized by rejection, 'old people are boring and selfish and totally unrewarding'; denial, 'I just can't imagine what I'd be like in old age'; or aggressive defence, 'I hope I'd be run over by a bus before then'; pejorative responding may indicate an active repression of personal older age. As the submerged Self, the shadow also represents potential that is as yet unused, to fly from it is to limit and devalue the future self. It is thus avoided at considerable personal cost.

Attempts to find a socially acceptable balance between different potentials and the suppression of other parts into the shadow can take a variety of forms (Henderson, 1990). First, if an idealized ego takes shape, contact with other parts of the Self becomes more tenuous. Shadow parts then take symbolic form, persons in dreams, for example, that seem to act autonomously and can become 'extraordinarily real' and threatening. Second, if one 'plays for safety' from the perspective of maintaining the ego, '. . . one is haunted by the uncanny aspect of what would (otherwise) seem a perfectly harmless personal shadow.' (Henderson, 1990: 66).

An example of this can be drawn from Freud's essay *The uncanny* (1919) in which he describes seeing 'an elderly gentleman' in his travelling compartment. Freud recalls (Freud, 1919: 248): 'I can still recollect that I thoroughly disliked his appearance'. Freud had in fact seen his own unrecognized reflection in a mirror. The suppressed parts of the Self lurk behind psychic corners, of which the conscious actor, trying to be a 'good' pillar of his or her particular community, is dimly aware, and has to be on guard against.

Finally, the threatened ego can respond by projecting unacceptable parts, that may partially characterize the unacceptable in the Self, on to other people. Personal antipathy, prejudice and persecution follow in varying degrees as individuals respond to the parts they have no wish to be as if they were located in others. Little more is being done than responding to a part of oneself, and little meaningful contact with the other as another individual with their own thoughts, feelings and intentions can take place. As others respond to this unfair treatment, they may activate their own defensive strategies as a result. Projections may then become self-sustaining as individuals react to what they think they see in others. Hinshelwood (1986) proposes that projection does not occur willy-nilly. Persons on to whom one projects unacceptable parts of the Self are likely themselves to have qualities that correspond to those rejected parts, which act as 'hooks' for the negative projection. Parts of the Self may have to be suppressed in everyday activity, such as when younger adults are working, and the fact that elders find it easier to express qualities that are inappropriate to a working environment increases the possibility of intergenerational conflict. If infirmity, lack of self-respect, or approaching death are associated with an imagined yet personal old age, and one works in an institution that requires these characteristics as qualification for receiving help, the client may easily become associated with a worker's projection of that feared potential. Following Brooke (1991: 133) it is now easier to see that menacing or despised figures are not the '... reason that the subject flees in terror but a self portrait of (personal) fear.'

This reading of the relationship between conscious expression and suppressed potential means that consciousness is always marked by the traces of the unconscious. 'Consciousness can be understood as the moment of desire to know, the desire for identity and wholeness and the unconscious as that which undoes identity.' (Game, 1991: 49). Interaction is inevitably entwined with the defensive products of attempts to maintain an unreal version of oneself.

Persona

The need to present a socially acceptable face not only banishes some parts of the Self into the shadow, it also leads to the creation of a persona, a social mask in order to confirm conformity to stereotyped expectations. Over-identification with the persona is seen as a particular danger during the first half of adult life, when the youthful ego is developing a social identity (Samuels *et al.*, 1986). According to Jung (1967, 7: 303).

> The persona is a complicated system of relations between individual consciousness and society, fittingly enough a kind of mask, designed on the one hand to make a definite impression upon others and on the other to conceal the true nature of the individual.

Although this description holds with our discussion of ego and Self, it is important not to confuse ego, a self-consciously aware actor, with social acceptability. The persona is, in fact, used by the ego for the purposes of impression management.

The persona is required by social organization in so far as it makes relations with others predictable and reliable, and its maintenance bestows a certain status in conformity. As such, it is, as Samuels (1985b) indicates, the outer layer of the personality that one first meets in another person, and without it strong and punitive impulses would make social living difficult, if not impossible. However, the concept of the persona has not been of great interest to contemporary Jungians, presumably because of its peripheral relation to the psyche. Jung does not help matters by identifying the primary emotional consequence of maintaining it as being merely irritability in public life and duplicity in private. Jung (1967, 7: 158) sees it as primarily symptomatic:

> When we analyse the persona we slip off the mask, and discover that what seemed to be individual is at bottom collective, in other words, the persona was only a mask of the collective psyche. Fundamentally, the persona is nothing real, it is a compromise between individual and society as to what man should appear to be.

However, the persona makes an interesting psychological link with the social construction of reality, as a personal correlate of Berger and Luckman's (1971) common-sense reality. The rigidity of social expectation, its value in channelling social discourse, contributes to a mechanical playing out of roles that can prejudice actors against the unexpected and the non-conforming. The appearance of two people, each responding to the other's social mask, begs the question 'What do they perceive?' Because personae encourage stereotypical behaviour, that is not necessarily humanly real, personae may themselves become empty spaces that can be inhabited by stereotyped images. The possibility for misunderstanding, for projections to 'stick' on the other that is already presented as caricature, must surely increase. Factors that enhance the smooth running of everyday expectation would then amplify the mechanisms of nihilation identified by Berger and Luckman (1971), namely trivialization and incorporation into one's own perspective, through to segregation and marginalization of others whose mask is not complementary to one's own. It begs the question of how far actors in intergenerational communication must maintain professional and age-related caricature in the service of smooth running, but superficial, social exchange. Similarly, if actors fail to conform to expectations, will the encounter be invalidated as various forms of disqualification come into play? Biggs (1989a) has hypothesized that social behaviour is itself 'gerontized' and, in general, people are more familiar relating to others who share common age-stages. Behaviour that contravenes stereotyped norms, or is simply different to relating to age-peers, would then be classified as deviant and be disqualified as an example of 'type' alone.

Archetypes

Thus far we have examined two features of the relationship between the psyche and the social world, namely tension created by attempts to balance ego and shadow and the development of a persona or social mask. The psyche is also structured in ways that help to locate new experiences through the existence of archetypes (Jung, 1972). It would now seem timely to pay greater attention to the concept of archetype, which in Jungian psychology are manifestations of the intrapsychic world of particular interest.

Archetypes may be human images or processes that arise repeatedly from the unconscious and give it a common form. They could be thought of as generic images, such as 'mother', 'rebirth', or 'spirit' which do not depend upon a particular known instance to give them vitality and a sense of familiarity. Jung believed that archetypal forms are inherited in a very general sense, and are common to all humanity as part of a collective unconscious. They are thus a component of the psychic world, which is independent of personal experience having existed prior to individual existence. 'It seems to me . . .' says Jung (1967, 7: 108):

> . . . that their origin can only be explained by assuming them to be deposits of the constantly repeated experiences of humanity. . . . The archetype is a kind of readiness to produce over and over again the same or similar mythical ideas.

The word 'myth' intimates that Jung is talking on a grand scale, which some post-Jungian thinkers (Hillman, 1983) have amplified into an explanation of all psychic phenomena. Shelburne (1988) has disputed the reduction of psychical experience to the mere reflection of archetypes, pointing out that it is a form of idealism, impossible to penetrate with counter arguments. This use of archetype will not be pursued here, partly because of the difficulty of convincing non-Jungians of the validity of the concept, flying in the face as it does of the highly individualistic values of self-determination current in Western culture.

So, archetypes manifest forms and processes that are commonly held and prefigure an individual psyche. They are a sort of blueprint, helping to locate experiences in psychological space.

The question thus arises of how personal and cultural experience mediate an archetype, and how different forms of experience modify the 'raw' archetypal form. Again, we can turn to Samuels (1985a) who, when examining the role of fathers in psychosocial development, points to three factors that humanize the paternal image. First, there is the real father in the outside world, the father as seen and experienced as an autononous individual with intentions, behaviour and personality. Second, there is the archetypal father, an embodiment of fatherliness, including positive and negative qualities, the protector or the patriarch, facilitator or castrator. Finally, we have the father as a partner to the Self, as a member of one's family with whom one has a shared history. The father observed, epitomized and experienced:

> The flavour of one's image of 'father' depends upon the personal father's mediation of the archetypal father . . . the degree of humaneness in the image of the father and the ease with which the image can be related to a child depends upon the success of the personal father in humanising the archetypal images. (Samuels, 1985: 24)

So the actual father is archetypal to some degree. If the balance is manageable, given the expectations that personality and context allow, the father becomes another human being in the mind of his son or daughter. If relations fall on stony ground and archetypal patterns become dominant, the image may become extreme and it would difficult to achieve a meaningful connection with the actual father and other fathers one may later meet. 'Given an excess or serious lack of simple emotional qualities in the personal father the individual can only relate to a heavily archetypal image.' (Samuels 1985: 24). Following Samuels, it would seem that the psyche abhors a vacuum and, if lived experience cannot fill psychic space, the archetypal stereotype takes its place.

The quality and degree of personal contact, encompassed by culturally accepted norms for role-appropriate behaviour, therefore feeds the development of an archetypal image, which may be activated when similar others are met over a lifetime. The internal image becomes a symbol for those thoughts, feelings and actions that are associated with other examples of the type. This influence extends to include not only the imaginal archetype, projections on to others and the content of dreams, but also more subtle psychological processes. In the case of the

father, for example, it might influence the actor's own exercise of authority, tenderness or will to achieve. Whether or not opportunities exist
to humanize psychic images is central to understanding interpersonal
relations and will be returned to throughout this book.

Archetypes and age
Archetypal figures also have developmental characteristics. Brooke (1991)
lists a number of polarizations that reflect lifespan and include, child–
mother, mother–father and trickster–wise elder. Archetypal themes of
youth and childhood include 'puer aeternus/puella aeterna', the eternal
present of early years. Adult images include the mother and father, hero
and heroine, representing nurturance and boundary setting and the
struggle to achieve in the outside world. Finally there is the wise elder
who reflects a capacity for reflection, insight and wisdom.

Each theme also has a negative side. The optimism of youth may
degenerate into selfishness and omnipotence, whilst the heroic imagery
of the 'prime of life' may give way to a driven quality or an inflated
sense of self-importance. Images of old age can equally represent rigidity,
conservatism and smothering the potential of others. These images are
experienced differently, depending upon the degree of ego-development,
both over a lifetime and during therapy:

> A particular image may be returned to again and again each time
> with new significance. The old man's helping hand in a dream
> shows the contempt a person experiences in his parents' attempts
> to treat him as a child, later it shows his dependency, then it shows
> his own resources that helped him in times of need, later still it
> shows his capacity for humility in the face of God. (Brooke, 1991:
> 152)

Samuels' analysis of meditation of the archetypal image has implications for perceptions of older people, particularly as we move from the
personal realm of parent and grandparenthood to the more public domain
of professional relations with elders. It is perhaps unsurprising, given
the predominantly negative vision of older age current in Western society, that the shadow manifests itself in dialectical opposition to the
public stereotype. The Jungian archetypes of old age – the wise old man
and woman – are seen as a positive and potentially transformative psychic
force. Here the wise elder, when she or he appears in dreams, is often a
'transitional' figure (Samuels *et al.*, 1986), a harbinger of change who points
to a potential future and offer themselves as a guide to a wider understanding of the Self. They are saying 'we have been there, it is possible'
and can appear as powerful emotional images.

A transition is possible when '... one dares to act against natural
instincts and allows one's self to be propelled toward consciousness'

(Jung, 1933: 103). The intrapsychic image acts as pointer to imbalance in the life one is currently living and often highlights the opposite to what is consciously apparent. However, confrontation with an otherwise hidden part of the Self is a challenge that can be accepted or rejected. For example, Samuels *et al.* (1986) note that at first, if the content is projected, it may seem as if the other is actually preventing self-development. In other words, individuals or groups who trigger a potentially transforming image may be experienced negatively, giving rise to unpleasant feelings because persons experiencing intrapsychic associations sees these qualities as an impediment to the state they are presently in. Elders in real life may suffer doubly, first as characterizing shadow parts of the younger person and second as containers of an unconscious message that things can, indeed will, change. A not uncommon response follows if these intrapsychic projections cannot be humanized, namely 'blaming the bringer of ambivalent news' (Biggs, 1989a: 47).

Shelburne's comments (1988: 57) are interesting here, as a description of how these emanations are experienced:

> Archetypal images (when they emerge in consciousness) characteristically have an alien, impersonal character so that they do not appear to be the contents that were once conscious and then forgotten or repressed.

There is, then, a moment of personal choice, to embrace or to reject, to begin a path toward transcendence or to seek to maintain the psychic status quo. As has been argued with fathers, an important determinant of whether the imaginal elder is embraced or rejected would be the degree of flexibility within the context of meeting real older people. Biggs (1989a) has identified a number of factors that make humanization of the archetype less likely when younger people and elders meet, which include, the status difference between age cohorts, the institutional setting and the personae adopted by actors in professional encounters.

How the ego relates to emerging images and their associated energy as they seek realization in an individual's life is therefore a core issue for personal and interpersonal development. An objective power imbalance between parties may take a particular form, called inflation.

Inflation happens when an archetype takes the form of a superhuman figure of the same sex as the actor. The same-sex figure has been referred to as a manna-personality (manna being food from the gods). Danger lies in the possibility that this intimation of power is used to fuel a heroic persona that draws on, rather than combats or attempts dialogue with the archetypal message. The person recognizes it as part of the Self by attempting to take on the qualities of the archetypal image directly, whether or not this conforms to their personal circumstances. The power of the image is mistaken to be the power of the person who experiences the image. Fordham (1956: 60) outlines the consequences 'When it is awakened, a man may easily come to believe that he really possesses the "mana", the seemingly magical power and wisdom that it holds.' For women, the archetype may trigger:

> Infinite caring capacity for understanding loving and caring and (she) will wear herself out in the service of others. She can however also be most destructive, inviting (though not necessarily openly) that all who come within her circle of influence are her 'children' and therefore helpless or dependent on her to some degree. This subtle tyranny, if carried to extremes can demoralise and destroy the personality of others. (Fordham, 1956: 60)

Unfortunately, these phenomena are not uncommon amongst the helping professions as will be examined in Chapter 7.

INDIVIDUATION AND THE SECOND HALF OF LIFE

So far it has been argued that there is competition between different parts of the Self, which influences the potential that any individual can express at any one time. In addition, the psychic world is itself structured archetypally and associated images crystalize into developmentally recognizable forms. Some of these forms will be allowed expression depending upon pressure exerted by the social world and the degree to which unacceptable parts can be suppressed. When ego and shadow come into conflict, considerable tension arises for the individual, who may accept or reject the intimation for change that the shadow holds.

According to analytic psychology, this changing relationship between ego and shadow is of great importance in explaining human development, and refers to the concept of 'individuation' whereby, throughout life, contradictions and constraints upon the personality are increasingly withdrawn so that a more complete Self can emerge. It is possible then, that as this struggle takes place over a lifetime, older people are more likely to be able to allow different parts of the Self into conscious awareness and thus influence their social behaviour, whereas individuation may be less developed in younger people. Elders may therefore exhibit parts of the Self that younger people are trying to suppress.

Jung proposed that individuation is a primary psychic task of the 'second half of life', although he does not identify a specific chronological age, the lifespan is divided into younger adulthood, middle adulthood and later life. To understand why individuation and increased acceptance of the Self are products of ageing, it is necessary to examine the different pressures on the ego at different times of life. The 'first half of life', spanning early adulthood up until middle age, is seen as a time in which the constraints of childhood are thrown off as part of a process of creating a socially competent self-image. Achievement in the outside world is at a premium as younger adults define their own domain. Experience is broadened and consolidated in the service of the personal will. 'It is enough . . .' Jung (1967, 9: 114) says '. . . to clear away all the obstacles that hinder expansion and ascent' whilst 'To win for oneself a place in society and to transform ones nature so that it is more or less fitted to this kind of existence, is in all cases a considerable achievement.' (Jung, 1966, 9: 771). However, the polarities of the first half of life ultimately result in a period of mid-life crisis, when a struggle takes place between new and 'younger' projects. This is in part a reaction against a 'diminution of the personality' that Jung identifies with work, individualism and external achievement in this first half and has continued influence throughout middle-age.

As these needs diminish, the psyche enters another developmental phase. For, as mid-life approaches, the actor becomes increasingly entrenched in attitudes and positions. 'We suppose them to be eternally valid, and make a virtue of unchangeably clinging to them. We overlook the essential fact that the social goal is attained only at the cost of a diminution of the personality.' (Jung, 1967, 9: 772). 'Passion now changes her face and is called duty; I want becomes the inexorable I must, and the turnings of the pathway that once brought surprise and discovery become dulled by custom' (Jung, 1967, 4: 331).

As existence becomes stale, a stock-taking occurs, a re-examination of priorities, which if successful ushers in a second stage of development in which parts rejected to date take on new significance. For Jung, it is a necessity for older persons in this second half of life 'to devote serious attention' to themselves as psychologically distinct, developed and spiritual beings, which itself requires that the Self is divested of the 'false wrappings' of the persona. Similarly, an important task for this second stage is that projections onto others are gradually withdrawn and owned again as part of the Self. The assimilation of previously suppressed parts in turn strengthens the ego as consolidation both extends the circumference of consciousness and frees energy previously used in suppression itself. If individuation is successful, 'The person becomes conscious in what respects he or she is both a unique human being and at the same time, no more than a common man or woman' (Samuels *et al.*, 1986).

The active subject, having addressed life's project of critical self-scrutiny and developed personality, is, in Jungian terms, prepared to leave it.

This formulation of radically different priorities for the first and second halves of life, indicates that the projects of elders and the not-yet-old may require quite different resources, have different objectives and contribute to a different commonsense understanding of social reality.

Unfortunately, embarking on the process of individuation is not unproblematic. The same pressures that make it difficult for images of elders to be humanized in the minds of younger actors, affect the degree to which circumstances enable older people to address this important life-task. For rather than encourage self-development in older age, associated projects are given low status and priority in a social world channelled by the imperatives of the first stage. Indeed, it is ironic that just as the older person is psychologically prepared to expand self-understanding, social pressure conspires to close this process down. This analysis helps to give shape to the conflicts that might emerge in intergenerational encounters, as it would seem that older people may naturally be expected to address human potential that must be suppressed by others, even if this contributes to a diminution of the younger personality. The 'future self' that a younger person sees in the elder is not simply, then, an intimation of an unwelcome reduction of current potency, but evidence of a project that attempts to integrate the very potential to which she or he is unable to give voice and banishes to the personal shadow.

Disengagement and activity in the second half of life

Jung's emphasis on individuation in the second half of life should not be mistaken as a form of disengagement. Disengagement theory, put forward by Cummings and Henry (1961), proposes that older people progress- ively withdraw from social interaction as a preparation for death. Victor (1987) has shown that disengagement in this sense implies a triple loss, of roles validated by society, restricted social contacts and a reduced commitment to social mores. It is seen as functional for wider society in so far as it facilitates the smooth transfer of power from one generation to the next.

It is worth stating Jung's words that most closely correspond to disengagement 'An old man who cannot bid farewell to life appears as feeble and wretched as a young man who is unable to embrace it.' (Jung, 1967, 9: 792). Forgiving his dated equation of 'man' for 'humanity', let us follow Jung's argument, 'From the middle of life onward, only he remains vitally alive who can *die with life*' (Jung, 1967, 9: 800; Jung's italics).

First, it is important to note that 'dying with life' is to recognize the reality of one's situation and to actively engage in understanding its meaning for lived experience. Second, when analytic psychologists talk of the tasks of later life, they refer to a re-establishment of equilibrium within the personality. Individuation requires the awareness of more parts of the Self not less. As such it engages in a radical critique of the very values that disengagement takes uncritically as normative in earlier life where only rigid work, family and gendered identities are allowed to flourish. From a Jungian viewpoint, disengagement theory itself could be seen as an example of an uncritical validation of partial development, an imperialistic child of the 'first half of life'. Third, Jungian thought does not anticipate a reduction of social contact, rather, a qualitative change in relationships between generations and the continuation of them amongst peers. In intergenerational terms, this arises as a wish to use experience to assist those 'who are still developing', thereby indirectly influencing the working or family world (Deickmann, 1985). This position intimated a readjustment to changed social status, informed by expanded wisdom, but for only part of an older person's social life. Jungian theory is problematic in so far as it is unclear whether this indirect influence is part of a natural process or not. A case could be made that, as this reflects the facticity of an ageing body, it is simply realistic. However, in considering older persons as active creators of meaning and the authors of projects, disengagement would be rejected.

The second half of life and activity theory

'The second half of life' should also be distinguished from activity theory (Havinghurst, 1963). As Victor (1987: 36) points out this perspective:

> Maintains that successful ageing involves preserving for as long as possible, the attitudes and activities of middle-age. Thus, to compensate for activities and roles the individual surrenders with ageing, substitutes should be found.

As we have seen, for Jung, middle age has few values of its own. It is rather a period of different tensions, some of which, erroneously to this view, attempt to maintain the values and activities of earlier life. Other values, which compensate for earlier distortions in the personality, would begin to develop via the process of individuation. Mid-life, then, is a period of transition and increased awareness of alternative ways of being. However, mid-life may vary from the commonly held notion of 'middle age'. Jaques (1965) located mid-life 'crisis' as early as 37 years, in the middle of the lifespan. Middle age has come to represent later working life, overlapping with, but generally finishing shortly after retirement at aged 60 to 65 years. Activity in middle age may therefore approximate the beginning of 'the second half of life' in Jungian terms. However, this distinction only accentuates conflicts about whether one should fight to maintain, or develop beyond the values and behaviour of this period. Put bluntly, should one consider as adaptive the older person who relinquishes the activity of 'middle age' or the one who still clings on to it without qualitative change? New activities, according to analytic psychology, should not take the form of 'substitutes' for preferred younger activity, but enhance the personality as it continues to develop in its own right.

Jung is quite adamant on this point, saying 'It is a delusion that the second half of life must be governed by the principles of the first' (Jung, 1967, 9: 139) and 'The very frequent neurotic disturbances of adult years all have one thing in common, they want to carry the psychology of the youthful phase over the threshold of the so-called years of discretion.' (Jung, 1967, 9: 139).

For him the later years are just as meaningful as the the younger ones, but the meaning and purpose are different.

The arguments outlined above extend the paradigm of analytic psychology to include a consideration of its implications for older age and intergenerational communication. A perspective emerges that prioritizes active psychological development in older age, which takes a different form from that which has preceded it in other periods of adulthood. If, as has been suggested, repression of parts of the personality is related to age and associated life tasks, then it is reasonable to conclude that contact between elders and others presents an opportunity for hidden and contextually inconvenient parts of a younger worker's own self to be tickled into consciousness. This may contribute to increased distance between ages as a result of the defensive processes that then come into play.

CONCLUSIONS

It would seem that both outward and inward understandings of how dominant realities maintain prominence and conspire to make alternative perspectives hidden can contribute to an analysis of older age and intergenerational discourse. It may now be possible to outline a number of themes that characterize the construction of later life in advanced industrial societies.

Contemporary existence gives the impression of choice between a multiplicity of roles whilst paying less attention to limiting factors on human activity. This holds particular relevance for older age as a period in which limitations become increasingly more pressing. This multiplicity itself inhibits the development of a stable sense of Self and brings with it a fear of psychological fragmentation. There emerges a need to continually reconstruct personal identity, which is habitually assumed to be under threat and in need of maintenance.

However, personal meaning can be created through engagement with socially mediated but essentially self-directed existential projects. The degree to which projects associated with later life can achieve fruition depends upon how far opportunities arise for them to be recognized and given voice. This would require a relatively hospitable interpersonal space, allowing resources for projects to take shape. This itself depends upon opportunities to humanize stereotyped images and it is here that certain differences between younger and older age gain significance. First, it has been proposed by analytic psychology that projects for the first and second halves of life may be radically different. Second, social value is unequally attributed to age-specific projects by prioritizing the reality of the not-yet-old. These inequalities are reflected at different levels of discourse. At the level of large social groups, such as organizations, bounded areas of commonsensual agreement mark out the limits within which projects can be fulfilled legitimately. As social policy and caring agencies are generally dominated by the beliefs of the not-yet-old, this may marginalize the concerns of older people. At the interpersonal level, attempts to maintain an acceptable self-image may be sustained by defensive mechanisms that distance the Self from recognition of the different requirements of others. Gerontized projects may increase difficulties in intergenerational communication if those of older age include the development of parts of the psyche that have to be actively suppressed in earlier adult life. Each level, common-sense reality, interpersonal discourse and psychological process reflect and reinforce each other in a dance that marginalizes the concerns of older age in the eyes of the not-yet-old.

3

Body, time and image

INTRODUCTION

Previous chapters proposed a number of differences in perspective and power between older and younger adults, which might influence the degree to which shared understanding can take place. An attempt is now made to discover what, specific to older age, contributes to social and psychological defences that might come into play. In older age there are two special factors that affect personal expression and understanding in ways more pressing than at earlier periods: (i) the body becomes less able; and (ii) time begins to run out. Both increasingly impinge on the art of the possible and need to be taken into account in projected activity. To this can be added how understanding older age is mediated by other messages at large in society. Body, time and image thereby give some insight into the fears younger people might associate with older age, which give grounds for the rejection of certain qualities in self and others. Each is conceptually distinct, yet come together to locate older people within a certain meaning domain outside positive social value.

BODY

To be located in one's body means to look at the world from a unique point of view. According to Woodward (1991), Freud went so far as to equate ego with body. As the body becomes less effective with increased age, 'Old age is thus understood as a state in which the body is in opposition to the self,' as a '. . . narcissistic wound to the ego' (Woodward, 1991: 62). Freud, therefore agrees with de Beauvoir to the extent that one must keep one's active integrity in spite of old age.

The body, then, is part of facticity. It puts limits on human potential, but is at the same time our gateway into the world.

'Through the body . . .' says Maquarrie (1973: 67) '. . . I perceive the things and persons that make up the world. Through the body I am able to act on them and conversely, they are able to act on me.'

To the able bodied, these observations are so obvious that it is difficult to conceive of a world in which it is not the case. The body is transcended as it is used as a tool to effect the environment. One 'has' rather than 'is' one's body. Like common sense, it generally only enters awareness once it is stretched to its limits or when obstacles become too great. This 'fitness' of the body as an intellectual and physical tool significantly affects other sources of value. Most important of these are productive and reproductive capacity, which are used to locate the individual within dominant definitions of social usefulness. Because chronological age is used to exclude older people from the workforce (Phillipson, 1982) and maturity changes the ability of women to have children (Greer, 1991), signs of bodily ageing are an easy shorthand by which to place people within this value system.

Several writers (de Beauvoir, 1970; Sontag, 1977; Woodward, 1991) have noted an increasing disjunction between a personal sense of continuity in older age and the discontinuity of the ageing body. The Self grows and develops, whilst the body increasingly lets it down. Dittman-Kohli (1990) indicates that the boundaries of possibility become increasingly circumscribed as 'the world within reach' diminishes and with it external sources of reward and satisfaction. Woodward (1991) goes further, proposing that the body becomes a register for the successive subtraction of meaningful objects in the environment, and a coming to terms with their 'slipping away'. For Featherstone and Hepworth (1989) bodily, most notably facial, ageing becomes a mask that is impossible to take off. Others then respond to what they associate with the mask, rather than the personality obscured by it. They see some hope because these associations are socially constructed, 'The images with which we struggle do not have a fixed shape or meaning, they change over the years and can be manipulated and modified within certain limits.' (Featherstone and Hepworth, 1989: 261). To accommodate this new situation, Dittman-Kohli proposes that ageing raises the question of creating positive meaning through coping in the face of adversity. However, it is a depressing thought for most able-bodied persons that, as Bromley (1991: 35) puts it, the role of social and behavioural sciences has become largely one of 'retarding or ameliorating the adverse effects of ageing' or rejecting 'an inevitable process about which nothing can be done'. Rather, that is, than assisting in the creation of positive identities and new projects.

It is important to recognize the body as political, as a means of assessing identity and, by constructing idealized images that contribute to the physical and social world order, disadvantage people who do not conform to the ideal image either by appearance (Woodward, 1991) or disability (Oliver, 1990). People may be categorized, assessed or disenfranchised simply because of their bodily appearance. In some cases, the body may itself become a signal to be 'disattended', as for example when an able-bodied person notices, then guiltily ignores, someone with a disability. It is as if the disabled body replaces and disqualifies the active other as a social being. It is worth remembering here that 70 per cent of disabled people in the UK are aged over 60 years (OPCS, 1988).

Oliver's (1990) critical analysis of social and medical models of disability extends this analysis. Disability is, he says, characterized by a 'personal tragedy' in the minds of professional helpers whereby an unfortunate accident disqualifies disabled people from participation in everyday life. The 'personal tragedy' at the same time individualizes the disabled person's predicament and allows practitioners to relate to parts of the disabled person. If the disabled person is only addressed through dysfunctional parts, he argues, then disability becomes denied as part of that individual's lived experience.

Chiriboga (1990: 13) locates a similar phenomenon in research on stress in later life:

> In these studies, subjects were identified who had experienced, or might experience some condition that most would agree was stressful. The goal was generally to examine what actually happened to the subjects, how they coped with the situation and how they ultimately fared.

This research model, in addition to mainstream medical and welfare practice, plots the effects of one part of an individual's experience from the point of catastrophe, or approaching catastrophe. Individualized responses may then be collated by the researcher. The problem with this is that it again tends to ignore the experience as one affecting a whole individual. What is seen by the other as a defining characteristic may be experienced as partial by the active subject, for whom it may simply be a facet of life to be taken into account when executing various projects.

To some extent all models will be specialized. A problem lies in the fact that resulting literature skews professional understanding toward that partial reality. Oliver argues that little space is left to examine how the social and physical worlds are then constructed on that basis. So, even if disabled people manage to gain physical access to an institution, there is no guarantee that they will be treated as active participants once they arrive. Others may either pretend the disability does not exist or only see the disability (Miller and Gwynne, 1972). Both interfere with accurate empathy. The former might lead helpers to work toward impossible goals for the actor, thus assuming built in 'failure' or severely under-estimating global ability. In both cases mutually constructed discourse is avoided.

For Sontag (1977) and Woodward (1991) sex and age contributes to a doubled marginality of the Self as eclipsed by the body. The general characterization of the body, as an object for sexual attraction, is marked by spectatorship. One is judged, as Sartre (1943) and Schutz (1967) point out, by the appearance and behaviour of one's external shell, responsibility for which is attributed to personality rather than circumstance.

Adults, according to Woodward (1991), measure their own age by comparing differences between their bodies and the bodies of others. Is my body ageing better or less well than his or hers, than that picture in the magazine and so on? That bodily portrayal in magazines consists of younger women and men portrayed in 'older' roles or clothing (Pezeshgi, 1989) would reinforce the potential for negative self-attribution. One is not encouraged to compare like with like, but the older self with younger models masquerading in more mature roles.

Woodward (1991) uses the metaphor of masquerade to explain how people cope with bodily self-presentation in older age. There is a conceit, whereby women, in particular, are expected to conceal their ageing, which others will go along with in so far as masquerade is accompanied by behavior judged to be age-appropriate. Woodward hypothesizes that it is age that becomes the dominant category over time, and there is some support for this from research. Not only are women more likely to be judged negatively, based on bodily ageing, with increasing age (Kogan, 1979), but ageist stereotyping has been found to achieve dominance across sex, occupation, and race (Bassili and Riel, 1981).

The facticity of the body, then, is not simply a matter of the 'body letting us down' in a mechanical sense, self-presentation and self-expression are radically constrained by social constructions. Both may become exaggerated in older age and may lead to conflict between aims to preserve existing achievement or engagement in the creation of new meaning.

Summary

The changing body has almost come to signify age and related status in a society where image, or surfaces, have become a means of locating people who might otherwise be relatively anonymous. It is also used as an index of successful ageing through comparison with others. However, this success is almost universally conceived of as absence, that the signs of ageing are not so obviously etched on the personal body as they are on other people's. An implication of such signification is that other forms of meaning in older age are eclipsed by physical characteristics. So, if elders are largely defined by age-status (as other sources of value in the public sphere, work and family, are reduced) and that is itself based on the body, the communication based on superficial characteristics would be a predictable result. Opportunities to go beyond outward appearance to deeper levels of engagement would be less likely if the other is seen as an example of bodily type, a process reinforced by the not-yet-old's anxieties about ageing.

TIME

A second limiting factor on existence is the facticity of time. Time allows us to be open to developing possibilities, however, our 'allotted span' is universally limited and eventually closed. Foresight is restricted as existence itself is limited by death. Projects, then, as the creation of meaning by projection of intention into a future state of being, are affected by a contraction of temporal possibility in older age. Time available is therefore a qualifier of existence that can be taken into account or excluded from the calculations as far as possible.

Ageing and death

Death is the ultimate limit set on both active involvement and self-understanding. As Maquarrie (1973: 151) points out, 'We can be sure of such a date, but from our present point of view we cannot tell whether our actual existence will extend as far as our anticipations of the future.'

Responses to the fact of death vary. For de Beauvoir, for whom identity is essentially created by action upon the world, death becomes a brick wall, and is associated with the biological determinism that she rejected in the same way as she repulsed conservative notions of the biologically determined status of women. In *The second sex* (1972) she argued 'There is no justification for present existence other than its expansion into an indefinitely open future'. The answer, accordingly, is heroically to continue with projects and activity in the face of finitude.

For Maquarrie, death very much enters into the story as a qualifier of possibility and as such requires reflection on how time has been used. Looking forward, it is necessary to anticipate death, to take it into account as a boundary to one's plans. This consideration is taken up, with what could almost be thought of as enthusiasm, by Frankel (1969), an existential psychotherapist. By posing the opposite question, indefinite existence, Frankel (1969: 75) links finitude with a fundamental motor of activity and the construction of projects:

> If we were immortal, we could legitimately postpone every action for ever. It would be of no consequence whether or not we did a thing now; every act might just as well be done tomorrow or the day after or a year from now or ten years hence. But in the face of death as absolute finis to our future and boundary to our possibilities we are under the imperative of utilising our lifetimes to the utmost.

Frankel defines a maxim for existence: 'Live as if you were living for the second time and had acted wrongly the first time as you are about to do now.'

The recognition of a personal end to time therefore opens the possibility of reassessment and active consideration of potential.

In darker vein, Schutz (1945) also recognizes the hidden hand of death in everyday working activity. This he calls the 'fundamental anxiety' – 'That I know I shall die and I fear to die'. Schutz drops this into a discourse on multiple social reality in a quite unexpected way. It leaps out from the page, as the anticipation from which all others originate, but which is not referred to, although it is fundamental to action. Fennell *et al.* (1988) cite studies indicating that death may be commonplace in the passing thoughts of many Americans. Death, they say, 'May be more of a taboo topic in the public domain than in private thought.' A denial of death during working life might also reduce the degree to which workers question the importance, the personal meaning, that work gives them. Although it might arise in asides such as 'Why am I wasting my life doing this?', these can find no real place in a common sense that requires a relatively even role-performance in a continuous present.

Death, then, is conceived as a hidden motor behind action, which all people will inevitably experience only from the outside in terms of reflection on the fate of others, but influences anticipation of it happening to the actor. This analysis of finite existence raises the question of how people cope with its relative imminence – What strategies are adopted?

Awareness of death is not uniform across the life course. In Western society at the time of writing, death in earlier life is the exception and one is encouraged to consider oneself as immortal. In mid-life, as grandparents and then parents die, awareness of finitude increases, but is primarily important because of the changed position it brings in generational terms. When the same sexed parent dies one becomes aware that one is at the top of the generational tree. There is no one to act as a buffer between the Self and this universal truth. Recognition of this can, as Pincus (1974: 210) tells us, from her rich experience of family therapy, be liberating:

> There was a need for self-assertion, for taking the dead parent's place both in relation to the surviving parent in the family and in relation to the lost parent's position, his work, his creativity ... The loss of a parent rouses the need to progress, to mature, to be potent.

Pincus links this to a lifting of repressed and defeated childhood rivalry with the same-sexed parent.

Jung (1933: 122) discounts awareness of death as a primary motivation for the mid-life crisis, 'As a rule death is still far in the distance and is therefore regarded somewhat in the light of an abstraction.' However, as mid-life continues, 'Instead of looking forward, one looks backward, most of the time involuntarily, and begins to take stock.' Schroots and Birren (1990: 12), following a research review, largely support this view, 'Sooner or later . . .' they say, '. . . a confrontation with time occurs in life promoting a change in time perspective from time lived since birth to time remaining until death.'

The experience of the death of others in earlier age, and more pressingly in mid-life, may occasion a qualitative change in perspective with respect to time. As life continues and death reduces the number of peers and contemporaries, it becomes more familiar. Widowhood in later life may be more easily accepted than at other ages. Studies show that younger adults confronting bereavement have more intense reactions than if death is experienced in older age (Pincus, 1981; Ferraro, 1990) and although some writers have proposed that stress is more difficult to cope with in older age (Eisdorfer and Wilkie, 1977) this may be less so in bereavement. Ferraro (1990) suggests that an important variable in determining ability to cope is an ability to anticipate personal distress and social disorganization, in particular, through supportive networks, which both protect and allow expression of grieving. This would suggest that age peers in later life may be more open to, and less threatened by, bereavement than the younger bereaved. The relative intolerance of younger people toward bereaved peers is evidenced by Crockett (1979), who found that a 76-year-old widow was viewed more favourably by student subjects than a widow of 36, even though both showed similar characteristics under controlled conditions. Whereas the older person was perceived as alert, interesting and involved, the younger woman was thought to be depressed, inactive and dull. Dittman-Kohli (1990) found that younger Berliners (mean age 24) made far fewer references to death, which lacked detail and specificity, whereas in older people's (mean age 74) responses, references to death were both more common, rich and differentiated. An example from the writer's own experience would confirm age-related differences in tolerance of death as a subject. An age-exchange theatre production, staged in an old people's home in East London, began with a coffin being carried in, an occasion for funereal jokes. Although residents found the performance most enjoyable, it caused considerable disquiet amongst staff, who were of course much younger. The troupe was not asked back.

Returning to Jung, it will be remembered that, to the psychotherapist, an elder who cannot bid farewell to life appears as unwell as a youth that cannot embrace it. This is not to trivialize the sense of loss and emotional longing that older people undoubtedly suffer. However, increased familiarity plus a need to come to terms with one's own imminent departure, may make death less threatening in older age. A coda needs to be added here on changing cultural attitudes to death. For many people, now in their 80s and 90s, death has been a companion from their earliest years. Poverty, infant mortality and world war would have made death a more familiar occurrence. The cultural denial of death, currently so persuasive in Western culture, is a recent phenomenon that leaves younger adults without socially sanctioned strategies to deal with it, especially in the public sphere. The same may not be true for survivors of a previous age, where ritual and social norms for behaviour recognized the importance of a final transition.

Ageing and time

Although death, as the final point of corporeal existence, is of great importance, awareness of its imminence may also change attitudes to time across the lifespan. Schroots and Birren (1990) have noted that psychological time passes more rapidly with advancing age. How often, for example, has the youth squirmed uncomprehendingly at their elder's remark 'It doesn't seem yesterday that you were a baby'? Two explanations have been put forward for this common phenomenal experience. First, that in terms of lived life, one year at age 10 is 10 per cent of one's life, at 60 it is only 1.6 per cent, so the backcloth on which passing time figures varies in length and variety. The relative dominance of past, present and future also changes in the consciousness of the individual, as more memories become logged in experience. Second, there is some evidence that the internal clock, circadian rhythms themselves, slow down with age as measured by metabolic rate, thus affecting the perception of passing events, which seem to happen faster, as the experience of internal time is less tightly coiled. Fraisse (1984) indicates that as a result, with increased experience, events are less novel, more easily categorized and thereby less vividly perceived.

A changed experience of time, that it is at once running out and seems to be passing more quickly has certain strategic effects on everyday experience. 'The contribution of meaning in old age can no longer be based on a denial of finitude and infinity if this runs counter to what is perceived as reality' says Dittman-Kohli (1990: 291) 'Adversity is rendered less oppressive by its integration into a different framework of cognition and valuation.' Efforts to achieve in the outer world become replaced by hopes that positive attributes can be conserved and maintained. This runs close to Jung's observation, worth repeating here in full, that in psychotherapy:

> Our task in handling a young person is different from the task of handling an older person. In the former case it is enough to clear away all the obstacles that hinder expansion and ascent, in the

latter we must nurture everything that assists the descent. (quoted in Storr, 1983: 125)

Strategies to maintain the positive also extend to the social sphere. Lee and Shehan (1989) propose that the maintenance of self-esteem amongst older persons hangs on an ability to terminate social relations that are viewed as including 'negative reflected appraisals'. Whereas peer friendship was perceived as involving choice and enhancing self-esteem, relations marked by obligation were not.

An awareness of finitude plus a positive use of capacities is reflected in Hildebrand's observations of older persons in psychotherapy. Older persons, he says, understandably, often prefer brief psychotherapy, but within that exhibit '. . . a good deal of capacity to delay gratification, allow problems to resolve and to take the long view. Moreover they often have much greater self-reliance than do younger people and can be left to get on with things by themselves.' (Hildebrand, 1986: 22). Each of these points identifies an important difference between younger and older projects and the salience of different forms of psychological potential.

Summary

If death is an increasingly important existential question associated with ageing, but is either inconvenient to institutional common sense or threatening to the personal integrity of younger people, a key part of experience in older age may find it difficult to find a legitimized voice. It must be remembered here that personal death is the primary issue, and not bereavement, which is more easily addressed through counselling. Changes in the perceived relevance of passing time would also change life's priorities, forming a specific instance of difference between first and second halves of life. Whereas bodily ageing has come to represent the whole ageing process, time, and its association with mortality, would seem to have become eclipsed in spite of its potentially transformative character.

IMAGE: MEDIATED MESSAGES ON OLDER AGE

In the preceding sections, body and time were examined as important, though not exclusive, causes of changed perceptions between generations. They indicate a doubled difficulty in achieving personal expression. As the body comes to replace the wider Self in locating elders within social space, temporal awareness is suppressed by those same social constructions, even though it is of increased importance for existential strategies.

The particular form that cultural interpretations of older age take, and the means by which bodily and temporal limits are marginalized in the wider consciousness, can be discovered through an examination of media images of ageing. This section looks at the mediation of age through the mass media, as one of the most potent means by which definitions of appropriate behaviour are maintained and disseminated.

A consideration of mass media is relevant to self-perceptions of older age because it indicates how the 'common sense' of older age comes about. If the gap between actual experience and the stereotype is great, then other material can mediate, to humanize the image in certain directions. This may work in two ways. To signify the hooks by which projections can legitimately be attached and to influence expectations in interaction between age-groups.

Nielsen (1975) points out that the US media gives an image that is generally stereotypical and often either perpetuates myths about ageing or does little to dispel them. A study for the BBC (Mullen and Von Zwanenberg, 1988) concurs that TV '... tends to mirror social beliefs about old age'. Lambert *et al.* (1984) in a study for the University of the Third Age, Cambridge, UK, found that over a 2-week period over 50 per cent of programmes transmitted included persons over the age of 60. However, once world leaders, who were mostly older males, were taken into account, non-current affairs programmes for the most part failed to depict older people. When they did appear they tended to be complementary to main characters, often acting as a foil to deepen these other roles. Davis (1988) found that older males appeared every 22 minutes on US TV, whilst one would have to wait 4 to 5 hours to view an older woman. 'Anchor' women presenters tended to be in their mid-30s and were found in less important positions with increasing age. Davis notes that TV also distorts age so that the relative youth of older persons is emphasized. A similar trend has been observed in advertising (Hobman, 1990) where agencies avoid using models of 50 years and above, even when an older part is required. Given that the power of advertising extends beyond commercials themselves to the financial purpose of commercial television programming (Siegel, 1982) their influence may be broader still.

A 'perpetual middle-age' seems to populate UK soap-operas, according to Mullen and Von Zwanenberg (1988), where older people are almost universally omitted. Sit-coms (Marshall, 1990: 31) on the other hand promote the ends of the stereotypical spectrum. Older people are either '... enfeebled, vague and forgetful, or at the other extreme cantankerous old battle-axes'. Kubey (1980) found evidence of 'reverse-stereotypes', whereby the older person is portrayed as unrealistically able and youthful, which audiences have tended to interpret as comical 'exceptions to the rule'. More recently, the mass media has consciously promoted an active image of ageing (Nussbaum *et al.*, 1989), the athletic extended middle-ager, which corresponds to an increased awareness of the 'young-old' as relatively affluent consumers. However, these authors note a corresponding lack of concern for the problems of older age and ageing. When problems are portrayed, they come as single events or catastrophies and scandals. Enduring problems are unlikely to be newsworthy as they '. . . take place over time, with no easy examples or quick fixes' (Nussbaum, 1989: 45). Similarly, when the disadvantages of older age are portrayed, the chosen motif emphasizes frailty and vulnerability (Age Concern, 1985). Rodwell *et al.* (1992: 7) conclude their study of British television by saying:

> There was no dominant emphasis on passivity or dependency. If anything, there was a tendency to present a selective view of old age that played down the possible connections between old age, disability, ill health and death. The more frequent and dominant images tended to have strong positive elements . . . The most common negative characteristics often involved some combination of complaining, interfering, being miserable, bad tempered, gossiping and being a kill-joy.

These studies would suggest that whilst a positive active image is portrayed, concerns are stigmatized or ignored.

Williamson (1978), Sontag (1979) and Biggs (1983) have noted the way in which people freely accept media images as they are presented. Sontag has called this 'knowledge at bargain prices' because these 'carefully manicured fragments of social reality come to represent the whole social world'. She sees them as helping the viewer define what is really worth perceiving in an overwhelming world full of potential bits of information. One of the products of the media version of reality, as Williamson has shown in her study of adverts, is that the image is unattainable in everyday terms. It leaves the viewer dissatisfied and needing to consume more. Williamson (1978: 13) argues that we are being sold '. . . something else besides consumer goods; in providing us with a structure in which we, and those goods, are interchangeable, they are selling us ourselves'. She claims that although people's conscious attitudes to such images will usually be one of scepticism, there is an unconscious tendency to absorb an underlying message, which offers a mirror to the viewers own social relationships. For example, the older person may not believe that Brand X will make them feel younger, but will internalize and feel a certain security in the relationships expressed within the television peer group portrayed. Biggs, (1983, 1991a) has examined the way in which editing and the conventions of 'stagecraft' contribute to the creation of a tacit language for televiewing. If these rules are broken, viewers will complain that the message is 'not real' even though the portrayal itself is unrealistic in everyday terms. So, an older viewer may accept the somewhat peculiar image of old age on the screen and reject other versions if their expectations of the TV world are broken, even when these fail to correspond to their lived experience. Younger viewers with very little personal knowledge of older age and none of its experience, may accept the message wholesale.

So, the image of ageing, and older age in particular, is at best unrealistic and at worst a confirmation of negative stereotypes. Is this, however, important to older people and is such material used by them? Bliese (1982) and Unruh (1983) indicates that it might be. Both say that televisual material is used as a surrogate for interpersonal relations and provides topics for conversation amongst older people. What little research there is on the effects of viewing is equivocal. Gerbner *et al.* (1980) found that increased viewing was correlated with an increasingly negative view of elders and their quality of life. Wober and Gunter (1982) only found a relationship between perceptions of elders in reality and televisual images in the case of news, documentaries and game shows. These contexts actually showed real people but, as we have seen, were only a partial reality. Gunter (1987) calls for more research in this area. Considerable research interest was shown in the 1960s into whether children copied behaviour shown on TV (Bandura, 1965), however this research has not been expanded across the lifespan.

It was mentioned earlier that self-esteem can be affected by comparing signs of one's own ageing to that of one's peers. If advertisements and entertainment use younger actors and actresses to play elders, then positive self-attribution is unlikely to result. The reference group has been rigged, a fact that the viewer, taking for granted the common sense of televiewing, is unlikely to be aware of. This possibility is not ruled out by Wober and Gunter's findings, as the players may be legitimately used for reference purposes independently of the plot. Biggs (1980) has shown that the normal courtesies of attending to social behaviour (Goffman, 1971) are easily waived for persons observed on TV, viewers feeling free to comment on any part of the body or non-verbal behaviour shown. Negative self-reference could easily follow. Older people receive a double message. On the one hand, the use of younger players in older parts says 'you don't compare well', on the other hand, such players model a younger, middle-aged, ideal, through subtleties of appearance and ease of movement. This underscores a polarization of positive and active younger elders against vulnerable or laughable senility. Concern with body and time then become an occasion for derision or shameful anxiety.

Summary

The mass media would, then, seem to be selling a marketable image of older age, corresponding to the continuity of middle-aged lifestyles into later life. Although this might contribute to a common-sense definition of 'positive ageing', promoting an ideal type beyond its shelf-life might also have negative effects for elders in relation to their active projects. These activities would, if the media criterion were accepted, over-estimate the capacity of the real age-peer, leading inevitably to failure through the setting of goals that were too high. Marketing also raises questions about in whose interests projects are constructed in the first place, as the need to sell certain commodities may not correspond with the actual requirements and life experience of older age.

In terms of projects, then, it is not at all clear that the image seen either originates from older people's construction of meaning or realistically addresses questions of facticity. As a transmitter of intergenerational role expectations, effects are likely to be uniformly negative. Stereotypes are confirmed or standards of performance set too high whilst non-conformity has been provided as the signifier of an exception to the rule. A result would be that the ego-self becomes externally defined, relying to an inappropriate degree on the persona for legitimated expression. This means that there is considerable pressure to conform to an artificial image of older age – its social mask – if the presentation of Self is to receive social value. This process requires that the real Self has to be constructed in between, either as an undercover activity or submerged into the shadow. Many of the questions central to individuation, the ageing body, limited time and approaching death are simply eclipsed in the televisual world by an alter-image of able-bodied and timeless individuals, or of the international elite.

CONCLUSIONS

Body, time and image influence the way in which older age is construed by younger and older people. Their importance lies in the degree to which both the content of personal projects is affected and their location in socially defined space. Some projects in older age may simply not be accessible to the not-yet-old, whilst those defined by younger people may be too restrictive for the priorities of later life. Whereas bodily ageing is an overt, but superficial indicator of age-status, questions arising from limited time available in the lifespan through greater awareness of death, are almost entirely eclipsed as existential questions. The mass media further slants what is legitimately expressed away from key issues in later life. It would seem that questions around limits to body and time are resolved by focusing on a perpetual middle age. Whilst this would support the exhortations of activity theory as described in Chapter 2, serious doubts have been expressed as to whether this allows elders the space to address significant existential issues. The degree to which older people accept the image or subvert it as the priorities of experience might dictate, will be explored in Chapter 4.

Section 2

Perspectives

4

Self-perception and older age

INTRODUCTION

The argument pursued so far has suggested that self-presentation in older age does not exist in a vacuum. It is influenced by a pre-existing 'common sense' that defines the parameters of acceptable behaviour. This is eased by the development of a personal persona, which lends social acceptability and helps interaction conform to mutual expectation. Individuals would need to achieve a balance between these expectations and an ability to stay true to their own beliefs and experience. Those parts that are more easy to express are less likely to be submerged into a personal shadow and thus restrict human development. Older age might be a time when more, rather than fewer, parts of the personality could achieve expression. A core issue in older age would be how far issues surrounding facticity, of body, time and image, can be recognized whilst still allowing the creation of active meaning, thereby maintaining positive self-esteem. The form that strategies for self-presentation take in older age will shed light both on the social construction of ageing and how elders deal with it.

SELF AS EXPERIENCED

The experience of older age has most elequently been described by de Beauvoir (1970: 315), in the following manner:

> When we are grown up, we hardly think about our age any more: we feel that the notion does not apply to us; for it is one which assures that we look back towards the past and draw a line under the total, whereas in fact we are reaching out toward the future, gliding on imperceptibly from day to day, from year to year. Old age is particularly difficult to assume because we have always

regarded it as something alien, a foreign species: 'Can I have become a different being while I still remain myself?'

A number of similar reports have been noted by Woodward (1991) in her
study of old age as portrayed in literature, whilst the phenomenon is
common enough in oral history for Thompson *et al.* (1991) to call their
book in that field *I don't feel old*. What is this description trying to tell us?
Although chronological age is common to all (de Beauvoir was 62 when
she wrote the passage quoted above), private experience may not be
experienced as social expectation would lead us to believe. There is a
lack of fit between what an observer sees, and therefore imputes, and
what the intention and construction of meaning may actually be like.
This is, of course, common to all attempts to understand another person
and share social experience with them. One does not respond (Turner,
1991) to persons on the basis merely of their immediate presence, but
also to complex associations with the groups the person is assumed to
belong to and one's attitude to those groups. In older age the body is an
important signifier to others, and to the Self, of passing personal time,
qualified by the socially constricted definitions associated with that image.
    The imperatives of older age are therefore pulling in two directions at
once. On the one hand, there is an inner urge to preserve continuity in
the face of constraint in the outside world, on the other hand, new
requirements might lead to different ways of relating to the world,
which again has to come to a workable compromise with the dominant
social reality.
    A number of factors have been identified which might influence how
self-perceptions emerge. de Beauvior was particularly concerned with
the projection of activity into the future and paid little attention to
reflection (Woodward, 1988). This perspective would emphasize continued self-development through participation with others. Schutz (1967)
reminds us that memory is also subject to reconstruction in the here
and now. Memories become the raw material drawn upon by self-
presentation in the service of current needs. This focus on active construction also points to a tension between an orientation to the future
and limiting circumstances facing the older person. For example, Jungian
approaches would point to some form of discontinuity between projects
at different ages as individuation progresses. This would go beyond the
signifying body, although influenced by it, to suggest that qualitative
differences emerge in the nature of projects themselves. Because we are
talking about psychological processes, change may influence the way in
which meaning is created, as well as its content. Increased personal integration of experience and individuation, accepting previously denied
parts of the Self, would mean that elders may be more likely to come to
terms with new internal and external events than younger people, finding

them less unfamiliar, and less threatening. This is not to deny the anxiety experienced when facing change that is objectively threatening to existing lifestyle, and beyond personal control (for example residential relocation or illness), but distinguishes it from disruption of a relatively integrated core Self. Finally, the relation between shadow and Self provides a mechanism that allows different potentials and different projects to emerge at different ages. It would be expected that a negative value is given to the qualities attributed to old age, not only because these may be at variance with personal experience, but also because of attempts to distance oneself from the shadow-self, where currently unacceptable potential resides. Each of these processes would be present for older and younger people. However, some characteristics of old age may be valued positively in older age itself, as a result of individuation and in the service of enhanced self-esteem. All of these processes take place against a backdrop of a social construction of old age (Phillipson, 1982) characterized by negative stereotyping, or at best ambivalence, which shows little ability to tolerate ambiguity.

A number of points arise from the above. First, the Self as experienced in older age may not correspond to the Self as observed. Second, judgements about the Self and others begin from a number of associations that are already signified as denoting relative age. Third, the degree to which characteristics are found to be personally acceptable may vary between age groups, whilst unacceptable ones may be hidden in the shadow of the personality. Each of these factors will help determine how self-presentation strategies and projected action are constructed from the point the active subject occupies.

Attitudes to the Self in older age, therefore, are complex phenomena dependent upon the interplay of personal integration, Self as reflected by others and socially constructed prefiguration, each of which affects the preoccupations of the individual. Unfortunately, for current purposes, research has rarely approached self-presentation from the perspective of the active subject, whilst empirical evidence that takes account of unconscious processes seems to be virtually non-existent. Much of the evidence on self-description has arisen from questionnaire surveys, which are prey to a fairly coarse-grained collection of data and subject to whatever the respondent wishes to present. They are, however, a valuable snap-shot of attitudes at one point in time, with wide generality. I have also attempted to include a number of smaller studies, which have pursued questions in depth, although in both cases these should not be taken as comprehensive. Descriptive 'oral histories' can provide raw material for analysis, however the authors' selection of material means that such studies rarely report exclusively. Researcher bias may simply be more difficult to detect. The approach taken, then, has been to look for trends in data, often designed for other purposes, from which inferences might be drawn. Particular attention will be paid to the degree that negative social constructions are associated with the Self, differences between the expectations of older and younger persons and tension between continuity and discontinuity.

POSITIVE SELF-DESCRIPTION

In 1987 Barbato and Feezel asked younger (17–44 years), middle-aged (45–64 years) and older (65 years plus) Americans what they thought of a number of descriptors of old age. Ten nouns were used, including 'mature American', which was preferred by the youngest group, and 'senior citizen' and 'retired person', which were preferred by the middle group; no descriptions referring to old age were chosen by elders themselves. Other nouns included 'aged', 'elderly' and such charmers as 'biddy', 'fogie', 'old-timer', 'golden-ager' and 'aged person'. A study by British Gas (1991) in the UK found that whereas those aged between 16 and 24 years generally called older people 'elderly', younger elders (55–75) preferred 'retired' followed by 'senior citizen', whilst persons aged over 75 overwhelmingly went for 'senior citizen'. There preferences are interesting in so far as both attributions do not refer to old age so much as social status. For people aged between 55 and 75, relation to their former working role would seem to be more important than at later ages where citizenship is preferred. Both studies concluded somewhat unsurprisingly that care is needed in using terms referring to older people.

Ward (1984), discovered that only 20 per cent of Americans aged 60 to 69 described themselves as old. By the age of 80, 33 per cent rejected the label, describing themselves as young or middle-aged, whilst 66 per cent thought of themselves as old. British research has uncovered similar trends. For instance, Age Concern (1990) found that most people perceive themselves as fit, well and active in older age, which was thought to begin at around 68 years. Paradoxically, the older the respondent, the more likely they were to count themselves as middle-aged. Victor (1987) reports that older people generally describe themselves as friendly, wise, alert, adaptable, open-minded and good at getting things done; in fact, in ways little different to possibly idealized self-attributions at any age. These findings are striking in so far as they go against social expectation and perhaps indicate that some older people have intuitively taken up the exhortation of activity theory to maintain the persona of middle age for as long as possible. Such findings are not universal. Palmore (1970), in a longitudinal study, reports that the older a person is the more likely they are to see themselves as aged, and that this was not greatly affected by sex or social class. However,

Afro-Americans were significantly more likely to see themselves as older than their chronological age. Victor has associated this difference with health problems, and says it may not be due to differing perceptions of age as such. Harel (1987) found that the 'life perspective' of black Americans is somewhat higher than that of white homebound elders despite the greater social deprivation experienced. He suggests that this is a result of more extensive kin and community networks. However, Markides (1988) suggests that what little research there is on racial differences in life satisfaction is inconclusive.

Kaufman (1986: 11) concludes her interviews with six Americans, selected from a sample of 60, by saying:

> Not only are the biological and social changes that occur with time relevant for the analysis of identity and ageing but more important, it is the ways in which these events are interpreted by individuals in relation to the passage of time that have the greater potential for exploring the process of change and continuity in later life.

She characterizes the self-disclosures of older age as emphasizing continuity of an 'age-less Self', which develops across the lifespan. Ageing *per se* was not found to be a substantive issue, rather, older people deal with issues as they arise in the light of themes established earlier in life. They meaningfully connected past experience and current circumstances.

Older and younger perceptions of old age

One major survey has been particularly influential in gerontological circles. This is the Harris Poll, undertaken by the National Council on Ageing (NCOA) (Harris, 1975) in the US, which compared older and younger people's perceptions of ageing.

Three times as many older people reported life to be better than expected, than felt otherwise. This proportion was found to be no different from that of other respondents aged under 65. When the actual responses of those under and over 65 are compared, it emerges that several factors that younger people saw as being characteristic of older age were not experienced that way to anywhere like the same degree by older people themselves. Of the 'very serious problems' expected in old age, four of most common stereotypes showed discrepancies of over 44 percentage points. Loneliness, thought by 60 per cent of younger people to be serious was only reported by 12 per cent of older respondents, money worries by 62 and 15 per cent, respectively, feeling needed by 54 and 7 per cent and lack of job opportunities by 45 and 5 per cent. The two highest categories that older respondents saw as 'very serious' were crime at 23 per cent (as opposed to 50 per cent attribution by younger respondents) and poor health at 21 per cent (and 51 per cent). It would seem from these figures that the collective experience of older age in older age disconfirms the fears that many younger Americans hold. These findings are again reflected in the Age Concern (1990) study, which contrasts the views of elders with the response of most Britons that they would rather die than endure an old age supposedly marked by poverty, disability and disease. Concern about this presumed negative future was found to be most pronounced between the ages of 35 and 44.

The NCOA's conclusions suggest that many elders interpret the different messages coming from self-experience and social expectations:

> It is not the young alone who have negative expectations of old age. The older public themselves have bought the stereotypes and myths of old age, and, recognising that life is not so terrible for them, consider themselves the exception to the rule. (Harris, 1975: 111)

Kearl (1982) has gone so far as to suggest that stereotypes may be psychologically and socially functional for older people to believe, by proposing a theory of relative advantage. If elders feel that peers are worse off than themselves, they should exhibit higher life-satisfaction by comparison with that reference group.

A problem with self-disclosure of the type reported above is the difficulty in determining how far people respond on the basis of how they would like to be seen. Idealization would enhance the persona and thus personally positive stereotypes, which are to some extent superficial. Evidence on the accuracy of elder self-disclosure is sadly lacking, although Rogers and Herzog (1987) report that for some kinds of information, accuracy was no more of a problem than for any other age group. They compared questionnaire responses to administrative records, census information, maps, voting behaviour and the characteristics of neighbours. When differences were compared, the most elderly (70 years plus) were sometimes more accurate than both the under 60s and those between 60 and 69 years. As increased accuracy is also a consequence of eroded psychological defence, it would be an expected consequence of individuation, although the link here is tenuous.

FEARS AND CONCERNS

A British Gallup survey (1988) compared the responses of people aged between 65 and 74 with those of people aged 75 and over. Respondents were asked 'Which of the following statements about living longer and the rise in the number of elderly people do you agree with?'

The problems included, in order of perceived importance, shortage of income, lack of NHS resources to keep older people fit and well, less respect, need for part-time work, family obligations to the elderly and lack of activities and entertainment. The order of concern was the same across age groups, but in each case the older age group showed marginally less concern. As responses ranged from 74 to 30 per cent average concern, it would seem that British elders are relatively more worried by issues in older age than their American counterparts, with two provisos. First the Gallup study asked only about problems, and second, it asked questions about issues that were largely dependent upon societal provision. British Gas (1991) also compared younger and older people's perceptions of problems in older age and found considerable agreement in so far as financial difficulty, declining health and loneliness were prioritized by both groups. These findings are encouraging as they indicate a closer degree of intergenerational understanding than shown by Ward (1984). However, both groups showed considerable ignorance of the actual circumstances of elders in some areas. For example, neither age group knew that elders were less likely to be the victims of crime than other parts of the population. The findings are difficult to interpret because ages 55 to 75 and above are summed on these questions, which therefore confound later, middle and older age.

Croake *et al.* (1988) compared the fears expressed by older men and women to those of working adults and college students. Although women expressed greater fearfulness than men, across all age groups, gender did not affect the way fears were prioritized. Croake *et al.* concluded that there were no quantitative differences in overall fearfulness between age groups. In fact, older people's scores were lower, with the exception that older people gave far greater emphasis to ageing and sickness. A re-examination of Croake *et al.*'s figures reveals that elders reported substantially less fear than other groups. Whilst ageing and sickness showed only a 1-point difference from other groups, less fear was expressed on the economy (4-point difference), politics (2) and ecology (7). However, none of the differences reported reached statistical significance.

Warner (1989) has reported some evidence on the incidence of negative life experience amongst students as compared to people aged between 53 and 90 years; the numbers of reported experiences were greater for his older group, as they had been alive for longer. Whereas the older group reported death and personal injury most commonly, students showed no experience of death and only some of injury. Students were more concerned about negative experiences with teachers and parents. No great surprises there, then, but it does show that there are qualitatively different experiences at different ages.

CHANGES

This chapter began by examining de Beauvoir's observation that the Self as experienced, as an active subject, is in conflict with bodily ageing. Some consideration, then, needs to be given to what effects changes in age identity. Woodward (1991), who strongly identifies perceived ageing with bodily change, notes that although the first signs, wrinkles and so on, accumulate slowly and continuously, the social definition of older age status is sudden and discontinuous. Victor (1987) has reviewed factors that precipitate dropping the label 'middle age' and adopting older age. She indicates that whilst in good health, difficulties in walking and driving, tiring easily and reduced hearing and sight contribute to awareness of ageing, changed status is more likely to be linked to a fall, stroke or heart attack. Changes in physical health have been shown to be a significant indicator in the US (Ward, 1984), UK (Henwood, 1990; Victor, 1991) and Europe (Vischer, 1978). Health and physical activity are closely linked and have knock-on effects for maintaining social networks (Williams, 1988). An inability to pursue what are perceived as normal activities may, according to Victor, stimulate the development of a revised age identity.

Knight (1986), drawing on his experience of psychotherapy, notes an important difference between work with younger and older patients. Age entails an increasing relationship between physical and psychological problems as the body increasingly influences the mind rather than the mind influencing the body. Bodily complaints, he says, should not be interpreted as predominantly psychosomatic as would be the case with the able-bodied young, as they directly affect the elder's physical and psychological reality.

A second factor concerns changes in ascribed role. For those who have regularly worked, retirement (Phillipson, 1982; Laczko and Phillipson, 1991) not only reduces income and increases financial dependence, it marks the withdrawal of a central role in life, which cannot be fully replaced by leisure activity as this lacks social value (McGoldrick, 1990). Although health may be grounds for retirement, McGoldrick finds no evidence that retirement precipitates declining health and may even improve it.

Victor (1987) says, however, that for some cohorts of older women retirement has no real meaning. Widowhood (Ferraro, 1990) and other family events such as children leaving home or the appearance of grandchildren are more significant markers of increased age. This is not to say that family life is unaffected by the retirement of one member, which may cause tension if existing roles have to be redefined or are contested (Ruszczynski, 1991). Unfortunately it is unclear from these studies whether role-change leads to changes in self-definition and the adoption of 'old age'. They may contribute instead to an existing intrapsychic debate over conflicting priorities arising during mid-life.

STRATEGIES

As has been noted elsewhere, changes associated with ageing may also lead to a reassessment of strategies, particularly in relation to the maintenance of self-esteem (Kearl, 1982; Lee and Shehan, 1989; Dittman-Kohli, 1990).

An increased awareness of temporal and bodily facticity, lead to projects that maintain the positive rather than ones driven by fears about achievement:

Within the existential constraints of older age, positive meaning is created by older people through various cognitive and affective strategies. For instance instead of maintaining high expectations for life realisation and self-development, the elderly change their standards, becoming more self-accepting and value more highly what is still available. (Dittman-Kohli, 1990: 278)

Dittman-Kohli's study of sentence completion tests is particularly valuable for its use of 300 subjects, a large number for research of this type.

Rott and Thomae (1991) followed a cohort of 221 residents in Bonn born between 1890 and 1905, from 1965 to 1980. They found that although attitudes to housing, income, family and health remained consistent over a 15-year period, individuals responded differently in different situations. This effect was most marked for family relations, where they report active strategies that not only took account of changed circumstances, but were applied consistently to situations with common characteristics.

Keller *et al.* (1989), whilst lamenting the lack of data on lived experience in the literature, found a number of coping strategies being used by older Americans. In addition to strategies that maintain existing competency, they found that compensation, finding different means and different ends, and involvement with peers were commonly adopted. These found favour over attempts to manage stress directly or altering the meaning of existing beliefs. Although elders in this study found older age to be generally positive and meaningful, health changes were seen as uniformly negative. Ill health was again a predictor of 'feeling old'. Keller *et al.* conclude that for many, classifying oneself as 'old' is not a permanent state. They would agree with de Beauvoir that although old age is often identified with illness, the two experiences are quite different. However, whereas de Beauvoir sees old age as a definite threat to the active subject, the three studies above indicate that projects are not negated so much as redefined to fit changed circumstances.

Lynn and Hunter (1983) indicate that perceiving oneself as potent has much to do with how locus of control is attributed. Elders with a predominantly internal locus experienced themselves as younger than same-aged subjects whose personality reflected an external locus. In other words, if a degree of personal integration has been achieved, the stings and arrows of circumstance had less of a negative effect.

As might be expected these changes have also been discovered during the close scrutiny given to self-experience in psychotherapy. Hildebrand (1986: 30) observes differences in the strategies adopted by older and younger psychotherapy patients, 'Older people do not have time to hang about contemplating their navels, they want to get on with things – but different things.'

He points out that developmental advances necessitate readjustment to novel needs and identifications and cites as an example Malan's (1978) study of brief psychotherapy, where younger men were found to be more concerned with traditional oedipal conflicts whereas older men were increasingly raising questions about dependence and independence. Knight (1986) points to the prevalence of what Neugarten (1977) calls 'interiority', a tendency toward introspection and concern with the meaning of life, an expected consequence of increased individuation. He found that interiority is not related to social interaction or other levels of activity, and should not be confused with introversion.

CONTINUITY AND CHANGE

This chapter has so far pointed to two different trends in research findings. On the one hand there is evidence of continuity, on the other a marked difference between the orientations of younger and older actors. An explanation lies in the focus and methods used. Reports that noted changes referred to observation and specific tasks designed to examine strategic thinking. Those that reported continuity tended toward non-directive interviews or questionnaires to elicit self-reporting by older people. It would seem that when older people are asked directly, the content of what they say emphasizes links between their current situation and previous experience. It is more likely to access conscious projects, thoughts and feelings associated with those links. When researchers focus on the process of thinking and feeling, differences between strategies become apparent. Rather than being an artefact of investigative design, it seems that different levels of activity are being tapped. Older people may thus be conscious of personal continuity, but that consciousness operates differently at different ages.

It is interesting in this light to note an observation from Erikson *et al.*'s

(1986) interviews with subjects from the Berkeley longitudinal study, one of the few to cover almost an entire lifespan. When interviewing people in their 80s:

> Our subjects spoke clearly and interestingly about their lives, not seeming to hold back. When, however, we later learned about some of the crises they had met, the major challenges they had faced with their children and one another we marvelled at the quiet, rather bland way in which they had presented these experiences to us, if they mentioned them at all. (Erikson *et al.*, 1986: 26)

Here, memories of important events had been washed over. The length of the study allowed actual life history to be compared with current preoccupations and self-definitions. Memory or significance of earlier events had been lost, indicating changed strategies in the service of present projects whilst maintaining a sense of personal continuity that confirmed a positive orientation to life.

LIFE-REVIEW AND REMINISCENCE

Elders' new consciousness of the limited time left in older age has led a number of writers to hypothesize that life review and reminiscence are a natural project for this time in life. Two points arise from the current debate, which would influence a consideration of this view. First, there would be a need to recognize that memories and reconstructions do not simply happen, but are constructed from a particular point in personal existence and would reflect current projects. Second, as both Jung (1933) and Deickmann (1985) recognize, reflection about their life-course serves at least two functions for an older person: (i) the passing on to and indirect influence on new generations; and (ii) adaptation to new requirements arising from individuation.

Life review has been found at all ages (Butler, 1975; Coleman, 1986a, 1988; Bromley, 1988; Schroots and Birren, 1990) as a precursor to major developmental change (Butler and Lewis, 1977; Knight, 1986) thought to occur in late adolescence, mid-life transition as well as in old age.

Butler (1963) was much influenced by Erikson's (1963) views on developmental stages, which place the relationship between integrity and despair as a central task of older age that, if successfully resolved, results in wisdom. In older age individuals are said to take an overview of their lives up to that point and accept or reject the narratives they have constructed previously. Butler was careful to emphasize that, as a therapeutic process, life review would not be easy, as it involved the retrieval of previously repressed events that required resolution. The results might be painful and not necessarily positive. Life review thus focuses on change as a normal occurrence in older age and suggests a view of what constitutes a desirable model of psychological integration at that stage.

Life review and reminiscence have also been employed as a therapy tailored to older age, both individually (Knight, 1986) and in groups (Coleman, 1986a). In this context, Coleman (1988) outlines a number of positive functions that reminiscence might have. It contributes to the maintenance of self-esteem in the face of declining physical and intellectual ability, the preservation of identity as a continuing platform for security and the transmission of culture as a contribution to wider society. Bromley (1988) has pointed to its value in ensuring continuity when older people are faced with residential relocation or disorienting institutional care.

Whilst Butler and his followers have maintained the psychotherapeutic element, others (McMahon and Rhudick, 1964) have focused on its informative and teaching potential. Moody (1988) has added a historical/political function to the list, as a record of grass roots people's history.

The need for reminiscence as an intervention indicates that life review may not be an inevitable consequence of ageing. Butler himself referred to patients who blocked, who would not remember certain events. Macquarrie (1973) notes that when faced with the facticity of time, it is equally possible to refuse the challenge. This may take the form of a paralysis in the present, whereby the previously active subject is unable to plan and act. Security in the 'not-present', dwelling on the successes and failures of the past, might prove a way of avoiding current existential questions. Or, by dwelling in an eternal present, people might behave as if they had no will of their own and simply respond passively to pressures and stimulation. Coleman (1986b) looked at the way reminiscence was used. Some elders saw the past as a treasured possession, some compulsively returned to areas that they could not repress, others saw no general value in it, whilst some deliberately avoided it because it made them depressed. In summary he found (Coleman, 1986b: 180) that 'the large group of those who reminisced valued their memories highly and found them helpful in coping with old age.'

Unless workers understand the role of reminiscence it can easily be dismissed as incoherent rambling that does not address the point, in professional terms. Coleman notes (1986a) that until recently the memories of older people were often summarized as good for long-term but bad for short-term recall, and thus formulated as dysfunctional. However, it may simply be that different retrieval strategies reflect the priorities of youth and mid-life (the majority population in memory experiments) when compared to those of later life.

Conway (1990, 1991) has analysed the special qualities of autobiographical memory, which differ from factual and conceptual remembering.

Autobiographical memories are marked by direct and strong self-reference, are subject to vivid perceptual and environmental specificity and have a duration measurable in years, which makes them quite different to experimentally induced retrieval. Rather than being irrelevant to the professional's objectives, reminiscence can provide a rich vein of information for community-based intervention (Corrigan and Leonard, 1978). Wright (1984: 60) gives an example of how reminiscence can be integrated into daily practice:

> My initial reminiscence-work consisted of talking to older people about their past . . . whilst delivering bath aids, seats, mats and rails. I found elderly people more than willing to be engaged in recall when I asked, 'How long have you lived here?' 'What work did you do?' 'I suspect that you have seen a lot of changes?' Although these were fairly basic and unimaginative questions they always led to an enjoyable discussion about the past and, sadly, often much bitterness over the present.

Because older people are often deeply embedded in their local community they can help the worker understand why things are organized as they are, the history of struggle and past of an area. Rememberings also provide insight into the role of labour mobility and why children may have moved away or be unable to maintain regular contact. Corrigan and Leonard (1978) are careful to stress that helping professionals should take an active part in working with older people to use that knowledge. This fits well with the criterion that an older person's contribution would be aimed at transmission rather than remembering for its own sake. However, whether this is a common occurrence is open to doubt.

Two problems might arise here. First, life-review itself gives a set of rules for relating to older people in a culture that is marked by omission in that regard. The purpose might be for the younger person to listen tolerantly to storytelling because that is what you have to do with elders, rather than using content as intrinsically valuable. Giles (1991) has reported some evidence of this happening, which will be explored in more detail in Chapter Five. Second, if reminiscence occurs in the service of transmission across generations, it is important to ask to whom and for what purpose. Disch (1988) argues that the use of life review for research purposes, high school projects or as a timetabled event in day or residential settings, may have more to do with the projects of the others involved than the spontaneous requirements of elders themselves. Such interventions would not characterize the distance and respect required for genuine understanding and may be experienced as intrusive or simply a reqirement to be helpful. Bromley's (1988) suggestion that life review may be shaped by behaviour modification would be a case in point.

That an older person '... can be lead by means of suitable rewards to express opinions about personal matters, past life or present circumstances which are conducive to good adjustment' (Bromley, 1988: 279), seems to both misunderstand the value of reminiscence to the rememberer and beg the question in whose service 'good adjustment' is to be achieved.

Others (Moody, 1988; Woodward, 1988) have questioned the undoubted enthusiasm of many workers for the method. If Moody is correct, negative aspects of life review are too regularly eclipsed by a need to promote a positive and optimistic vision of old age, which he labels a cultural myth, intimating possibilities of personal renewal:

> Whether natural or unnatural, we care about it for reasons we find hard to address because they reflect our deepest hopes and fears. Is reminiscence an activity somehow induced because we, the young ones, fear to find nothing more in that empty space of old age beyond an imaginary story, a story that was never told, a silence that frightens us as an anticipation of our own old age? (Moody, 1988: 8)

A danger lies, then, in the possibility that professionals will impose their own image on late life development in ways that analytic psychology would identify with misuse of the power of the archetype, rather than letting elders define their own experience. Similarly, oral history and transmission are prey to nostalgia on the one hand and a progressive view of history on the other. Moody (1988: 15) again: 'The present is better than the past, we know more now than we knew then.'

Reminiscence methodology could then itself be seen as a product of a superior present. At least we now know how to respect older people. The subtext, however, reads 'your past is inferior to our present'. Woodward (1988) has criticized what she calls 'controlled group reminiscing'. 'That's my life in a nutshell' said one older man to her, which she says reduces personal experience to a collection of entertaining stereotypes.

Gubrium and Wallace (1990) report that rather than simply regurgitating reminiscence as a stream of 'consciousness-past', old people were concerned to provide the 'right' response. Indeed a request to tell one's life story posed considerable conceptual difficulty, as it would for anyone at any age:

> Before the story could be told, respondents were at pains where to begin and what to include. It was not clear what the margins of a life were for the telling. In other words, the boundaries of the subject had to be constituted before its substance could be conveyed. (Gubrium and Wallace, 1990: 140)

It was quite possible to obtain different life stories depending on the cues given by the interviewer. Similarly, Coleman (1986b) found varying attitudes to reminiscence, depending upon the phrasing of the question asked. Whilst only 25 per cent of his population of elders responded to 'I live in the past more and more', 66 per cent said that 'I like to think about the past'. In both examples it is relatively clear that the older person's project was to assess the question and inform the interviewer, and thus it was important to them to discover the latter's interests and requirements. This would correspond to an active construction of meaning in the service of indirect influence on the next generation as embodied by the researcher. It also questions the uncritical use of life review interviews as a means of supporting a particular theory of adult development, as has been employed by Erikson *et al.* (1986).

The intention to pass on experience to the next generation also has implications for reminiscence in groups. There may be little point in setting up a 'reminiscence group' so that older people can pass on their wisdom to each other, the younger professionals presence being simply that of 'organizer' or 'group leader'. Although elders often prefer the company of peers (Lee and Sheehan, 1989), this would not be the purpose of the group. If life tasks depend partly on 'passing on' and the group leader is the sole representative of the younger generation, to engage her or him in reminiscence activity is not necessarily dysfunctional. Similarly, for participants to focus on the response of the younger organizer is not necessarily a sign of pathological dependence. In an environment of relative scarcity, such attention would be an adaptive response in line with age related projects.

Summary

A lack of correspondence between the Self as experienced and social definitions of older age, may result in a particular presentation to a public audience. Awareness of age-related limitations lead to an active reconstruction of Self, which both emphasizes continuity of content and reflects changed processing in the service of circumstances older people find themselves in.

Reminiscence, or life history, fulfils one objective for some people in older age. When older persons spontaneously remember or require specialist help to negotiate past events, it may overlap with their projects at that point in time, as such reminiscence is a tool for the creation of meaning and not the circumference of created meaning. There is a tendency, when reading Butler and Erikson, to assume that reflection during the 'final' stage of development somehow marks the end of personal history. This review gives some indication that although elders often take care to transmit information accurately to younger people, this is itself part of a project and is constructed for certain purposes. These projects would transcend transmission in itself as greater self-understanding and selective memory act in the service of increased self-esteem in order to relate more humanly to the world.

CONCLUSIONS

This chapter has examined a number of factors influencing self-perception and self-presentation in older age. Firstly it would seem that whereas many elders do not experience ageing as uniformly negative, younger adults expect old age to be so. Secondly, elders might interpret their well-being as a sign that old age has not been reached and that they are exceptions to the common sense of normal ageing. This results in adherence to the label 'middle-aged' as a signifier of successful ageing.

As might be expected from the type of research reviewed, there is no direct evidence for hidden parts of the Self. However, perceptions of age and its relation to self-esteem did show a tendency to polarize around difference, and there is evidence that perceptions differ markedly between the first and second halves of life, with a peaking of anxiety in chronological mid-life. However, it is unclear how far this reading of age enhances an ability to tackle questions arising from older age itself, as opposed to maintaining those associated with middle age. Younger people evidenced an unrealistic view of old age that was predominantly negative. Even amongst the young-old, negative attributions seemed to be shunted into an older age. Negative aspects of older age were clearly 'not me'.

Older people themselves, or those older people who did not respond with denial, seemed to have a different, reality-based view of their predicament, which was accompanied by a different set of priorities and constructions of meaning. Such would be predicted by moves toward individuation. This was not at odds with perceived continuity in so far the projects of older age might legitimately include life review as an appropriate task and did not imply disengagement from current social events. A concern for continuity, accompanied by different strategic thinking in later life, indicates increased personal integration of both content and process.

Loneliness was, unexpectedly identified, not in its traditional sense of social isolation, but as an existential distance from other elders. The personal experience of ageing appeared atomized and estranged from that of other older people, as others were occasionally reported as being used to register one's own relative youthfulness.

5

Intergenerational communication

INTRODUCTION

It has been proposed in previous chapters that people at different ages have different projects. That is to say, existential endeavours, hopes, fears and activities vary across the lifespan and most particularly between the first and second stages of life. Although the age at which change in aspirations takes place varies from individual to individual, it has been suggested that at least three periods are characterized in adult life. Early adulthood is marked by need to achieve in the external world and extraction from the preoccupations of childhood and adolescence. A middle period is at the same time 'the prime of life', with maximum involvement with work and family, whilst intimating the facticity of a limited lifespan and awareness of an ageing body. This tension can provoke a 'mid-life' crisis that takes a number of years to work through. A third period, older age, accommodates to bodily limitations and closeness to death by individuation, review, transmission and preparation to leave life, and notes a marked change in relation to the everyday world. During each phase a case has been made that the active subject chooses, consciously and unconsciously, whether to embrace or reject the challenges that arise.

BARRIERS TO UNDERSTANDING

A number of factors may contribute to intergenerational misunderstanding. Age differences would influence communication depending upon the degree of overlap between younger and older people's projects, thereby allowing mutually constructed meaning and action to emerge. It has been argued that complications arise because age-related projects are not valued equally as productive and reproductive contributions to society. Generally speaking, the projects of older age are afforded less priority and status than younger people's. So, even when intentions overlap, openness to communication, whether what is on offer is valued or is perceived as a worthwhile use of one's time, will depend upon the age-related status of the interactants.

A second factor is the degree to which people of differing ages are organized into cohorts. A cohort refers to a group who share certain life-experiences by virtue of having a similar age, in other words, are part of the same generation. It has been noted (Chudacoff, 1989) that since the middle of the nineteenth century, Western industrial societies have shown an increasing trend toward peer organization along age lines. Schooling, work and retirement have ordered life in such a way that people are not only very conscious of their stage in life, but also tend to encounter and value contemporaries to the exclusion of other groups. This is particularly true of the public sphere where these institutions exist and may thus be expected to influence the perceptions of working adults and older people requiring services.

The existence of age-related cohorts raises the question of how much contact occurs between generations. It was noted in Chapter Two that, if there is little contact, it is easier for communication to become stereotyped when meeting takes place and for those encounters to be interpreted as examples of type. It may almost be possible, as Giles and Coupland (1991a) suggest, to talk of generational cultures existing in the divergent communication styles of different ages. This tendency to perceive oneself as part of an age-related group also contributes to the development of 'in-groups' and 'out-groups', whereby members are able to cohere their own collective identity in contrast to and at the expense of people who are different to themselves (Tajfel, 1969). So, the structuring of cohorts by age could lead to a denigration of other groups in the service of developing one's own group identity.

A third factor concerns the ability to have experience of an older age. Direct experience is, by definition impossible, as one cannot know what it is like to be 75 when aged 35 by drawing on personally lived experience. These empathic difficulties would be less acute when meeting or working with people of an earlier or similar age to oneself. It may be easier, for example, to identify with an adolescent because one has, generally speaking, 'been there'. Similarly, encounters with same-aged peers would allow actors to assume a certain common sense in interaction as a variety of aspirations and terms of reference would be shared, making identification with the other's circumstances that much easier. The aims, if not necessarily the contents, that arise are thus relatively easily understood and do not challenge assumptions about the world and correct behaviour within it. Unfortunately this very commonality may become something of a blind spot, leading to problems when people with different priorities are encountered. If, as Biggs (1990b: 51) has pointed out, helpers are trained and work mostly with people of a similar or younger age:

Unspoken factors that underpin the majority of interactions that such a helper would have, would not necessarily fit for elders. The cornerstone of social encounter becomes shaky, if not completely dislodged, and is thus problematic. Where work with older people forms a minority of cases, it would be relatively easy to see deviation from an expected framework as evidence of resistance, deviancy or sheer cussedness.

Luckily, personal experience is not the only source of information about the circumstances of other people. It may be possible to draw on that kind of human experience, such as similar situations that the worker has been in. Indeed, this has been proposed as an aid to groupwork for ageing-awareness (Itzin, 1986; Biggs, 1989b, 1990b). A partial empathy might then arise, and can be used to develop what has been called 'enlightened self-interest' on the part of the person who will become aged (Biggs, 1991a). Both writers note the need to check-out any insight gained with the actual experience of elders to make sure conclusions are not simply the product of a younger imagination.

Another source of empathic information would come from someone the actor knows or is close to. This often hinges on relations within the family and in particular with grandparents or ageing parents. It can lead to problems if attempts are made to generalize to other older people with different life circumstances or are in a different relationship to the actor. Over-association with family history could lead to misattribution or avoidance of the other if they evoke memories of difficulty in those relationships.

The position of an older person attempting to communicate with someone of lesser years is somewhat different. Firstly, they would have had personal experience of other life phases, although this will be affected by the historical and normative context in which the original experience took place. So, although the projects and feelings of work-life may be understood, the way that these were allowed expression may vary dramatically across generations. A desire to pass on accrued life-experience may be received as obsolete or simply not valued because of low status associated with older age. Alternatively contents may be valued as historical information about family and culture but not relevant to current events. Repeated experience of miscommunication would be discouraging to both parties and lead to a sense of impotence and frustration. Finally, attempts to generalize from known younger people, grandchildren or children, would be subject to the same constraints as outlined above. Media stereotypes of youth, race or any other example of type, would then influence the perception of 'other' with whom little personal contact was had.

Unconscious motivations will affect the way in which information about another person is interpreted. The balance between the consciously accepted self-image and unacceptable shadow parts will depend upon the nature and strength of identification with whichever age-cohort belonged to. Shadow parts would either be repressed or projected onto other people whose life-circumstances to some degree reflect those elements the ego is attempting to disown. As a part of this process, one party may distance itself from the other, either by avoiding contact altogether, by superficiality, or by confirming existing beliefs. If such a path is followed, the possibility of seeing the other simply as caricature increases.

Each of these factors influences intergenerational communication by determining how close one can get to another person and how messages are interpreted. It contributes, in Samuels' (1985a) terms, to the degree stereotypical or archetypal images can become human. A divergence of projects, identification with cohorts and an unequal balance of empathic experience each mediate the task of genuine communication. The degree of contact between generations and styles of communication therefore require further exploration.

CONTACT BETWEEN GENERATIONS

There is unfortunately very little information on the degree of contact between generations. The British Gas Survey (1991) asked questions of 16–24-year-olds and those age 55 plus. Of respondents aged 55 and above, 19 per cent reported that they tended to mix with people of predominantly the same age, whilst 80 per cent had a variety of contact across ages. These self-reports seem to indicate frequent intergenerational interaction, however, the survey did not distinguish between young-old and older old people, nor are we told the age of those mixed with and their relationship to the respondent on that question. Other responses lead to the conclusion that contact predominantly referred to friends and family.

When the survey distinguished between people aged 55–75 and 75 plus, neither group wished for significant changes in the contact that they already had, although younger elders wished for slightly more interaction with younger people. When asked about actual contact with the 16–24 group marginally more of this 'retired' group reported 'a lot' (43 per cent) than the elder group (30 per cent). These figures are influenced by race, as Asian respondents reported more contact than black or white groups. However, different levels of contact between generations did not seem to influence the degree to which older people enjoyed life.

Finally, the British Gas Survey asked the 16–24 group from what age they would think of someone as being old. Four categories scored over 20 per cent: under 45, 45–50, 56–60 and 61–70. For some unknown reason 51–55 and 71–80 scored 6 and 5 per cent, respectively. It would seem that youth's perception of age is surprisingly comprehensive and complements Baker's (1985) finding that in young Americans' opinion social status decreases linearly from 30 years onwards.

Several writers have commented on a widespread ignorance on the true nature of the ageing process (Comfort, 1977; Palmore, 1977; Prunchno and Symer, 1983) Peterson *et al.* (1988) looked at contact between generations as a predictor of accurate knowledge about older age. They found that, when age of respondents was controlled, more contact with old people led to better understanding of the processes of ageing. Although 'the mature adult's understanding . . . is actually rather limited' it increased with age, whilst women were more likely to be accurate than men. Contact, age and sex were thought to make independent contributions to awareness of the ageing process. They concluded (Peterson *et al.*, 1988: 131) that increased ageing:

. . . would heighten [other adults'] attention to factual information about its salient characteristics while diminishing their motivation to accept without challenge the negative stereotypes about which misinformation about ageing largely consists.

Knox *et al.* (1986) examined whether university students' judgements differed depending upon whether experience was based on contact with older people in general or from specific individuals. They found that these young adults used a variety of contacts in coming to a decision and did not generalize from one person. Quality of contact was more important in determining views held than status, length or frequency of contact.

Whilst there have been a large number of reports from the US on the supposedly beneficial effects of contact between adolescents and older people as an increasingly popular curricular activity (Disch, 1988), these have rarely been subject to experimental study. When Chapman and Neal (1990) examined attitude change as a result of such meetings, they found that only adolescents who had helped older people significantly enjoyed the experience and decreased in social distance between the two groups. These young people also thought that elders took a more positive view of youth as a result. The older people's attitudes, however, showed no change. Interestingly, these same helpers were less likely to want to repeat the experience than their non-helping peers.

Evidently they had now 'done' the elderly to their satisfaction and were ready to move on to the next novel experience.

A striking common thread throughout these studies is their focus on relations between relative youth and older age. This may partially be explained by the fact that it is comparatively easy for investigators to access populations who are at school, college or members of clubs and day facilities for senior citizens. A second factor would be an assumption that in some way these two groups have affinities that are related to their particular life-phases, such as lack of engagement in formal work-activity, a period of experiment with a variety of social roles (Fitzgerald, 1988), plus a relative ease of emotional ties through grand-parenthood, which is often not marred by the intensity of relations between parents and children (Knight, 1986). Relations between adults is more difficult to find and is often divided into professional activity and obligations between adult children and their parents. These will be examined in later chapters.

Some evidence on the degree of contact between working adults and older people arises from training exercises (Biggs, 1989b, 1990b). Two exercises are of particular value. The first considers the degree of contact between helping professionals and persons of varying ages. Results from ten such groups ($n = 124$) are surprisingly consistent. Regardless of a participant's age, contact tends to be cohort-related. Persons of approximately the same age are most frequently in contact with each other. This is particularly true of social contact, whilst workplace interaction tended to overlap with people immediately older and younger than the respondents. An exception was reported in the case of people with young families or other dependent relatives.

An interesting point is that even when work required contact with older people, this contact did not seem to be given the same priority, nor have the same immediacy and importance as contact with other groups. Whether this was because others were old or service-users was not investigated, however it was not unusual for workers to omit or under-estimate this form of contact when a subgroup compared actual reported contacts over the period of 1 week.

A second exercise asked participants to note different aspects of personal age, such as chronological age, felt age, ideal age and how old they would like to feel when aged 75. Although some participants reported their current age for all categories, women were more likely to distinguish between different questions than men and not be so 'hooked' on chronology. Reports also indicated an implicit desirable age – some time in the 'prime of life' as younger people often wished to be slightly older and vice versa. Both of these exercises were subject to group processes and took place in uncontrolled settings. However, they do supply anecdotal evidence that contact amongst the adult population is affected by cohort and that adults in working life are quite unsophisticated in using different indicators of ageing.

It would seem that intergenerational contact is somewhat limited and superficial, at least in the public sphere. If this is the case, then lack of genuine contact would be an important factor in maintaining stereotypes and reducing opportunities to humanize those images. However, contact is only a first step in communication which also depends upon impressions created when generations meet.

COMMUNICATION BETWEEN GENERATIONS

Ageing and physical barriers to communication

Bodily changes that accompany ageing will influence how messages are communicated and received. Presbyopia, changes to the lens of the eye, leads to a slow decline in visual accuity beginning from approximately 40 years onwards. Cataracts may also begin to reduce the amount of light that enters the eye, thus obscuring the perception of outside events. Reduced hearing would impair ability to receive information correctly, which then interacts with other decrements if these reduce the possibility of using other cues. Although glasses and hearing aids can be used to ameliorate the situation, communication increasingly comes to rely on the sensitivity and good will of others to modify their own communication. For example, Dreher (1987) notes that communication can be enhanced significantly if a partner arranges to have the light on their face, is positioned at the visual level of the listener, uses non-verbal cues to amplify meaning, speaks slightly louder than normal, uses short sentences and is willing to rephrase communication that is misunderstood. The list could be extended by adding that familiarity with the context of communication would ease the encoding and decoding of messages.

Physical changes also affect the muscles used to create speech. By the age 65, imprecise consonants and slowed articulation rates were found to be commonplace (Ryan and Burk, 1974), whilst the ability to make rapid repetitive movements of the tongue and lips (or diadochokinetic rate) was reduced (Pracek *et al.*, 1966). The quality of individual speech, including articulation, phonation, pitch and timing, is affected by increased age (Dreher, 1987).

Slowing down and a restricted range of expression make it more difficult for an observer to identify how an older person is feeling, whilst the elder requires more time to monitor communications coming from their younger partner:

Reduction in the emotional expressiveness on the part of elderly people means that younger people may misunderstand their state of mind. Their fixed expression may be misinterpreted; their relative lack of expression may be mistaken for lack of feeling and emotion. Conversely the failure of the old person to register the younger person's faster emotional expressions may lead to lack of appreciation. The stage is thus set for mutual misunderstanding between older and younger people. (Bromley, 1988: 274)

Nussbaum *et al.* (1989) comment that the simplification of speech, a strategy often used by younger people to enhance communication, may contribute to misunderstanding if not handled with sensitivity. Simplification can reduce the affective and relational components of a message, making the speaker sound unfriendly. Nussbaum also summarizes research that emphasizes the negative effects of such age-related decrements on others' judgements. Slowed memory transmission and production of speech sound is often incorrectly perceived as an indication of less animation, intelligence and extroversion, all of which are positively valued by Western cultures when present. The ability to recognize these cues and associate them with old age, simply from hearing sound recordings, has been shown by Shipp and Hollien (1969) to be commonplace amongst all ages. Giles *et al.* (1989) found that when open-ended questions were asked about a reported car accident, using a variety of speakers and speech styles, a driver's older-age and class produced a more negative assessment of their abilities. When subjects were asked to recognize reports amongst 'distractor' items, two days later, information relating to younger speakers was more accurately remembered. Moreover, a fast-talking elder was judged to be the most unbenevolent of that age group. These findings not only underline the negative status attributed to old-age, it shows that the disconfirmation of stereotypes is not always favourably received and may reflect the disruption of common sense assumptions.

COMMUNICATION STYLE

The preceding section outlined the effects of bodily limitation on effective communication between older and younger generations and the need for modified styles when a younger person expects that their conversational partner may not fully comprehend what is, for them, normal talk. Such modification presupposes a willingness to put oneself in the position of the other and value the resulting content. A consideration of conversational style might reveal the degree to which such accommodation takes place.

Giles and Coupland (1991a) have examined 'beliefs about talk' amongst

70- and 19-year-olds. Elders were found to be more positive about the recreational value of talking. Younger people recognized this tendency amongst their elders as small-talk '. . . with a strong tinge of egocentrism, and with an assertiveness not represented in the young's views of their own age-peers' (Giles and Coupland, 1991a: 161).

A difference was also noted in the conversational styles of young-elders and old-elders. Discussion groups consisting of the latter were marked by 'topic-flux' and simultaneous speech (Giles *et al.*, 1991: 164):

> Subtopics were developed piecemeal by various participants as talk rolled forward, in some respects tangential to the topic the researcher had established. Indeed the interviewer's multiple attempts to re-assert the (defined) topic were simply ignored by these groups, who seemed unprepared to fit her broader frame. . . . Much to her annoyance, it would seem as 'talking to animals for company' quickly lead, through a number of transmutations, to 'Scotland is lovely'. Speaking at the same time became such a problem that 'There were points during the discussions where the researcher found it necessary to intrude and ask for this to be minimised.'

This style of conversation seemed, the researchers report, to be well suited to developing personal narratives and simultaneous speech was not perceived by elders to be anything other than cumulative collaboration and quite creditworthy as a marker of having 'got on well'. Younger-elders, in common with other ages, stuck to 'thematic-cumulativity' whereby participants supported, modified or took issue with a dominant line of argument. Outcomes and discoveries were deemed more important than talk in itself.

The researchers did not elaborate further on the motivation of the older group, or whether conflict over age-related projects were in evidence. In terms of peer identity, elders certainly managed to retain control of the discussion, effectively excluding their younger facilitator. Whilst it has been reported that new, and in this case presumably short-term, relationships are unlikely to equal established ones with 'insiders' (Unruh, 1983), this seems unlikely to explain the degree of exclusion reported. The findings are reminiscent of LeRiche and Rowlings' (1990: 134) experience of feminist groupwork with older women, 'By making us feel reified, angry and powerless, they shared with us their feelings about their experience as older women.'

Similarly, Ezquerro (1989) found that groups with the 'pre-elderly' (55–67 years) were marked by envy of the younger therapist and a struggle for control that resulted in the group becoming 'a group of co-therapists'.

Giles *et al.* (1991) were not primarily concerned with the group as a context for information exchange. The influence of a clash of projects across generations, the need to enhance in-group identity and the opportunity to give the shadow sides of personality free play may explain the problems they encountered more fully.

In rejecting the younger researcher, perhaps these elders were using a particular strategy rather than revealing a characteristic form of communication. When in a collective situation, their tacit awareness of holding priorities and experience in common, which were at the same time different to the younger researcher, may have led to an acting-through and handing-back of disconfirming experience. As one would expect if this were the case, the younger-old group, who maintained the values of earlier existential projects did not respond in the same way. If differences between cohorts were themselves an explanation of differences in communication style, then one would need to explain why no-one had noticed this peculiar phenomenon amongst a generation as it moved through life to this point. Such an interpretation would change the status of this study, from an investigation of content, to one of how processes emerge as part of intergenerational dialogue itself. At first glance, these strategies would be in contradiction to any wish to pass on accrued experience to younger generations. The shadow of such a wish, the desire to exclude the younger other, seems to have come to the fore. This may itself be a response to a particular situation in which the group was called together and questions defined, not by elders themselves but for the purposes of research. If the elders in question had been subject to unrewarding exchanges in the past, their response may be more easily understood.

Observations of intergenerational communication have also identified two characteristics, which in other circumstances would be thought of as transgressing the norms of acceptable social conversation. These are painful self-disclosure (PSD) and overt reference to chronological age. Coupland *et al.* (1988) found that British upper-working-class elders (70–87 years) spent an average of one-sixth of initial encounters with women in their 30s relating PSDs. Details of health-related problems often arose spontaneously, and although listened to politely, even to the extent of being maintained by cues from listeners, were judged to be socially insensitive and evidence of elderly egocentrism. Giles and Coupland (1991a: 163) concluded that 'Talking to the old is perceived as a time-consuming duty and a necessary therapy rather than as relational development and broadening.'

A second characteristic noted by these investigators was the spontaneous telling of age. Although common in childhood, such disclosure is generally avoided in mid-life as the passing of age becomes associated with derogatory humour and decline rather than interest in maturation and development. Advanced age, however, seems to occasion either a positive assertion of health and independence of the 'Pretty good for

84!' variety, or the moral right not to have to undertake onerous duties, such as 'at 79, I think I deserve a rest'. Giles and Coupland (1991a) point out that these assertions claim credit against normative expectation and, as such, implicitly underscore the dominant perception of ageing as decline. The 'gift of praise' that is the acceptable intergenerational response ('You don't look a day over 60!' or 'Aren't you marvellous!') rewards in the short-term and provides a ritualized negotiation of an otherwise problematic encounter. Age-disclosure does not seem to generate the same negative response in listeners as PSDs, and may be an indication of the form that personae take in such interactions.

Both characteristics mark the encounter as one of difference. In this light it is interesting to note that Coupland *et al.* (1991) show, at least in the case of one 79-year-old woman, that content and expectation are quite different depending upon whether she spoke to an age-peer or a younger woman. Whereas her peer-conversation was marked by levity, differentiation from a relatively passive and dependent identity and 'a light-hearted perspective on life', cross-generational speech focused on decrement, an effect that was cumulative across interactions.

PSD and age-telling would seem to mark out communication between younger people and elders. Whilst PSDs allow elders some control over the content of conversation and disclosure of age may ease ritualized interaction, it is unclear whether either would lead to deepened understanding across generations. Rather, they maintain common sense and the social mask. They make exchanges predictable. It must be remembered, here, that evidence has arisen from studies of 'initial encounters' and although it is hard to say whether it is typical for sustained interaction, these strategies may influence identity formation and expectations for future encounters.

Most of the research outlined above concentrated primarily on the responses of younger participants in cross-generational communication. Evidence on how older people view these encounters is more sparse. In this context an existential position would emphasize the degree to which overlap exists between projects and the negative effects of culture. Jungians draw our attention to a need to pass on experience, plus balance between acceptable and unacceptable parts of the Self in the service of enhanced self-esteem. The previous section has shown that although younger people may be willing to engage with elders, there is no guarantee that genuine listening and mutual respect will result. Communication can easily become ritualized and unrewarding, causing both parties to show a different face in peer and intergenerational contexts. Avoidance of potentially conflictual areas, coupled with a tendency to reinforce perceptions of the other as a 'type', mean that the possibility of sharing projects and engaging in reciprocal exchange is reduced, allowing shadow sides of the personality to come into play.

JOHN RYLANDS
UNIVERSITY
LIBRARY

ELDERS' COMMUNICATION AS PROJECTS

It would be surprising if elders' views of relative youth were not coloured by this stony ground. However, the investigator is presented with certain difficulties here in addition to the limited interest shown by researchers to date. Firstly, the tacit dominance of any one party, as reinforced by social norms, ascribed status and physical potency, will influence how an encounter is defined and how participants manage the impression they try to create. If differences between in- and out-groups become emphasized, then perceived similarities within and differences between groups, such as those characterized by age, will be enhanced (McGarty and Penny, 1988; Tajfel, 1969). Turner (1991: 156–7) takes this analysis one step further. According to his self-categorization theory:

> As social identity becomes salient, individual self-perception be-
> comes depersonalised, i.e. people tend to perceive themselves more
> in terms of the shared stereotypes that define their social category
> membership and less in terms of their personal differences and
> individuality.

So, when age becomes a dominant aspect of interaction, it is increasingly likely that superficial expectations are exchanged. A second complicating factor is the evident irritation and anger that some researchers have seen expressed by older people in intergenerational conversation (Giles, 1991; Nussbaum *et al.*, 1989). An interesting insight into the frustration that can result from younger people's inability or unwillingness to take up the accrued experience of age comes from Tom Main's (1990) discussion of difficulties encountered when he, as a senior practitioner at the Cassel therapeutic community, attempted to pass on knowledge to the next generation of staff. He argued that the acquisition of knowledge from one generation to another was inhibited in three areas: (i) difficulty in understanding content; (ii) that ideas themselves become 'internal objects' with a life of their own in the learner's psyche; and (iii) that knowledge without experience is 'swallowed whole' and applied by formula rather than being used judiciously. From Main's (1990: 59) point of view, new knowledge should be valued, 'Not only because it gives the ego a tool for dealing with immediate reality but also because it gives hope – promise of future usefulness as an aid to mastering later situations.'

However, it soon became clear that new knowledge, or rather transmitted knowledge, engaged strong feelings as well as the intellect. Trainees began to take up positions with regard to the ideas that they internalized. Curiosity, distaste, guilt, or liking, became as great an influence as its truth or usefulness. Also, senior staff showed less willingness to allow time for experiment and mistake in the next generation than they had needed to grasp the concepts themselves. So, 'What had begun as a free ego-choice had grown into a fixed discipline' (Main, 1990: 64), and:

Anger of the old at the ingratitude of the young will lead to increasing forcefulness and the moral use of the idea resulting in the danger of helpless introjection and idealisation on the one hand or rejection and denigration on the other. (Main, 1990: 72)

Main concludes that knowledge can itself take up residence in different parts of the psyche depending upon its generational source, and be responded to differently between generations. This is an important insight because it goes beyond arguments about the relative obsolescence of 'old' material and indicates that the source itself affects how and whether experience will be accepted.

In assessing the value of these observations it should be noted that Main was senior physician in a workplace where a medical hierarchy prevailed, and power relations would be quite different to those between a retired elder and a younger worker. However, even in these favourable circumstances, the intergenerational transmission of experience was fraught with difficulty.

de Beauvoir (1970) notes that relations between adults, from early mid-life through to older age are marked by ambivalence and to a certain extent competition for the same space in the social hierarchy:

The characteristic mark of the adult's attitude to the old is its duplicity. Up to a certain point the adult bows to the official ethic of respect for the aged . . . but it is in the adult's interest to treat the aged man as an inferior being and to convince him of his decline. (de Beauvoir, 1970: 245)

An elder may slowly be displaced by a process of obviating any mistakes and blunders that are made and attributing these personally, rather than to situational causes. This wish to replace the older adult is often mirrored by fear of devaluation and erosion of independence and respect (Hess, 1987). Relations between older and younger adults are complicated if both parties are at different stages in resolving the contradictions of mid-life. An unconscious fantasy operating here (Jaques, 1965) includes a fear of personal fragmentation as existing priorities are questioned, giving rise to heightened sensitivity to persecution and existential doubt. Before resolution creates a new set of priorities, conflict can provoke increased rigidity in dealing with others as part of an attempt to shore up existing verities perceived to be under threat.

Ezquerro (1989) has analysed the processes at work in group psychotherapy for 55- and 67-year-olds, where power relations were quite different to those described by Main. Barriers to intergenerational communication were equally apparent, 'As it became clear that I was significantly younger than them, I was perceived as a threat: most of them were facing retirement or displacement by younger people.' (Ezquerro, 1989: 301).

The group was marked by two dominant phenomena, firstly a struggle for control and then mutual support and cohesiveness between participants. As participants increasingly became cotherapists for each other, to the relative exclusion of the therapist, they began to '. . . work through feelings of sameness, which had started from the appreciation of the similarities in their ages, and to see more clearly their individual identities.' (Ezquerro, 1989: 303).

A number of points are of interest here, the evident intergenerational antagonism arising from elders themselves and a seeming need to exclude the younger worker before the work of moving toward age-peer support and identity begins. Although the context of this study is specialized, group psychotherapy is a tool designed to examine the complexity of human relations, and may have implications for other forms of social behaviour. It should be noted that the ages of participants would place them amongst the 'young-old', whom previous studies have identified as having similar communication styles to younger people, perhaps a consequence of identification with middle-age. Both Main's and Ezquerro's observations may indicate that this is a period particularly prone to the frustrations of generational misunderstanding and issues of power. The rogueish behaviour of Coupland *et al.*'s (1991) octogenarians, might then be seen as a response to repeated negative experience based on age-difference emboldened by the perception of new and different priorities.

Additional evidence of elder's attitudes to intergenerational communication arises from the British Gas survey (1991). Elders were asked whether they thought older people were given enough respect. Over half (59 per cent) felt that they were not respected enough. Interestingly, the same survey showed that 12 per cent of younger people reported this as a problem, more so than elders themselves (7 per cent). As the question was asked amongst a number of other 'problems' of older-age it is possible that although elders view it as a problem, it is not a particularly pressing one if new priorities were at hand. (One is also tempted to surmise that almost any group, including doctors, social workers and even university lecturers would agree that their group was not accorded due respect.)

A number of studies have indicated that elders prefer age-peer company, because it is reciprocal (Ingesol and Antonucci, 1988), marked by choice and positive feedback (Lee and Shehan, 1989) and more satisfying (Chappell, 1983). Unruh (1983) notes the need for extensive shared pasts as a determinant of comparable levels of commitment and willingness to engage in long-term planning amongst the aged. He itemizes a number of stances that might be taken depending upon the degree of such embeddedness. Interaction with strangers may be superficial and detached, depending upon contextual cues rather than seeing the other as an individual. 'Tourists' enter in search of certain kinds of experience and are transient. Regulars are integrated but do not have the same status as 'insiders' with whom one can be intimate through shared identity. This is reminiscent of Goffman's (1963) work on stigmatized groups. Here only two groups could be trusted: 'the own', those with similar experiences to oneself and 'the wise', who are capable of making a limited creative leap into the experience of marginalization and can be thought of as allies. The latter '. . . are ready to adopt his standpoint in the world and share with him the feeling that he is human and "essentially" normal in spite of appearances and in spite of his own doubts' (Goffman, 1963: 31).

Assuming that Goffman would include women in this equation, and accepting criticisms made of 'stigma' as a concept (Oliver, 1990), the distinction is helpful in making sense of the caution evident in elders' reactions to intergenerational encounters. Matthew's (1979) study found that, to maintain a positive view of themselves, older women managed information given to younger people, trying simultaneously to protect their real selves and adopt an age-free persona. Again, she found evidence that 'the old woman has one definition for other old people and one for herself', indicating that even amongst peers self-protection is at a premium.

As has been shown, there is no guarantee that either age-group will embrace contact in the spirit of 'I–Thou' or 'I–You' (see Chapter 1), required for genuine understanding. The cards are stacked in favour of age-stereotyping, in-group enhancement and opportunities for unconscious manipulation. If elders are looking for 'the wise' they may have a long wait in store. Little surprise then that peers are preferred and others may have to prove themselves.

CONCLUSIONS

It would seem that questions of power and group identity are never far away from intergenerational communication, primarily in the public sphere, where relative strangers can be said to meet along continua of formality and contrived circumstances. This can result in ritualized behaviour of a superficial and predictable nature, which whilst it protects both parties, does little to humanize interpersonal perception. Common sense is kept intact through the use of social masks, a strategy itself characteristic of the first half of life. For younger people, implicitly characterized as the productive and valuable part of society, contact with elders is seen as a duty with little, at root, of value. Elders emerge as active strategists in the communication game. However, older people's frustration and resentment may spill over into competition and exclusion as experience accumulates. Much of this negative reaction may be a result of an unwillingness by youth to receive the wisdom of a lifetime's experience, thus invalidating the basis for intergenerational exchange from an elder's point of view. Older people are then left with the choice of relating to age-peers who 'know', or of maintaining a middle-aged identity for as long as is credible. If the latter path is chosen, social validation is bought at a price because this form of interaction relies on the adoption of the projects of a younger chronological age, with the accompanying difficulty of suppressing increasing parts of the Self in the shadow. Intergenerational communication can then become a limiting factor, as the transmitter of stereotyping into the personal arena. Some age-related projects would be more easily addressed through peer interaction, without the complications that intergenerational contact brings with it. Either way, the psychological need to individuate and assess one's lived experience in recognition of limited time left, may not find expression as a natural part of intergenerational communication, at least, not in present historical circumstances.

This is a bleak scenario, made more so because the mutual suspicion of age cohorts can so easily create a spiral of rejection and misunderstanding which, as younger people do not have much empathic experience to draw upon, is unlikely to spontaneously provoke the creative leap from outsider to the 'wise'. It may also be an unwelcome conclusion for many who study and work with older people and perhaps it is not accidental that many studies focus on relative youth and old age. Contact between consecutive age cohorts has rarely been addressed simply in terms of communication, tending to arise as reflections of work or family roles. These issues will be adressed in Chapters 7 and 8. Chapter 6 explores influences on the power that elders can express.

6

Power and oppression

INTRODUCTION

Theoretical and research evidence from previous chapters would suggest that although individuals attempt to shape their own destiny, they do not do so in circumstances of their own choosing. In some cases these constraints arise from facts about the human condition, just as ageing is limited by the effects of time on bodily functioning. However, such attributes are also signifiers of group identity, and are subject to evaluation by others. As power is not distributed equally in society, group identity, ascribed and achieved, will effect the likelihood of its members having access to resources that enhance their chances of living a satisfactory existence. These structurally created opportunities and limitations give rise to ideologies that both reflect the circumstances of social beings and contribute to the same patterns being reproduced. Dominant groups will contribute to dominant ideologies that both conspire to maintain their position at the top and convince anybody else that this state of affairs is both just and desirable. If this view achieves hegemony (Gramsci, 1971), the ultimate aim of the group whose interests it serves, then it becomes extremely difficult for competing definitions of social reality to find a voice other than within terms of reference that are already structured in the interests of that dominant group. In these circumstances, projects do not depend solely on the wishes of existential actors, as the ground upon which they act has already been organized in ways that may not reflect their interests. Dominance may express itself through age, disability, race, gender and class, or combinations of these in any one circumstance.

A second way in which dominant definitions survive relies on the amplification of differences between groups, either self-identified or categorized from outside, that are seen as a threat to the group with power. To some extent this process occurs in intergenerational communication, as evidenced in Chapter 5. Difference can both foster competition, particularly when resources allowed are scarce, and obscure the common creation of meaning across group boundaries. For those who have already identified with the dominant ideology, whether or not it is in their material interests to do so, the marginal position of other groups becomes a defining characteristic of their members. In this way, material marginality from the resources to achieve projects becomes reinforced by socially ascribed marginality, whereby requirements are given less value and priority, a state of affairs reflected in social institutions and personal behaviour. If members of marginalized groups are not actively conscious of their ascribed identities, then they will increasingly internalize these negative characteristics to the detriment of other potential selves (Freire, 1972; Leonard, 1984).

COMPETING DEFINITIONS

One result of the promotion of structural inequality in this way is that the active subject experiences tension between competing definitions of Self. This tension will be felt throughout the personality and will affect parts that are allowed to develop and those that are suppressed. However, even if the unacceptable is banished to the unconscious, there is no guarantee that it will obediently stay there, as such a warped presentation to the outside world will create its own psychic imbalance requiring resolution. Temporary solutions can be found in such primitive mechanisms as projection or denial. If social inequality is structured so that actors are encouraged to identify with one ideology and reject others, and that formation identifies marginal groups characterized as different, actors who to some degree rely on the status quo for their material and social well-being are provided with a ready target on which to train those parts of themselves that are rendered unacceptable by that same process of identification. The marginalized may either be disliked, as they seem to contain the very qualities that have been labelled unacceptable, be envied, because they seem to indulge in behaviour forbidden to 'normal' citizens, or simply have their needs ignored as irrelevant to the greater good of which the actors assume themselves to be a part. In the case of elders, this may include the attributed qualities of weakness or unattractiveness, increased leisure time without the responsibility of raising a family or working life and an assumed lack of productivity. To engage in dialogue from outside such a system would require the adoption of a diminished persona to complement the common-sense currency used by insiders. Where contact is sustained and unavoidable a more radical denial of one's own personal requirements might result as, little by little, the ego itself pushes other parts into the shadow. Once such a stage is reached it is relatively easy for a cycle of mutually disconfirming communication to become established, a dance to an alien tune that diminishes both partners.

It has been argued that the relationship between continuity and difference takes a particular form in older age. We have seen that actors value a sense of continuing identity, whilst at the same time increasingly coming to terms with identity change due to experience and to different priorities. Those who desperately hang on to earlier priorities, particularly those commercially identified with middle-age, may do so at the expense of adaptation to current circumstances. Earlier life phases are themselves structured into cohorts that largely accrue status depending upon the perceived potential for productivity and consumption. Elders become marginal as a result of lowered income and retirement. Similarly, one's rewardingness as a social partner has also been affected deleteriously by changed age status, even though needs to pass on and validate one's lived experience may continue undiminished.

AGEISM

The particular form of oppression arising from the social construction of older age has been called Ageism. First coined by Butler (1963), the concept increased in popularity with the growth of such social movements as the Grey Panthers in the US (Kuhn, 1977) and reflects its geneology as part of an impetus for civil rights, now recognized as a distinctive feature of the late 1960s. Ageism is defined, says Butler (1987: 22):

As a process of systematic stereotyping and discrimination against people because they are old, just as racism and sexism accomplish this for skin colour and gender ... Ageism allows the younger generation to see older people as different from themselves: thus, they suddenly cease to identify with their elders as human beings and thereby reduce their own fear and dread of ageing ... At times ageism becomes an expedient method by which society promotes viewpoints about the aged in order to relieve itself from responsibility toward them.

Butler's definition has certain qualities that help understand subsequent debates. It sees the issue as one of power imbalance between younger and disenfranchised older people and is not concerned with the question of 'adultism' (Itzin, 1986), which would include the oppression of children. Ageism is also closely linked to other oppressions, although the nature of that link is unclear. Elders are also placed in a passive relationship to social policy, whilst it is assumed that relations are marked by some form of dependency.

Ageism is now established, amongst gerontologists at least, as a starting point for nearly all investigations of older age and has given rise to a number of interpretations (Bytheway and Johnson, 1990; Biggs, 1992). In the UK context, much of this work has its roots in analysing structural inequality evoked by retirement (Laczko and Phillipson, 1991) and the unequal distribution of resources based on age (Townsend, 1986; Walker, 1986), which contribute to an artificially constructed dependency by older people on the state. Wilson (1991) has shown that the models used by policy-makers are indeed based on assumptions that bear little relationship to the lives of elders, reflecting a common Western European view that old age is a time of inevitable and increasing dependence. Evidence for such an assumption is widespread, as illustrated by this example from *Social trends* (HMSO, 1988):

> Although the size of the dependent population in 2025 will not be much higher than it was in 1971, its composition will be different in that there will be far less children and many more eldery people, so reducing demand for education but increasing the burden on health services.

One age's demand, it seems, is another's burdensomeness. Material deprivation and an enforced marginality from wealth production have been proposed as unifying factors in understanding the circumstances of elders (Phillipson, 1982) and the basis of all oppression (Leonard, 1984). However, these interpretations are increasingly open to criticism insofar as global explanations tend to blind the reader to the particular positions of distinctive oppressed groups, subsuming them within a class definition of society.

Attempts have also been made to show ageism's equivalence to other, more salient oppressions (Levin and Levin, 1980; Butler, 1987), although the value of these studies has been disputed (Hopkins, 1980) as this approach can diminish qualitative aspects of oppression. It has been suggested, as a means of relating inequalities based on gender, race and age, that the effects are additive. Thus Dowd and Bengtson (1978) refer to the 'double jeopardy' experienced by black elders, whilst Norman (1985) has called her book on the subject 'Triple jeopardy: growing old in a second homeland'. Unfortunately, debates between the champions of oppressed groups has tended to centre on the relative primacy of one oppression over another. Several writers have shown that older age is a significant contributing factor to the experience of oppression for women (Finch and Groves, 1985; LeRiche and Rowlings, 1990), black people (Patel, 1990; Ahmad-Aziz *et al.*, 1992), disabled people (Zarb, 1992) and lesbians (Macdonald and Rich, 1984). The existence of prejudice within groups has also been noted:

It is facile to suppose that (older people) might associate with one social group to the exclusion of others, that their deprivation is due to one characteristic rather than to a complex number of circumstances and that they are untouched, for example, by the ageism within the women's movement, the sexism within black organisations and the racism within pensioner organisations. (Bytheway and Johnson, 1990: 6)

A third stream of thought has questioned the validity of ageism as a concept at all. Kogan (1979) indicates that literature on ageism is fraught with problems of definition and methodology. Rarely do writers distinguish between beliefs, which change when accurate information becomes available, and attitudes, which include predispositions to accept or reject information depending on its source or content. Attitudes therefore include an emotional component that beliefs lack. Kogan also examined a number of studies to show that choice of experimental design can determine whether ageism is found. Between subject designs, where separate groups of subjects are assigned to different conditions (for example one group may be asked to rate younger and another older people), prejudice is negligible. Within subject designs, however, where age is a more salient feature because the same subjects are asked to make comparisons between youth and age, produce evidence of ageism. Schonfield (1982) laments the fact that, because so many studies rely on attitude data, it is hard to judge whether ageism is reflected in actual behaviour. When he reexamined McKenzie's (1980) 'ten myth-stereotype statements' outlining inaccurate generalizations about old-age by asking respondents to state opinions on exceptions, the ageist responding evaporated. Schonfield (1982: 269) explained this by noting that:

In everyday conversation, someone might say, 'Men suffer from gout', implying that gout occurs more frequently among men than women but not implying that all or most men have this complaint.

He infers that similar confusions extend to gerontologists themselves, who may have been looking for proof of ageism, rather than testing whether it exists, thus rendering many findings tautologous.

Unfortunately, these criticisms seem to have been ignored by mainstream gerontology, although this is not to say that counter arguments do not exist. Firstly, as Kogan and Schonfield themselves note, their critique refers to attitude studies, which do not extend to behaviour. It is quite possible that, rather than confirm their position, behaviour of younger adults really does exhibit prejudice on the basis of age, as evidenced by Giles and Coupland's (1991a) research on communication style. Secondly, neither of them looked at the self-reported experience of elders, although, as the British Gas survey (1991) showed, direct response to this question is ambiguous. Evidence on self-perception is complicated by the fact that few elders would categorize themselves as older than middle-aged and are more likely to attribute negative behaviour to peers than see it in themselves. Finally, the experimental paradigm used by both investigators tends to treat structural inequality as unproblematic, except when used as an experimental variable. None of the studies being criticized (see Kogan, 1979) distinguished between oppressed groups or socio-economic stati, thus treating elders as a homogeneous group and possibly obscuring such differences.

Three aspects of oppression are brought into sharper profile by the position explored in this book. Firstly, how socially constructed disadvantage places restrictions on projects that give both meaning and provoke action, and whether these restrictions vary between oppressed groups. Secondly, how perceptions of stereotyped groups lead to positions being taken by others that treat members as of secondary importance. Finally, how these processes affect the intrapsychic worlds of members of both dominant and oppressed groups, which can lead to feelings of contempt, envy and competition between the two.

As the effects of age are reflected throughout the book, this chapter will look more closely at the experience of women, black and working class people in older age. Particular emphasis will be given to the role of services as the position of elders as non wage earners throws them into a specific set of social relations with the state.

The economics of age

Disposable income is perhaps the most potent determinant of resources to engage in meaningful projects.

Schonfield (1982) points out, as part of his critique of ageism, that society has specifically put resources aside for elders in the form of state pensions, an altruistic act by the present productive population that belies the accusation that US society is inherently ageist. Barry (1985) has argued from the perspective of the British 'new right' that the working population bears no duty toward the welfare of past workers, if pensions are viewed a part of the current economy, and that provision for one's own old age is a personal responsibility. Given that most industrial Western societies do provide support for their aged populations, is this an indication that recognition is made of the needs of older people and that restrictions on projects are ameliorated?

Critics of pensions policy, most notably Phillipson (1982), point out that such provision is conditional. He argues that patterns of retirement vary with need for productive labour. In the 1950s and 1960s, when there were too few workers and immigration from the predominantly black commonwealth was encouraged, early retirement was rare. However, as younger people came of working age as part of the postwar 'baby-boom', older workers were squeezed out of the workforce. Although this increased the numbers of pension claimants, their lower productive value, affected by the speed of working conditions, the pace of new technology, and concern at the political consequences of youthful, able-bodied unemployment, more than compensated for any increased expense. Immigration also became restricted by a number of acts of parliament as a response to these trends. Phillipson (1991a) also shows that, historically, the provision of pensions owed more to pressure from below, than from the largesse of the state.

In periods of reduced economic growth, dominant groups show no compunction in pitting one group of claimants against another. In the US, Minkler and Robertson (1991: 1) report that reduced welfare spending has fostered a social policy debate on 'age-race wars' as:

> Attempts to frame problem analysis and policy deliberations within such an ideological framework are seen to be based on spurious assumptions concerning the relative financial well-being of the old, the role of elderly entitlements as a cause of poverty in minority children, and growing resentment of programmes for the old among minorities and youth.

Phillipson (1991a) notes a similar debate in Britain about generational conflict over welfare resources. Thus Johnson *et al.* (1989), characterize current and future cohorts of elders as a 'selfish welfare generation' who, having grown up in the welfare state, see it as their right to demand support from family and society. These observations would lend structural weight to difficulties noted previously in self-perception and intergenerational communication.

How, then, are elders placed economically within society? The British Gas survey (1991: 16) notes that:

> The gamut from extreme poverty to extreme affluence among retired people has never been so wide . . . Of the sample examined, 33 per cent were from households with an annual income of less than £4,500, Black respondents included 41 per cent of this category – marginally rather more than the norm.

The survey also showed that 45 per cent of respondents reported financial difficulty, with the exception of Asian respondents, who reported 25 per cent. The Department of Health's Family Expenditure survey (1988), shows a ratio of 30:70 over 65-year-olds below an income of £200 per week. Gallup's (1988) survey noted a substantial number of elders wished for some form of employment to reduce financial hardship. A number of studies (Leonard, 1984; Townsend, 1986; Laczko and Phillipson, 1991) report that fear of poverty is inextricably associated with old age for the majority of the population. It can be inferred that for a large number of older people scarce resources are an important determinant of choice. Their marginal position regarding wealth creation may also increase rivalry with other age groups.

SOCIAL CLASS

Different sections of the population experience different forms of financial restriction in older age, stemming from their collective histories. Members of the working class, particularly manual workers, rarely have access to occupational pensions to supplement state provision. Many occupational pensions also pay proportionally to previously earned income, thus extending financial inequality into retirement. Periods of unemployment, together with less disposable income restrict opportunities for saving in anticipation of older age.

A history of migration and settlement, plus the status of 'replacement labour' increases the difficulties facing black elders (Patel, 1990), most of whom are working class. The 'migrant' cohort of elders experienced physically demanding work rejected by the existing population, resulting in more unemployment in times of scarcity, plus greater disability over time, whilst reducing the length of national insurance contributions that determine entitlement. Furthermore, elders, predominantly women who came to Britain as 'dependents' to join their families, are not entitled to income benefit. It is unsurprising, then, that a Breadline survey in Greenwich, South London (1985) showed that 50 per cent of black elders, as compared to 15 per cent of whites interviewed, had insufficient money for day-to-day living; whilst one in four black elders in Leicester (Farrah, 1986) said they had difficulty in affording food.

Women, many of whom are now in their 80s and 90s, rarely worked once they married and thus depend upon the pension earned by their partner. A second disadvantage facing women who worked, now entering retirement, arises from reduced contributions to national insurance occasioned by periods spent in family care rather than at work. (Trades Union Congress, 1983; Finch and Groves, 1985).

Ability to use retirement, it has been argued (Seve, 1977; Leonard, 1984), also depends on the nature of previous working life. If work left little room for personal development, the older person would have few psychological and social resources to draw on later. For others, where working life allowed some form of self-development, retirement can come as a liberation and an opportunity to pick up on potential that was previously denied (Laczko and Phillipson, 1991). However, it is unclear how individual responses interact with these class-based possibilities. Victor and Evandrou (1986) indicate that social class affects income, health and the use of both statutory and informal caring networks negatively, as measured by the General Household Survey (HMSO, 1980). It is thus an important influence on quality of life in old age. However, Lalive d'Epinay (1986) reports from his Swiss study that working class elders, were more optimistic and less prone to nostalgia than those from an upper class background, indicating that perceptions of well-being may depend upon longtitudinal comparisons, as well as cross-sectional ones.

It would seem that at this most fundamental level, resources available for the completion of projects affect qualitative differences in oppression. If in no other way, the time and intellectual energy that survival on limited resources takes up would be expected to reduce opportunities for existential action and individuation.

However, the nature of projects does not rely solely on material resources. The way in which resources are made available and the differing experience of oppressed groups also affect the form that projects take and relations that emerge.

The degree to which discourse limits possibilities for self-fulfilment is particularly apparent when elders encounter the state. Mitchell *et al.* (1980) argue that, as a result of the capitalist state's ambivalence to welfare, resources are often made available in ways that are difficult to use and define users in ways that do not reflect their own understanding of their life-circumstances. 'All these things leave us wondering: if the state is not providing these services in the way we want them, it cannot really be doing it for us.' (Mitchell *et al.*, 1980: 9) and 'Although we are told that the welfare state exists to help us with our problems, it seems to be more concerned with the problem we are for the capitalist system.' (Mitchell *et al.*, 1980: 48).

It has already been noted that elders are often perceived as a homogeneous group for these purposes. Mitchell *et al.* analyse the structure of welfare to show that, to add to this contradiction, services respond on the basis of individualized need, which tends to obscure collective identity and reject collective responses. However, as the system seems to work for some individuals, some of the time, users are often hooked into a spiral of expectation and frustration.

BLACK ELDERS

Black elders face a number of additional problems, which restrict the projects of older age. It has been argued by a number of writers (Glendenning and Pearson, 1988; Patel, 1990; Sivanandan, 1991) that the 'common sense' of service provision is essentially 'white' and may not be accessible to minority groups. Attempts to use services, therefore, either require accommodation – the construction of a persona that conforms to perceptions dominant in that context – or run the risk of additional marginalization. Patel (1990: 42) identifies two features of a process she calls internal colonialism that distance provision and users:

> The economic and social conditions of black people (and for that matter the white unemployed, the working class) can be explained away by 'blaming the victim'. The focus of such arguments then shifts from individual pathology to family deficiency to cultural defects.

In addition to blame, black communities are paradoxically stereotyped as 'looking after their own'. This formulation compounds the fact that ethnic communities have often been forced to develop voluntary services themselves, with the implication that deficiences in that system are therefore their fault.

The myth of looking after one's own goes further than simply indicating a structural unwillingness to change eurocentric services. It interacts with liberal white fears of being labelled 'racist' by focusing the debate on the identification of difference. Hall (1991) has noted that a continuing feature of racism has been the need to eliminate different groups that may potentially occupy the same space, either material or psychological, that the in-group currently holds. An apparent contradiction between the liberal view that all people should be treated as individuals and structural racism has been explained in the following way:

> By denying, on a personal level, the hatred of those who are different, it becomes necessary for this primitive unconscious reaction to find expression elsewhere. Society provides that other place in institutional practices. (Davids and Davison, 1988: 49)

It therefore becomes 'the system' that is at fault and too great a psychological proximity to it pollutes the liberal ego. The stage is set for a number of interpersonal games that use difference to justify inaction. Kinnon (1988: 87) observed the following, when an Asian woman suffering from bereavement and isolation failed to receive appropriate services:

> All my attempts to initiate a reappraisal of need met with total failure. Each worker, in different ways, moved to Eric Berne's 'Yes, But' game, which he sees as most commonly played out when individuals or systems wish to avoid responsibility. Interestingly, their interactions also incorporated his 'See What You Made Me Do' game. Each worker kept insisting that the 'You' was the 'racist society', the 'racist institutions', 'other people who are racist', and within this context they themselves were playing out the 'Good Games'.

The community worker involved found herself being trapped in the role of 'specialist worker with Asian families', whose job it was to sort the problem out while other workers seemed paralysed. Looking after one's own, it seems, extends inside institutions as well.

Difference, then, can be used to justify an avoidance of commonsensual change. This is not to say that real differences fail to emerge in the restriction of projects. Firstly, overt racism continues to exist. A survey of day services in Birmingham (Bhalla and Blakemore, 1981), found that black elders were subjected to racist abuse and experienced hostility from white elders. Patel (1990: 39), following a review of the literature concludes that:

Sufficient importance may not be attached to instances of racial abuse in a home or a centre because staff involved deem it as insignificant or because white elders cannot be expected to change their behaviour! Hence black elders must put up with racism or not use the service.

Here ageism, exemplified in the belief that elders cannot change, is used to reinforce racism.

Racism in these forms is clearly not restricted to old age. Indeed, both Patel and Sivanandan point out that, in addition to a lifetime's experience of combatting prejudice to draw on, many elders will have an understanding of independence and labour struggles from their countries of birth. However, there is a particular restriction on existential projects that arises from the experience of migration itself which can become acute in older age, namely a wish to return and the increasing realization that this is unlikely to happen (Norman, 1985; Fenton, 1987).

When Bhalla and Blakemore (1981) asked elders what they thought were the differences between treatment of older people in Britain and the West Indies:

A strong sense of loss pervades the replies ... the loss of close family and community ties and of respect for the older person. Whether the characterisation of life in the West Indies was true at the time these people left, or is true today, is less important than the belief that it is so. The replies also carried a strong indication that the community spirit of the West Indies could not be recreated in this country. (from Norman, 1985: 26)

This factor can be expected to influence both an assessment of currently held projects and attempts to create a positive life review. If one's basic wish is to return, to something that may no longer exist except as a symbolic point of reference, and circumstances restrict the possibility of checking this out, a state of existential paralysis might be expected to result. If one finds oneself trapped in a different country, which itself in retrospect offered a promise it had no intention to fulfil, the situation begins to approximate that explained by Stokols (1975) as the psychological correlate of alienation. Escape cannot be made from a situation suffused by a thwarting of deeply held wishes. Unfortunately, there is virtually no evidence of the views of black people born in the UK, a reflection of the very few studies focusing on views held by black elders in general.

WOMEN

There is a conventional view of women's experience in older age, which is based upon continuity. This is partly seen as a consequence of a relative lack of disruption to traditional sex-role relationships caused by retirement and consequent exclusion from the workplace as a source of self-esteem:

> Generally speaking the elderly woman adapts herself to her stage better than her husband. She is the person who runs the home, and in this her position is the same as that of the peasants and craftsmen of former times – for her, too, life and work merge into one another. No decree from without suddenly cuts her activity short. (de Beauvoir, 1972: 261)

Similarly, Greer (1991: 10), talking about a different cohort of women, indicated bodily continuity during later life. She comments that:

> Women themselves had a better name for the period of the gradual cessation of the menses. They called it the 'dodging time'; they had no name for the time thereafter because it was generally agreed to be a time of 'settled health', much easier to manage than the dangers of repeated childbirth and the rigours of menstruation.

A focus on continuity can also be found in developmental theories of relations between women, most notably between mothers and daughters. Woodward (1991), following Bernstein (1979) in the US (and paralleling Eichenbaum and Orbach's (1982) thought in the UK), develops a theory of generational identity extending into older life. Because the mother's experience of her infant daughter is based on sameness, the process of differentiation, in the sense of establishing clear boundaries between one and other, is thought to be more difficult than with a male child. One consequence is that the little girl's development is more likely to be centred on a triangle of mother–daughter–baby, than on the gender-based and oedipal triangle of mother–child–father. Difference and aggressive impulses are replaced by similarity and caring as the basis for generational identity:

If generational identity is established in little girls before gender identity as sexual difference . . . and if little girls experience sameness or similarity in the mirroring relation to the mother, then we can see how generational continuity – the identity of generations over time – stems from generational identity. (Woodward, 1991: 99)

As the daughter grows up, the mother sees her own body reflected back to her, whilst as they both grow older, age shortens the distance between them and the daughter begins to see herself in the mother. In middle-age, Woodward proposes, 'The blurring of generations is at its most intense. The mother and daughter become intimate, peers, each other. Their interdependence is represented as truly reciprocal.' (Woodward, 1991: 100).

Woodward draws her examples from literature and does not explore development in the absence of younger siblings; yet, it would seem from these observations that women's ageing identity is closely linked to similarity, caring and continuity and, it must be added, ambivalence around those themes.

Arguments for continuity in women's older age have not gone unquestioned. Both Sontag (1977) and Hamner and Statham (1988) point out that because women are valued as youthful and attractive commodities, older age provokes a challenge as this diminishes as a source of self-esteem. Phillipson (1982) takes issue with the view that women are relatively unaffected by formal working life, pointing to the large numbers of women in poorer paid, less skilled and auxiliary occupations. Much of this work fails to provide an adequate income in retirement, reducing opportunities for leisure and independence. Even so, semi-skilled women workers have been found to be more resistant to retirement than men, as they gave greater priority to social ties formed within the workplace.

A partner's retirement may place intolerable strain upon established gendered roles within the family, leading the woman to cease work too. If both partners are at home, existing routines and responsibilities may come under threat. In most relationships partners need periods of intimacy, which they know will not become too obtrusive, plus periods of autonomy, which are not too tenuous that the partner ceases to be available when needed. In some cases, as both are suddenly thrown together, 'Husbands, feeling robbed of their jobs . . . appeared to go on and rob their wives of their role in the home' (Ruszczynski, 1991: 27). Alternatively, the husband became a shadow of his former self, getting in the way of his partner.

Finally, because women generally live longer than men, heterosexual female partners are also more likely to experience loss and isolation where relationships with partners had been good. The problems that arise through living alone would be reinforced by both physical disability and economic factors.

Intimations of intergenerational continuity do not correspond with the experience of at least two older women (Long, 1979: 16):

> Women often resent me and criticise me, or worse, avoid me, because I am of their mother's generation. A writer's evening . . . devoted a sizable portion of its content to relationships between mothers and daughters. In every case, the mother was at fault.

> Don't talk about your grandmother as the bearer of your culture – don't objectify her. Don't make her a museum piece or a woman whose value is that she has sacrificed and continues to sacrifice on your behalf. Tell us who she is now, a woman in process. Better yet, encourage her to tell us. (Macdonald and Rich, 1984: 75)

Macdonald, in an open letter to other feminists, rails against the way in which younger women have marginalized and invalidated their older sisters' experience and '. . . the ageism that continued to remain, undealt with, in the entire women's movement'. That a well known book on women and social work (Hamner and Statham, 1988), includes only one section on older women, and that that concerns the 'burden' of caring for an elderly relative, indicates that this tendency is alive and well over ten years since Macdonald wrote.

The role of carer seems to be a particular source of ambivalence for writers on the oppression of women. Hamner and Statham note that in addition to performing the bulk of caring, women are more likely than men to provide intimate personal care, care longer for adults with high levels of dependency and give up work to do so. Caring then becomes a new restriction on life when many women are looking forward to activity outside the home. This is especially true in middle age, as responsibility for caring for an elderly or handicapped relative increases with age reaching a peak around 50 years (Equal Opportunities Commission, 1980). However, a concentration on 'caring' has been criticized as reducing the cared for to the status of 'other'. As a disabled feminist, Keith (1991) is left feeling that 'Whilst it is the role of disability groups to argue for the rights of disabled people, feminists argue for the rights of carers'. The question with repect to elders is further confused by a relatively new study undertaken by Opportunities for Women (1991), which shows, contrary to established beliefs, that although there are more female than male carers (15 per cent as compared to 12 per cent of the total adult population), women have more access to respite care services. Further, of the most vulnerable carers, those aged over 75 years, are more likely to be men than women by a ratio of 5:3. Each of these observations raises the question of whether caring is a predominantly female domain in older age and whether the place of women as recipients of care has been seriously considered. The relationship between carers and practitioners is considered further in Chapter Eight.

The grandmother's role is often cited as a positive contribution and reward in older age (Elmhurst, 1990; Thompson, 1992). For de Beauvoir, grandmotherhood brings fresh possibilities and an antidote to 'total idleness'. Macdonald simply sees it as a continuation of gendered restrictions on self-development, which is at best 'a third-hand' identity, necessary in order to ward off active persecution. Caring for grandchildren, then, itself contains existential tension. Is it better to continue one's self-definition as carer, adopt different priorities to address personal individuation in the second half of life, or is grandmotherhood an adaptive response to changed circumstances? Unfortunately this debate seems hardly to have begun.

The debate on continuity in the experience of ageing women should not obscure positive potential for change with age. Release from work and family obligation, even through bereavement, can give rise to a new experience of freedom (Butler and Lewis, 1977). Greer (1991: 10) refers to the relative absence of sexual attention, which although bewildering to many heterosexual women, liberates the exploration of alternative identities:

> The idea that menopause is a tragedy has come from men, who cannot tolerate the loss of interest that menopausal women feel in their precious selves ... You will like yourself better than you have ever done before, but you may find that you like other people less. And you may be less afraid of telling them so than you used to be.

Greer's exhortation fits well with Guttman's (1988) and Schlossberg's (1984) findings that gendered behaviour becomes less stereotyped with age, and may even be reversed. It indicates how the tension between the imperatives of the first and second stages of life might constellate differently for women and men. Unfortunately, information and role-models on alternatives seem severely limited. As Jung has pointed out (see Jacobi, 1971) there are no schools for forty-year-olds, one has to learn as one goes along.

CONCLUSIONS

Whilst experience and aspirations in older age are radically affected by class, race and gender, oppression that relates to age seems to have one distinctive quality when compared with other forms. It is specifically focused on the passage of time and its effect upon the human condition.

Lived time is used to denote changes in ascribed roles, so that quite arbitrary categories are commonly used to place the social actor in relation to others. This characteristic has become institutionalized, and is used as a basis for self-identification between cohorts. Changes in status are influenced by each cohort's productive and reproductive value, whether this be reflected in the generation of economic surplus, or maturation as evidenced by the climacteric or menopause. As existential projects and potential for individuation also vary with accrued time, they are valued in so far as they conform to a common sense subordinate to the needs of younger more 'productive' groups. These are then used to place the other in terms of culture, ability, and interpersonal expectation. However, it is with ageing that the hegemony of other definitions of worth seems almost complete, rarely being given voice by the very group that it most effects.

An analysis of oppression in older age also exposes a common thread, which, influenced by race, gender and class experience, invalidates personal and collective meaning. Each marginalized group lives in the shadow of a dominant definition which maintains distortions between all parties. Forms of oppression are often internalized, to become what Friere (1970, 1972) has called the oppressor within. Victims have thus to struggle with their own thoughts and feelings, which have been socialized into accepting a negative self-definition. In terms of age this would include the maintenance of outmoded projects associated with earlier roles and requirements, the alternative being perceived as an acceptance of social worthlessness. Alternatively, recognizing oppression can provoke rage and retribution. A need to get someone else to feel the invalidation and injustice of one's position means that younger people in their turn may be excluded and denegrated. Neither strategy would free the victim of those same terms of reference that lead to oppression in the first place, as roles merely become reversed within an existing framework. At this level of analysis, the task would be to find a way of getting to a new identity, of disentangling the symbol from the real. For this to happen, opportunities that become available to humanize images, both for the self and the other, become central. As has been seen there are considerable obstacles to be overcome in order to both respect difference and recognize common interests. The rest of this book examines how far the contexts of care available to elders enhances or detracts from this possibility.

Section 3

Practice

7

Older people and practitioners

INTRODUCTION

There are certain differences between the everyday experience of older
people, who are generally not in work, and practitioners, such as doctors, nurses, social workers and home-helps. The older adult's time is
more likely to be structured by domestic and social routines, which may
seem relatively flexible when compared to the work discipline required
by employment. Priorities in older age focus on a maintenance of existing competence, such as mental and physical dexterity, social embeddedness and financial management, plus the maintenance of self-esteem as
these achievements begin to be eroded. This self-care extends to adopting new projects and priorities, which are better suited to the requirements of older age, finding a psychological parallel in reviewing lived
experience thus far and preparation for the imminence of death. Time is
not so much emptied of meaning, as it may seem to the casual observer
of another age, as a working through of vital issues in order to arrive at
a balance between continuity and change, which themselves slip in and
out of focus depending upon the immediate context that elders find
themselves in.

Although paid workers also have personal and social priorities, the
context in which they meet elders requiring services is primarily in the
public sphere of work. This brings with it a number of role-expectations,
which largely define the limits of valid discourse and acceptable behaviour independently of physical contexts, such as the office, institution or
home of a service user. Work itself is highly structured. Time is at a
premium in order to promote co-ordination with other workers, complete as much work as possible within the limits available, reduce
uncertainty and control the numerous demands that impinge on an
organization's day-to-day activities (Hassard, 1991). The worker's task
is thus to provide certain services in conformity with the common
sense of organizational, professional and legal requirements, a space

with varying degrees of opportunity for personal style, values and fulfilment to find expression within it.

Health and welfare services are also the gatekeepers for resources that elders need, which would influence the distribution of power whenever these parties meet. Although the worker may be perceived as being in control of needed resources, their daily experience may be quite different. The imperative to juggle with competing priorities, co-ordinate limited resources and manage a variety of personal and organizational boundaries conspire to construct a continual present in which other parts of one's life become excluded and may even be perceived as disruptive to effective task-performance.

This snapshot of the differing worlds of elders and professional helpers already gives some insight into priorities that would not overlap and require resolution. Much of the professional's time reflects a particular institutional common sense with its own limits and criteria for legitimacy, which will effect the sorts of projects that can take shape. Professions inevitably specialize, the nature of which will influence the rewards, pressures and protective defences available to them. Elders will be aware of some of these priorities, indeed, why visit the surgery, office, centre or clinic, if not to access certain services? They may be unfamiliar with the common-sense world that has to be entered at the same time.

The position explored in this book would point toward certain lines of inquiry. Firstly, can the projects of older age find a legitimate voice within the common-sense worlds inhabited by professional helpers? Of particular interest would be the degree to which differences between the priorities of the first and second halves of life can be recognized and elaborated. Secondly, how does the structuring of power relations in this public sphere influence the value attributed to these projects? Here, the way parties protect themselves via personal and institutional defences would determine those parts that are rejected and thus reside in the shadow of the psyche. Thirdly, what form does the context of created meaning take, what images are evoked and can these be made human?

Relations that emerge would reflect perceptions of ageing, rules of intergenerational communication and experienced oppression outlined in preceding chapters. However, precise forms would be influenced as they pass through the lens applied by any one professional common sense.

PRACTICE, BUREAUCRACY AND PROJECTS

It has been hypothesized that the structural role of bureaucracies is to integrate competing interests into the state, whilst at the same time creating a buffer between the Government and these interests (Palmer, 1985). Traditionally, public servants have been delegated power and resources legitimized by their technical competence in a particular area, which has a tendency to drain practice of power issues (Migliano and Misceraca, 1982). Each group also forms an understanding with interests who use their services, thus adding to perceived independence from the state. In a period of transition, institutional survival will depend upon a willingness to 'go along with' policy change plus the value placed upon them by wider social mores. In a period of attempted erosion of professional power (see Flynn, 1989; and Aleszewski and Manthorpe, 1990), practitioners may experience considerable stress in attempting to maintain their elected position as a force independent of competing demands, or an arbiter amongst them. The relative success of this professional project will vary, depending upon the resilience of the institutions in which work takes place. The position of different professional groups within society will form a backdrop to relations with their clients, a theme that will be returned to later in this chapter. Firstly, the relations between projects of practitioners and older service users will be examined in more detail.

The projects of health and welfare practitioners have a number of qualities that might be at odds with those of older service users. Amongst practitioners there is a wish to make things better, to inspire and maintain hope in the future and, in addition, a tendency to focus on short-term realizable goals. The first point helps maintain optimism in their task and can itself promote positive change, the latter reflects pressure on resources and is often found in professional slang, referring to service users with persistent needs as 'bed-blockers', 'heart-sinks', or 'difficult' cases.

Elders' perceptions of effectiveness may be influenced more by reducing the effect of diminishing performance and creating a positive view of themselves that does not rely so heavily on short-term achievements. Both of these points involve a longer-term perspective. An elder's concern with health and welfare may thus legitimately reflect concern to preserve existing powers, as much as the identification of a specifiable and curable problem, as a means to continued social and existential development. Both health and social problems faced by older people are likely to be long-term, with no obvious easy solution, and as such are unlikely to provide immediate rewards for a practitioner's time and effort. The temptation to see these problems as the inevitable and depressing consequences of ageing are therefore enhanced, especially if the professional perspective is focused on a partial reality of a specialism rather than a holistic view of the elder's life-circumstances.

PRACTITIONER'S PERCEPTIONS OF OLDER AGE

Biggs (1989a, 1990a, 1992) has identified a number of factors that might obscure practitioners' perceptions of older age. Firstly, lack of personal experience of older age may make empathy more difficult to achieve and add to a feeling that elders are a homogeneous group. This would be expected to create a psychological space that can be filled by social stereotypes and archetypal images. If practitioners are trained and work in situations where exposure to peers and younger people are the norm, then the different concerns of older age may be perceived as deviant. Unfortunately, Phillipson and Strang's (1986: 119) review of training for health and welfare workers indicates that this is likely to be the case, even though course content and caseloads primarily reflected work with children and families:

> It was characteristic of professionals to assume that they were in touch both with the emotional and material needs of their clients, and that they posessed adequate 'theoretical' knowledge about the social and biological construction of old age.

Secondly, power differences between older service-users and practitioners, brought about because the former needs something from the latter, would influence whose projects are addressed. As an elder enters the common-sense reality of a caring organization, projects need to be modified in order to 'translate' into a dialogue that the practitioner can legitimately respond to. This is common to all people who seek services and helps to explain why caring institutions are seen as providing services that people need in ways that they don't necessarily desire (Mitchell *et al.*, 1980). The situation is complicated for older users in the light of social legitimation given to projects of younger adults over their own. A double disadvantage thus emerges, based on age and context, whereby the projects of older age can easily be replaced by those of the younger professional.

Finally, it has been shown by a number of studies (Bender, 1984; Association of Directors of Social Services, 1985; Phillipson and Strang, 1986) that both the literature on old age and contact with elders requiring help skews professional understanding toward an unrepresentative sample of the ageing population, the most disadvantaged, distressed and unwell. Again the problem is doubled (Biggs, 1989a: 51), as firstly 'Workers mix with a disadvantaged group of old people and take this to represent the whole' and secondly:

> The 'taking-to-be-the-whole' freezes workers and makes it extremely difficult to confront an acceptable view of their own ageing. As this personal future would seem to be negative and inevitable, it is in the worker's interests to eschew contact with situations that will provoke recognition of this presumed future self.

Menzies (1970: 11) has pointed to the key role that institutional culture can have in defending workers from the anxiety generated by the helping task:

A social defence system develops over time as the result of collusive interaction and agreement, often unconscious, between members of the organisation over what form it shall take.

This is an important theme that will be pursued as the chapter develops, linking, as it does, the individual responses of workers to the commonsense of the system itself.

THE WOUNDED HEALER, HELPER AND HELPED

Relations between 'helper and helped' make factors that influence intergenerational communication take a particular form, giving rise to patterns that can enhance or detract from the helping endeavour. Estes (1979: 25) argues, for example, that helping can artificially increase dependency amongst older service users, 'Help rendered may be given from the purest and most benevolent of motives, yet the very fact of receiving help degrades.' Practitioners and service users '...belong to two basically different worlds and the asymmetry is not only of feelings and attitudes, it is also an asymmetry of power.'

The dichotomy between helper and helped, although a relatively accurate description of externally defined roles, skews expectations and limits the expression of potential between actors in ways that suffuse the helping situation with questions of power. In any interpersonal situation, one partner will try to make an object out of the other to some degree so that her or his projects or definitions dominate. This process is reflected psychologically as parts of the self are thereby disowned, reinforcing those trends within the particular context at hand.

A particular polarity has been suggested by some Jungians, constellated when a person requires help, and arises as a 'wounded–healer' archetype. Both poles reside in each party, but unequally, depending upon the formal roles that they adopt. Guggenbuhl-Craig (1971: 90) explains how this archetype can operate in health settings:

> The sick man seeks an external healer, but at the same time the intrapsychic healer is activated. We often refer to this intrapsychic healer in the ill as the 'healing factor'. It is the physician within the patient himself and its healing action that is as great as that of the doctor who appears on the scene externally.

It follows from this description that there is no single healer or patient and, for the regenerative process to work, both parts within an individual need to activate for successful healing to take place. Allowing the wound and the healer to find expression within the helper as well as the helped is necessary because if the archetype becomes split and separate poles become located exclusively within different actors, there is no space left for self-regeneration within the person requiring help. Pietroni (1990: 71) expands this theme in general practice:

> In time of illness, the doctor is seen as someone who with his knowledge and expertise will restore the patient's ability to regain control of his body or mind. It is because so much power is invested in him by the patient that the doctor or healer needs to be aware of his own powerlessness.

Unfortunately, Pietroni (1990: 72) contends that professional training often suppresses these facilities:

> The student is encouraged to dismiss them as signs of weakness, so that as he matures he adopts the mantle of only one half of the archetype; that of the healer/doctor with little or no perception of the opposite pole. This opposite pole is then projected onto the patient so that feelings of weakness, dependency and helplessness are avoided.

Before the non-medical practitioner dismisses this formulation as eminently accurate for doctors, but otherwise irrelevant, it is worth noting that what is being examined occurs at the level of phantasy as well as in practice. It can be extended to include other contexts once 'helper' and 'helped' are substituted for the same fundamental dilemma. The contention is that notions within the head of the practitioner preclude certain options for other parties entering into a common-sense reality where an professional ethos is dominant. Characteristics such as power imbalance, the 'wound' and power to 'make good' hold a universal quality for health and welfare in terms of the image that practitioners aspire to and how they make judgements about success or failure. The archetype will take different forms depending on particular professional circumstances and the debate take on different polarities, as witnessed by the concern over compliance/non-compliance with health advice and dependency/empowerment within welfare.

The point here is that considering the influence of the archetype is not the same as adopting a medical model. Indeed the conclusions are highly critical of institutionalized splits between roles, where the only part of the other seen conforms to the world view of the helping party and, in recognizing the helped's capacity for self-activity. The more that institutional pressure and self-perception divide power and passivity, the more difficult it becomes to take back projections of unwanted parts, which both allow self-regenerative powers to arise in the nominated patient or client and increase empathic sensitivity on the part of the practitioner.

Exclusive identification with helping or healing, the urge to be perfectly in role, might be seen in the nurse or doctor who cannot allow themselves to go sick, mental health workers who cannot express their own depression, anxiety or phantasy, or social workers who immerse themselves in activity so that 'something' is being done to an otherwise passive client. Each serves to create a manageable distance between helper and helped by locating its opposite in the latter. That the 'unprofessional' pole is often institutionalized as weakness would underline the power tacit in professional interaction.

Loosening the boundaries around ascribed roles would itself allow positive elements to emerge in a number of ways. Firstly, there is more balance in the parts of the personality that are allowed expression and thus the ability to see a more complete picture of the other is enhanced. Secondly, Guggenbuhl-Craig (1971) notes the importance of phantasy images of the other in helping to construct possible futures. A more creative relationship encourages each party to 'weave fantasies' around the other that help map out alternatives, 'actual lines of possible development', which, once given voice, can act as a new guiding principle for interpersonal development. It must be remembered, however, that such powerful visions would still take place within the overall structure of the archetype and thus the danger is always present of over-identification with one or other polarity. A practitioner may over-identify with the heroic in the healer/helper or the scapegoat in the wound, depending upon the particular common-sense world that they inhabit.

ARCHETYPES AND WORK WITH OLDER PEOPLE

It will be remembered from Chapter Two that meetings between older and younger people also gave rise to a particular archetypal form, that of the wise elder. This image differed from social stereotypes of old age in so far as the wise elder held certain positive qualities, the hope that transition to a more advanced state of personal being was possible and the qualities of wisdom and power that it could evoke. However, the ground prepared by stereotyping plus the tacit threat from intimations of change to familiar states of affairs meant that the image was not necessarily accepted by the younger person. When considering the role of archetypal images, or psychological guiding principles, in the helping situation, two potentially competing sets of images might arise simultaneously, one arising from the intergenerational nature of the encounter the other from its helping status.

The concept of elders as knowledgeable guides has particular relevance to relations between professional workers and older people. The opposite pole to wisdom – naivity, foolishness or unknowing – when constellated in the younger person would be unlikely to be accepted if part of the struggle of the first part of life concerns establishing autonomy. Acceptability of the archetype would partly depend on the age of the practitioner and their own tolerance of such ambiguity. In addition to this, the balance between knowledge and unknowing would seem to be reversed when the helper/helped principle is compared to the wise elder/naive youth. Both parties would enter an imaginal situation in which competition for the same space exists. Should the helper accept the elder as a more knowledgeable guide or should the older person bow to the professional expertise of the younger party? In everyday situations each party might find a working compromise to these opposing tensions. For example, it may be that the elder recognizes a circumscribed area in which the practitioner has greater specialist skill. The practitioner may respect the elder's lived experience, particularly where personal history influences the degree of success of the helping enterprise. However, it is quite possible for the image to transcend these rational territorial divisions, particularly with regard to guiding principles governing communication and the etiquette of respect. When this happens, the two sets of archetypal polarities may come together in a number of combinations.

A split archetypal situation raises questions about which pole is identified with. One pole would need to be suppressed in the interest of avoiding conflict and the release of powerful primitive feelings. This situation is complicated by the possibility that both poles exist in the psyche of each party. These possibilities will have implications for how practitioners construe elders in caring situations. When 'wisdom' is activated in conjunction with the healer/helper, the dominant party lays claim to power evoked by the archetype in order to consolidate their position, but without acknowledging its wider implications. This solution would be the psychic equivalent of treating the image of the other as an object in order to boost the personal ego, and is particularly difficult for workers to recognize because it also corresponds to formal power imbalance within the helping setting. An alternative possibility would be that whilst accepting one polarity, for example the healer, the alternative pole of the second archetype, naive youth, is also accepted. This would evoke considerable tension as the actor now has to contain opposing personal expectations. Helpers might then be overwhelmed by their unknowing and an unconscious expectation that the other will provide all the answers. They might avoid genuine participation by assuming that because the other is different, by virtue of age, gender or race, there is nothing that they can contribute. In a third situation identification with the wound and unknowing might take place, giving rise to feelings of helplessness and defeat. The worker would then become easy prey for the punitive projections of others. Finally, if the wound is identified with in harness with a sense of knowing, it is easy for practitioners to fall prey to righteous indignation on behalf of both the 'helped' and wounds within the Self.

That the psychological situation described holds within it alternative visions of the distribution of power also implies that a positive resolution based on mutual respect could flourish. For this to happen both parties would need to heal the split by recognizing that each holds within themselves all of the polarities and the potential therein. Action based on a realistic appraisal of what both can contribute and respect for the projects of both parties can then begin.

It has been noted in previous chapters that younger people do not have direct experience of older age to draw upon and that although archetypal forms exist in each person the particular image evoked depends upon experience and the culture they inhabit. The effect of this sense of absence is not easy to assess as other forms of empathic experience can be used and it is to the different ways that practitioners fill that gap that we now turn.

TRANSFERENCE AND COUNTERTRANSFERENCE

The helper–helped situation evokes projections that take a particular form, which are used to fill spaces in the emotional map of each party. They have most clearly been addressed in psychotherapy, where such processes are directly examined. Countertransference is a particular form of projection referring to associations and feelings evoked in the therapist by a patient as opposed to transference, the word used to describe the reverse process, concerning the projections of the patient onto the worker. Certain elements of one person's experience are thus transferred onto someone else because they are unconsciously reminiscent of other relationships that may not be appropriate to the one currently taking place. It is generally accepted that these processes also occur in the everyday world, but there they rarely surface into consciousness and are not given the opportunity to be understood. This is why people we meet, sometimes even strangers, can inexplicably evoke strong feelings that can only in part be put down to their actual behaviour. Something about them locks into the intrapsychic processes that we have and the symbolic situations they have come to represent.

When Freud (1910) originally described this phenomenon, he emphasized unconscious resistance against helping the patient deal with areas that workers found difficult themselves. Today, following the work of the Kleinian analyst Paula Heimann (1950), countertransference is more commonly used to describe conscious feelings that the worker has toward the other, arising from associations that are preconscious, that is to say available to consciousness given the right circumstances (Carpy, 1989). Whether misperceptions that arise are always a hindrance to real communication that should be eliminated, or are a form of information that can be used on the road to a deeper understanding of human relationships, has been a matter of debate since the earliest days of psychoanalysis. Freud took the former view, whereas Jung preferred a more flexible approach (Jacoby, 1984).

That relationships with older people give rise to particular forms of projection has only recently been acknowledged (Knight, 1986; Genevay and Katz, 1990), although as Sprung (1989) points out, the Committee on Ageing of the Group for the Advancement of Psychiatry in the USA listed a number of reasons for negative staff reactions to elders as early as 1971. These included workers' fears about their own ageing, conflicts about relationships with parental figures, that there was nothing to offer elders as their problems were untreatable, that they were near death and thus not really deserving attention, that the patient might die during treatment and that colleagues were contemptuous of interest shown in the elderly. The helper may respond by avoidance, by not providing services or speeding up the process by suggesting physical rather than directly interpersonal forms of intervention (Pfeiffer, 1971). Hildebrand (1982, 1986) has observed that even within counselling there is a tendency to focus concretely on short-term problems, such as bereavement, than on broader existential questions.

To enhance our understanding of how the psychological gap between younger and older people is filled, it is necessary to consider what associations are employed to humanize the archetypal contradictions noted above. Knight (1986: 132) notes that, 'With older adults the origin of the transference can come from any stage of adult life and especially from any of the family settings in which the older client has lived.'

Knight makes specific reference to identifying the worker as child, grandchild, parent, spouse at an earlier age, an erotic object and as a social authority figure. Similarly, workers may respond by reference to their own parents, grandparents or personal fears around the theme of death, ageing and dependency. Each of these associations would lend a particular quality to the relationship and two, which refer directly to intergenerational relations will be examined in greater detail.

If projections constellate around parent–child issues, Knight points out that 'child' takes on a different meaning for elders because their own children will be adult and could be older than the worker. So, concerns may focus on '. . . whether the child will be there to help when help is needed or will take charge of the client without good cause' (Knight, 1986: 134). The worker may '. . . become overly committed to seeing the client change, become irrationally angry, become involved in a struggle for control of the session, or feel very wounded by the client's questioning of the therapist's expertise.' (Knight, 1986: 142). The worker might also ignore symptoms such as paranoia or allusions to suicide, which are too threatening to recognize in an 'as-if' world where the client and the real parent have become confused. If the worker is having to confront similar problems with ageing parents in her or his own life an over-attatchment to one particular course of action might emerge, which the worker needs to see work in the client's life as well.

Grandparental projections are less intense than parental ones. Often the possibility of what Knight describes as 'fairly honest' emotional communication can exist. However, relations may become idealized and alliances formed to the detriment of the middle generation. Alternatively, both parties may find themselves competing for the attention of or protecting the sandwiched parents or whatever person or group comes to stand for them.

Finally, there is the relationship between the helper's own phantasized personal future and the elder's life circumstances. It was suggested earlier that this projected future state is likely to be a negative one given the nature of social stereotyping and the skewed circumstances in which older people and the helping professions generally meet (Biggs, 1989a). The degree to which the worker accepts or rejects these internalized assumptions would also influence how far elder's confirming or disconfirming experience can be recognized. Unfortunately, literature on the nature of the personal future and thence its influence on the quality of intergenerational helping is extremely sparse. Whilst both Knight and Sprung point to a number of the areas that older people might wish to explore, but are inhibited from doing so because they are considered inappropriate for younger workers to be prioritizing (for example the nature of death and its meaning for personal existence), the conscious construction of future but older selves may simply be blocked (Biggs, 1990a).

This review of transference and countertransference phenomena indicates some of the ways in which intergenerational issues interact with the helping endeavour that may or may not be open to conscious scrutiny. It is now time to examine professional common-sense reality to see how different helping professionals respond to elders as service users.

HEALTH AND WELFARE

So far, general trends in relations between elders and practitioners have been examined. A key factor influencing how these trends operate would be the context against which they are played out. Of particular interest would be the assumptive realities generated by health and welfare services, which although not comprehensive, provide guiding principles for a number of related helping activities. Each legitimates the space available for dialogue between worker and service user, which is reflected in professional expertise and reasons why that agency has been chosen as a source of help.

Health

Health services cover a wide span of interventions and settings in which older people are amongst the largest group of users (Victor, 1991). Even so, a number of studies have reported that the health needs of this part of the population often go unmet (Department of Health, 1989; Faraquar and Bowling, 1991). As this section has been concerned with the interpersonal relations between practitioners and users it is necessary to briefly review the common sense of medicine and nursing to examine trends that might contribute to that process. Issues arising will differ depending upon the position a practitioner holds in the institutional hierarchy, whether work is ward based, takes place in a nursing home or via community visiting and it may be better to see them referring to a continuum of health care rather than located rigidly with any one role.

A guiding principle behind most health care is the issue of life and death and thus diagnosis and cure. Status within specialisms often reflects their closeness to this fundamental aim (Pietroni, 1990). The ability to maintain hope in the institutional task also depends upon identifying and contributing to a cure (Stokes, 1991), and it is here that difficulty first arises for the older patient. Much work with elders centres on care over a long period, where diagnosis is often complicated by lengthy medical histories, drug interactions and the presence of multiple problems (Adelman *et al.*, 1991). Clarity of task and achievability of objectives is therefore less straightforward and more difficult to maintain. The guiding principle lends weight to questions of certainty and uncertainty, particularly for general practitioners (Adelman *et al.*, 1991; Woodhouse and Pengelly, 1991) who feel directly responsible for accurate diagnosis and fear 'missing something'. The weight of responsibility is often managed by referral within medicine. Physicians may feel powerless and uncertain relative to work with other patient groups when, as Adelman *et al.* point out, an 'aggressive curing instinct' is not always an appropriate response to the needs of elders.

In the light of the above it is worth examining the communication between health practitioners and older patients in more detail. Adelman *et al.* found that physicians gave better information on issues that they raised and were more supportive to younger than older people on issues raised by patients. Elders were believed not to desire information, even though research by Greene *et al.* (1986) has indicated that patients of different ages express an equal desire, but elders were less able to articulate it. Adelman *et al.*'s study found that physicians were more abrupt, condescending or indifferent to older people, and often mistook their lack of assertiveness for lack of interest.

Nussbaum *et al.* (1989) have noted that whereas nursing is often conceived as having a greater emphasis on psychosocial need, interaction tends to depersonalize patients and disconfirm patient's feelings in an attempt to be reassuring. More recently, Giles (1991) has emphasized the importance of 'attuning' to successful health communication if the patient is to feel supported, whilst Nussbaum (1991) has found that elders' recovery was linked to intimacy and friendship with staff. However, health staff often over-accommodate to the communication deficits of older age, which can be experienced as infantilizing. Coupland *et al.* (1991: 207) found that nurses soon became adept at deflecting protestations from patients and concluded that 'Nurses may well be immunised against chronic sickness and pain, and if they have low expectations of the quality of their patients' lives, this may well be a reflex of the general institutional arrangements.'

One trend in intergenerational communication has a particular effect on health issues. It will be remembered from Chapter Five that younger people tend to explain an elder's behaviour in terms of health and competence and that in older age painful self-disclosure is used by some elders to control intergenerational communication, even though this is disliked by younger listeners. When health is the explicit reason for seeking help, these same factors, Giles proposes, may actively work against meaningful communication as complaints can be dismissed as age-related or symptomatic of a gerontized communication style. Weiman *et al.* (1990) observed, following a review of health communication, that elders' need for affiliation to confirm encounters does not fit well with practitioner's task-based reasons for interaction, and is often ignored. This is of particular interest to the present argument because it suggests that the potential mismatch between projects during the first and second stages of life can directly influence medical care. Confirming evidence also comes from Adelman *et al.*'s finding that physicians found it easier to relate to younger than older patients, whilst Nussbaum *et al.* (1989) note that elders were generally not happy with the quality of communication with health care professionals and experienced them as unfriendly, even when practitioners thought they were being friendly. Whilst Miller (1987) proposes that medicine actively contributes to the illegitimacy of any ageing role that is not defined by illness, Adelman *et al.* (1991) propose that health workers should always be mindful of two agendas, that arising from their professional role and that arising from the position of the older person.

So far, health has been examined as the subject of communication between parties where a defining characteristic is that of age. A number of writers have also examined the form that contact takes.

Woodhouse and Pengelly (1991), in their study of interprofessional collaboration, noted the role that closeness and distance played between GPs and patients. The intimate nature of contact between parties has lead to practice that both depersonalizes interaction and requires the maintenance of firm boundaries around the intimacy of the pair as evidenced by strict rules of confidentiality. This is highly functional, as it protects both parties from tresspass and misunderstanding in what could otherwise be the occasion for strong erotic and libidinal wishes. The boundary between self and other is therefore scrupulously maintained, and the patient is reassured that information divulged in this setting will not find its way into other arenas.

However, this arrangement also reinforces a sharp divide between the wounded and the healer as it places considerable constraints upon the health practitioner's field of self-expression. A tendency toward omnipotence easily follows given the common sense of 'life-and-death', the wish to reduce uncertainty and the projected wishes of the sick patient to externalize the illness and cure. This may be particularly threatening in older age if Knight (1986) and Weiman et al. (1990) are correct and elders are particularly concerned to maintain control, fearing that younger adults will inappropriately take charge of their lives. This arises because concerns about physical decrement are easily generalized in the minds of helpers and patients alike to competence in other spheres. 'The point is that negatively valenced communication strategies coupled with normal health decrements can encourage the elderly to see themselves as unable to manage their environments.' (Weiman et al., 1990: 231).

It is then but a short step to what Giles and Coupland (1991b) have referred to as 'instant ageing', whereby in order to complement what has been identified here as the practitioner's archetypal position, the elder takes on characteristics of greater age and infirmity than is actually the case. As can be seen, it is relatively easy for a spiral of mutual confirmation to develop, which reinforces both the task-based common sense of medicine and, at an imaginal level, the split between wounded and healer.

Over-identification with the heroic healing archetype, a form of inflation identified in Chapter Two, may interact with the image of an internal wise elder if the practitioner becomes sufficiently distanced from the real older person. What Fordham (1956) calls the 'mana-personality' and Sprung (1989) the 'messiah complex' may then come into play. Biggs (1989a) has suggested that taking the power of the image is a relatively common phenomenon amongst helpers and its seductive power might be visible in the early writings of the psychiatrist Goldfarb (1956; Goldfarb and Turner, 1953). Goldfarb advocated a collusion with 'delegated parental authority' during what is referred to as 'psychotherapy' with aged and dependent mental health patients. He notes 'the opportunity to foster the illusion that a protective parent has been found is ready made' and can be used by the practitioner to increase a patient's self-esteem by fostering the perception that a powerful ally has been made. He advocates that patients are seen twice within the first week of this intervention, and thereafter 'as infrequently as possible'. This exposition would not be generally understood as psychotherapy and does little to create balance in the relationships described, rather the reverse. It may, however, illustrate how workers can be seduced by a combination of their formal position and the power drawn from an archetypal situation.

A second factor arising from the exclusive pairing of practitioner and patient concerns the boundary between this and other parties. Woodhouse and Pengelly (1991) have found that whilst practitioners recognize that problems often extend to wider issues and other relationships, there is considerable resistance to extending the circumference of a session to include family or non-medical professionals as this increases uncertainty in an already uncertain situation. Adelman *et al.* (1991) note that in 65 per cent of cases in their sample, elders were accompanied by a third person, who might take the role of advocate, passive recipient or be antagonistic to the patient. They hypothesize that this unfamiliar presence in the practitioner's space would inhibit bonding, intimacy and confidentiality. Both sets of writers lament a lack of literature on this point. If the current hypothesis that similar age-related projects are more compatible than those across generations is correct, this would increase the possibility of collusion between age peers to the detriment of the priorities of older age.

The context in which health professionals meet older patients is not limited to paired interaction. Menzies' (1970) seminal study of nursing in a general hospital outlines a number of ways in which institutional practices serve to distance patients and practitioners in the service of containing anxiety generated by health-related tasks. Here the factors that place each firmly on opposite sides of the wounded/healer fence were found to include depersonalization, the use of uniforms, reference to dysfunction rather than persons, attempts to eliminate decisions by the performance of ritualized tasks, the use of repeated checking and delegation of responsibility to superiors. An extensive review of nursing literature on attitudes to old people (Ingham and Fielding, 1985) could come to no firm conclusions on the different factors affecting their responses, as studies often confounded a number of personal and contextual variables. Robertson (1991) has studied the close relationship between morale and quality of care of dementing elders across a number of regimes. He found that high levels of satisfaction were related to high quality care as evidenced in higher levels of non-instrumental interaction with both patients and staff initiating conversation. Both morale and care quality were mediated by ward management practices and in particular the approachability and perceived fairness of senior staff. It would seem from this that an ability to humanize stereotyped or archetypal responses in clinical settings is dependent on a complex of personal and institutional variables that deserve further study.

Summary

This albeit partial review of clinical settings leads to a number of conclusions about the common-sense world that elders enter. Firstly, strong boundaries are required to defuse misunderstandings arising from the intimacy that health issues entail. Secondly, clinical practice is firmly task-based, which serves to reinforce these self-protective boundaries. Thirdly, health relies on the maintenance of hope, which is sustained by practitioners and patients alike and can be therapeutic. Each of these points, whilst necessary for effective treatment, can give rise to problems in work with older people when their priorities differ. Elders' requirements may be complex, long-term and focus on care rather than cure. They may place more emphasis on the affiliative nature of discourse than on tasks. The common sense of health services may make it difficult to step outside these boundaries to address the different priorities of older age and associated interactive styles of older people. There may be a particular danger when experience and understanding of these projects is lacking. Archetypal priorities, reinforced by an imbalance of power may strengthen trends in clinical settings that accentuate difference and inhibit self-regeneration.

Welfare

In the UK the development of systematic welfare is a relatively recent occurrence when compared to other professional groupings. Its bureaucratic legitimacy is therefore less than for health, and some have argued that social work has been less successful in deflecting political attacks upon it (Biggs, 1990a; Aleszewski and Manthorpe, 1990). Shortness of training, a generic skillbase that discourages specialism and the large numbers of welfare staff who have received no formal professional training (Barr, 1988) have left expertise a weaker justification of professional activity when compared to clinical practice. The process of social work has, perhaps as a result of the above, relied upon developing 'the use of self' in recognition of the attitudes and personality of individual workers as a central tool for the helping endeavour.

Practice is most often justified in terms of statutory responsibilities devolved to local authorities. As the local state depends for its legitimacy on local politics, statutory powers are subject to political interpretation and account. This combination of factors lends a fluidity to the common sense of welfare, which not only requires social service workers to respond directly to social issues (Biggs, 1992), but can also require them to act as a point of last referral for seemingly intractable problems (Woodhouse and Pengelly, 1991).

It should come as no surprise, then, that a number of writers have identified stress and problems of setting boundaries to be considerable difficulties in this field (Mattinson and Sinclair, 1979; Waddell, 1989; Woodhouse and Pengelly, 1991).

Welfare practitioners find themselves at the centre of a number of competing pressures. The personal pain aroused by exposure to people in desperate situations is compounded by political decisions on the availability of resources, which are largely beyond the practitioner's control. They are also subject to displaced responsibility from wider society to address social problems that that society creates. The worker is thus at one and the same time an agent of the system that generates seemingly insoluble problems and to which strong personal reservations might be held (Waddell, 1989).

A number of institutional phenomena have been observed, which suggest how defences against this contradictory situation arise. Bureaucratic proliferation (Waddell, 1989) and a heavy reliance on adherence to procedures (Ernst, 1989) have been noted as ways of distancing workers from the distress of service users and anxiety arising from responsibility for potentially life-threatening situations of others. Challis' (1990) study of social service departments, found that reorganization was a continuing phenomenon, often given as a reason for delay or inaction. There was, however, no national consistency in the direction of these changes, which, whilst reflecting a lack of professional consensus on good practice, also suggests that reorganization itself may fulfil other functions. It is perhaps easier to influence structures that can be controlled than address chaotic and seemingly insoluble social problems in the outside world. Waddell (1989) also observed a tendency to take on excessive work suffused with a sense of urgency and a difficulty in saying no. Waddell (1989) and Biggs (1990a) have identified these behaviours with a need to be seen to be responding, 'to do something', indicative of a lack of clear boundaries around the practitioner's task.

Finally, Woodhouse and Pengelly (1991) report that although social workers were amongst the most open to self-criticism and advice in the context of interdisciplinary learning, when institutional issues were raised they were the quickest to close ranks adopting a uniform and unchanging stance toward external comment. This they refer to as a 'siege-mentality' whereby internal dissatisfaction, often deeply felt, was split off from feedback from external sources. It is perhaps instructive that although social workers had participated enthusiastically in these learning groups, none of their employing authorities would consent to inclusion in this research. The process of follow-up and dissemination of findings, it was said, would take time away from the real business of providing a service. Although this response seems at first to have moral force, it belies a narrowed definition of task and wariness toward reflective practice.

Waddell (1989) characterizes social work as being torn between poles of activity and passivity, either in the rush to action of some sort or the reliance on institutional inertia. Both, she proposes shield individual practitioners from feeling and reflection. Adherence to the 'latest fashion' for correct values and method (Woodhouse and Pengelly, 1991) are coupled with concentration on information rather than digested meaning. These attributes, whilst functional in the service of equity and the statutory nature of the work, can also become dysfunctional. If active helping becomes the sole preserve of one party in the helping endeavour then space for the internal helper within the service-user would be curtailed. This trend can easily reinforce the latter's anger at having to request the most basic necessities for living. Both parties then mirror for each other their desperation to make an impact whilst neither's project is truly heard.

Each of the writers mentioned above comment on social service staff's strong identification with their clients, sometimes bordering on narcissism (Waddell, 1989). There is a temptation, here, to substitute a worker's judgement for the user's presumed experience of life. Paradoxically, this can emerge as an inability to help because differences between the two become over-emphasized. For example, black people cannot be helped because of the eurocentrism of the worker, elders cannot be helped because they are disengaging from life anyway. These processes must be distinguished from adaptive recognition of the cultural experience and life tasks of users, where they are used in the service of a partnership to develop an appropriate service response to requirements. As Mattinson and Sinclair (1979) point out, these issues may then be played out at different levels throughout an organization. For example, managers can become treated as if they are personally responsible either for restraining activity or not providing resources, whereas in reality they are subject to the same institutional restraints as the workers themselves. An additional defining characteristic of social services is the way that work takes on a moral dimension. Woodhouse and Pengelly (1991) report that agencies operate by 'continually exporting and re-exporting blame', which they link to an inability to contain both positive and negative qualities in the same psychological space. In Jungian terms this would mean that the opposite pole is hidden in the shadow or projected onto others. As boundaries are that much more fluid in social work than in health, these processes can extend to the partnership between helper and helped, or whole communties giving rise to perceptions that both worker and user are 'good' whilst the system remains 'bad'. The same authors note that social workers were more likely to see disagreement by users as a personal attack on their competence than were other practitioners.

Each of these observations raise questions about the effectiveness of boundary management at both individual and institutional levels. The statutory nature of social work, the tensions that being an agent of the local state entails, plus lack of clear technical expertise, may inflate this moral quality in social welfare. Guggenbuhl-Craig (1971) proposes that action against the will of the client requires that the actor be certain that their own ideas are right. As such action is predicated on motivation to help others, he says that power is often constellated in the shadow and leaks out when the user disputes the action being taken by the practitioner. Punishment is given by making the user conform to the professionally defined project regardless of its appropriateness to actual circumstances. This inflated response may arise differently, depending on the worker's gender. Whilst the above is characteristic of 'masculine' work-styles, Ernst (1989) and Marks (1991) report that women can unconsciously create a closed system between themselves and an infantilized client, as 'through projective identification with the object of her care, in phantasy, she meets her own needs and is omnipotent' (Ernst, 1989: 105). Both approaches exclude the other's reality through parental imagery, either by patriarchal domination or matriarchal smothering.

Pietroni (1991) found that social workers often collectively occupy the role of scapegoat, arising from society's willingness to transfer collective guilt onto someone who will bear it. Both of these forms, scapegoat and controller, may come into play at different times depending upon which polarity of the power archetype is in the ascendent. If the dominant form of defence centres on practitioner activity, this would run the risk of engaging the power of the archetype without understanding its influence. If it centres on passive identification, workers may see themselves as victims. Neither of these extreme positions would allow dialogue, as in both cases the worker defines priorities in line with an internal agenda that presumes knowledge of the other's projects, but fails to check them out.

Given the contradictory nature of these demands, a lack of clear boundaries to the professional task, and the resultant tendency to lurch between inflexible institutional responses and personal identification with distressed others, it is necessary to re-examine the role of 'use of self' as a defining characteristic of the welfare project. Use of self may contribute to confusion between the professional role and user requirements, by blurring the origin of agency in a situation that is already ambiguous. If the practitioner believes that they themselves are the primary tool in achieving change, it is but a short step to blaming oneself for inability to improve situations where the relationship between helper and helped is only a small part affecting social deprivation. It is relatively easy to accept the displaced projections of others, that one is in some way responsible for those original circumstances. When successes are achieved, it is unclear who possesses responsibility, or how it can be shared. Both scenarios open situations to inflation, over-identification or over-reaction, if confused boundaries between self and other lends particular force to the workers feeling of knowing what is best.

The positive elements of permeable personal boundaries should not be lost in this discussion, as they enhance the practitioner's ability to contain conflicting pressures and thereby contribute to their resolution. If they can enter into the world of the other and return with that knowledge to inform a mutually negotiated task, rigid distinctions between helper and helped are eroded and projects to some extent shared. The possibility of doing so depends upon a common sense that allows role flexibility and other projects to be voiced.

Social work and older people

As with health, the hidden majority of welfare service users, approximately two-thirds, are older people (Age Concern, 1990). However, their requirements are often given low priority, are serviced by low status and poorly paid staff, are routinized and are subject to set procedures.

A number of writers have noted an absence of older people from the caseloads of qualified workers (Rowlings, 1986; Phillipson and Strang, 1986; Biggs, 1989a). This reflects a belief that the problems of elders require a practical approach, the provision of aids to mobility and communication. However, a belief that work with elders lacks the legitimizing force of statute, for example in cases of elder abuse, has been shown to be groundless (Biggs and Phillipson, 1992) and its low institutional priority cannot be explained in these terms.

In general, work was marked by 'stoic acceptance, much the same as the fatalism expressed by many elderly people themselves' (Rowlings, 1986: 10), taking the form of surveillance visits rather than active intervention. Heycox (1989), speaking from an Australian perspective, notes that the perceived passivity of the user group was reflected in the passivity of the workforce, who at the same time found it necessary to feel responsible for older people's lives. Leslie and Fowell (1988) found that home help organizers classified cases as being either demanding or straightforward. Straightforwardness was associated with the simplicity of the required task, whereas more complex requirements were viewed negatively. Above all, elders were evaluated in terms of whether they expressed gratitude and said that others were really in more need than themselves. The authors comment that these judgements were made at a very early stage of intervention and affected subsequent strategies. A study of student attitudes (Jones, 1986: 29) also found that elderly clients were viewed as satisfying because they were grateful, however:

Many of the views expressed by students reflect their personal anxieties about this work. This is seen in comments such as 'Older people are not saveable like children, its downhill all the way from where they are'.

This was in spite of a commonly held view amongst both teaching staff and students with experience of work with older people, that institutional barriers inhibited creative work with older people, rather than interpersonal relations.

These and similar observations (Phillipson, 1982; Biggs, 1989a) indicate that the dominant form of common sense operating in welfare is marked by denial and passive omission. The absence of personal experience, dominance of child care practice and the primacy of habitual procedure eclipse the projects of older age in favour of undigested stereotypes, which reinforce the helper–helped divide. Marginalization takes place if workers vicariously identify with a seeming passivity in older clients. The worker then mirrors this passivity back in their own inability to respond. The active helping pole can also lead to marginalization if activity is premised on what the workers own experience tells them should be the experience of old age. In both cases passivity is located within the user, as both inflated action and passive identification attempt to 'fit' the latter into a discourse, the rules of which have been decided in advance.

Summary

Common-sense boundaries that encompass welfare possess a fluidity arising from the multiple pressures upon that system and its position regarding wider social issues. Workers within it therefore have to juggle with a number of competing concerns. This inevitably causes considerable stress in interpersonal relations, even though these are thought to define professional expertise. Difficulties result in a simplification of work with elders who are not seen as an institutional priority. Pressure on limited time and resources may make it easier to justify avoidance of the projects of older people, who must be 'fitted in' to circumstances defined by other age-related objectives. This combination of factors can give rise to an inappropriate use of self, where both activity and its avoidance become identified with the worker's own intuitive sense of what is required. Unfortunately, as the basis for accurate empathy is weak across generations, there are few constraints on confusing these assumptive priorities with those of workers themselves.

CONCLUSIONS

Each of the common-sense worlds described has given rise to a number of distinctive qualities, which, whilst highly functional in providing an environment where defined tasks can take place without exposing workers to intolerable strain, can, in excess, work against those same helping endeavours. Work with older people is particularly prone to valuing professional common sense above that of aged projects. This situation is complicated in health and welfare settings by the existence of competing archetypal images that contribute to the construction of individual assumptive worlds. Both the helper/helped and the wise elder/naive youth raise questions about the location of knowledge and power. In addition, a younger worker's insight into old age is limited and can be filled by a number of potentially inappropriate projections from other, similar relationships.

A solution to the problem of competing interests has been suggested by Adelman *et al.* (1991), which entails the worker making two lists prior to any intervention. One would outline the professional's needs and objectives, the other those of the elderly service user. The present analysis suggests that this would require considerable application if the worker were to decipher their own contribution to the older person's agenda. This task would need to extend beyond the immediate context in which the two interact, in order to assess whether a sufficiently facilitative environment could place social and institutional attitudes in parenthesis. Although this chapter may seem to cite a litany of avoidance and frustration, certain positive conclusions do emerge.

It would seem that environments placing less emphasis on rigid distinctions between users and providers of services are therapeutically positive. The readiness of differing residential regimes to enhance participation will be examined in Chapter Nine. It is also clear that a balance needs to be struck between fluid and rigid boundaries, so that practitioners can be confident in their own contribution, whilst also allowing space for negotiation in line with a user's requirements. Both personal and institutional boundaries should facilitate a partnership from which a truly human perception of the other can emerge. Such an environment would place a high priority on the withdrawal of projections and an owning of shadow parts of the Self, which have arisen because of age difference and assumptions about the formal task.

Secondly, it is clear from the above that success does not simply depend upon the circumstances of the older person but requires an examination of the reactions evoked in the worker. It has repeatedly been shown that when workers think they are acting in accordance with the wishes of the other, they may be doing so on the basis of their assumptions alone. Contributing factors are complex and exist on different levels, such as avoidance of intimations of personal ageing, archetypal images and assumptive realities operating throughout institutions. Clarity of communication and an acceptable communication style are important factors in ensuring that user requirements are heard.

Institutional space for continuing reflection and debate cannot be over-emphasized in this context, if stated objectives are to be meaningfully fulfilled.

Finally, personal miscommunication often appears in harness with powerful institutional constraints, which are often beyond individual control. The question would be how to improve institutions whilst recognizing that change itself can mirror an avoidance of chaotic and seemingly intractable problems. Any change should therefore be grounded in continued debate with service users, whilst taking cognisance of the views of other constituencies. This process would need to be distinguished from single consultative exercises on a grand scale, which are often used by an institution to justify internal priorities. If collaboration occurs as closely as possible to the point of use and allows both service users and workers to identify common agendas, it might have a chance of maintaining freshness and relevance, which in itself would begin to humanize the image of the other.

Developments in community care have defined the relationship between practitioners and older service users in particular ways. These will influence which projects can be achieved and how alliances are made, concerns that will be addressed in Chapter 8.

8
Older people and community care

INTRODUCTION

Different groups in society will emphasize different aspects of the community, depending upon their own projects, and will set boundaries around common-sense understandings of what the resulting image contains. This is particularly true of notions of care and what 'care in the community' comes to stand for. Community care as a concept arose largely from an analysis of institutions, evidenced in Goffman's (1959) study on asylums in the US, Townsend's (1962) empirical work in the UK and the Psychiatrica Democratica movement in Italy (Bassaglia, in Schepper and Lovell, 1988). The writers identified the artificial and coercive nature of institutional care, but rarely presented a coherent picture of the advantages of life outside. The practical objective became to get people out of the institution, often with little consideration of what community living might entail. Community emerged from a negative definition of its opposite, as a reaction against exclusion from it and is often referred to as 'the community alternative' in literature of this genre.

This conceptual vacuum has quickly been filled by competing political definitions. Whilst commentators on the left (Hadley, 1982; Leonard, 1984; Bornat et al., 1985) have emphasized the caring potential of networks in everyday life and the collective identity that this could enhance, the right determined a desire to free individuals from dependence on the welfare state and underscore family responsibility (HMSO, 1989). It was soon noted by a number of feminist writers (McIntosh, 1981; Finch, 1984; Dalley, 1988) that both positions located community care within the family and therefore had an important role in perpetuating and strengthening women's dependency within it. Dalley (1988: 25) succinctly summarized the image of community care held by policy-makers when she said:

> Propounders of the familist ideal favour it because for them it embodies notions of the family as haven, as responsibility and

affection and thus a private protection against a cold, hostile, outside world.

It also became clear that the community imagery emerging was peculiarly eurocentric (Patel, 1990; Mirza, 1991). It rarely took cognisance of the differing needs, under-use of traditional community-based services and pre-existing supportive and defensive networks operating within minority ethnic groups. Community care, in its turn, became a repository for negative attributions, either as coterminous with the restrictions of family or as the exclusive domain of culturally dominant groups.

As the boundaries have been redrawn, the requirements of other groups, such as people with disabilities, added new voices to the debate. Morris (1992) criticizes the negative vision of caring from within the feminist camp, pointing out that the debate on the family locates women exclusively as carers and ignores the position of women who require support. She argues:

> Insult is then added to injury by the assumption that for a disabled person to aspire to warm, caring human relationships within the setting where most non-disabled people look to find such relationships is a form of false consciousness. We are to be denied not only the rights non-disabled people take for granted, but when we demand these rights we are told that we are wrong to do so. (Morris, 1992: 32)

She goes on to point out that 'caring for' has been confounded with 'caring about', so that the latter is eclipsed and interdependence lost as a powerful alternative to the family–institutional polarization. Interdependence is also key to Kuhn's (1977) thinking on the development of alliances between older and younger people and other oppressed groups.

The boundaries of community care, as variously described, denote where systems of formal and informal care begin and end. What individuals take from competing common-sense understandings, will impose limits to what is seen as being legitimately within and without those boundaries. These will influence the compatibility of projects arising between elders, carers and workers when attempts are made to enter another common-sense world. Perhaps more than any other factor, community care is about exchange across public and private worlds, the negotiation around that boundary and how systems are affected by such exchanges.

The common-sense view arising from the positions of different interests therefore influences the circumference set around notions of community, and points to a number of issues. Firstly, it is important to determine elders' requirements of care in the community, and whether these over-lap with social policy initiatives. Secondly, the degree of congruence between severely disadvantaged elders', carers' and professional helpers' expectations of each other within community settings, must be expanded, particularly in the light of the ownership and suppression of parts of the self. Finally, the mechanisms used by helping institutions need critical scrutiny to see how certain images of community are perpetuated and their impact on the social construction of older age.

OLDER PEOPLE'S REQUIREMENTS

It is important to begin by exploring how older people perceive commu-nity care. Whilst reviewing elders' expectations, Phillipson (1992) notes a change from the received orthodoxy that families are first turned to for help, then neighbours and lastly formal support when informal sources either lack the necessary skills and resources or are simply unavailable (Wenger, 1984). He concludes that older people increasingly prefer the support of professional carers if they have extensive care needs. This suggestion finds support from a number of studies in the UK (Phillipson, 1990), Norway (Daatland, 1990) and Sweden (Lagergren, 1991).

A community survey from three contrasting areas of Scotland (West *et al.*, 1984) indicated much less preference for care by the community than care in the community and an unwillingness to place the major burden of care on family members. These conclusions were based on evaluations of hypothetical vignettes, and do not take the age of re-spondents into account. It is therefore unclear whether they reflect the expectations of people who might anticipate being carers or being cared for. That older people themselves prefer formal care is indicated by a Gallup (1988) survey of pensioners in Britain, where 57 per cent be-lieved that responsibility for their care should shift toward the state. 98 per cent of Salvage's (1989) survey of people aged 75 and over, living in South Glamorgan, agreed that retired people should be maintained in their own homes for as long as possible, whilst rejecting the view that daughters should be expected to give up work to care for their ageing parents.

At least two conclusions can be drawn from these findings about the projects of older people who may either be in receipt of community care, or expect to be in the foreseeable future. Firstly, changes in the circum-stances of their immediate kin, such as daughters who work, the rec-ognition of the contemporary demands of child care and increased geographical mobility (Wicks, 1982), have been reflected in the expecta-tions of elders, which no longer rely exclusively on family support. This conclusion would indicate the flexibility of elder's expectations. It also reflects the increasing trend for elders to live separately from kin in all sectors of the population except the Asian community (British Gas, 1991), with numbers living with others falling from 44 per cent in 1976 to 19 per cent in 1985 (Grundy, 1992). Secondly, although many older people have expressed reservations about residential options, coming from a generation where institutions were designed to punish as much as care (Finch, 1987; Morris, 1991), this perception may be changing. Lee (1985), in a review of the US literature, is more provocative. He proposes that many older people turn to their families only because the alternatives are not perceived as available or viable. Thus family care may not represent an active choice at all, but rather the result of 'A succession of default options exercised because of perceptions of limited alternatives' (Lee, 1985: 33) and 'The elderly's sense of independence [is] threatened less by dependence on government than by dependence on children.' (Lee, 1985: 35).

A preferred option might be for elders to live near enough to kin to maintain contact whilst far enough away to retain independence, what Rosenmayer and Kockeis (1963) call 'intimacy at a distance'.

Developments in social policy in the late 1980s go some way to recognize changes in home ownership and the wish that elders be maintained in their own homes (Griffiths, 1988; HMSO, 1989), however, it is unclear whether these developments took full account of the wider wish not to become a burden on the next generation.

FAMILY: THE PRIVATE SPHERE

The discussion above requires further consideration of intergenerational relations within the private sphere of family life and how this corresponds with common-sense worlds created by social policy.

Social policy considerations of community care for older people are driven by two assumptions, which are also reflected in research literature to some extent. Firstly, the growth of residential care, particularly in the private sector where it is largely paid for through welfare benefits (Biggs, 1987a, 1987b), increased concern that familial obligations to care were breaking down, with a corresponding pressure on the exchequer. The perceived lack of commitment of younger generations to care for the elderly was used to paint a picture of rivalry between generations and between potentially competing groups of welfare users, both in the US (Minkler and Robertson, 1991) and the UK (Phillipson, 1991a). Thompson (1989: 44) argued that:

The young, whatever their income levels, have been learning some important lessons about the welfare state in the 70s and 80s – that

it does not deliver, and that it has no intention of giving them what older citizens once enjoyed.

As a result a 'welfare contract' between generations was, at least in the public sphere, breaking down. This concern translated into a wish to ensure that family obligation was reinforced and 'that responsibility is placed as near to the individual and his carer as possible' (Griffiths, 1988). Renewed interest in supporting carers followed in the form of a number of Government-sponsored guidance documents (Haffenden, 1991; Richardson *et al.*, 1991).

A second assumption – that elders are passive recipients of care, marked, as a group, by their increasing dependency (Wilson, 1991) – is obscured by social policy rhetoric on personal choice. However, it has been argued by Biggs (1987b, 1990a) that participation by elders was in fact eclipsed by a tendency to perceive choice solely between different sectors of the mixed welfare economy. The exclusion of service users from decision-taking, and a concentration on recourse to complaints procedures once services had been received, reinforced this definition of choice.

This exclusion, coupled with a change of focus to the needs of carers, corresponds closely to the perception of intergenerational care in older age as role-reversal. Role reversal, originally conceived by Rautman (1962) to explain 'neurotic and immature' relations whereby children find themselves 'parenting' their own parent in later life; has been described by Seltzer (1990: 7) as a 'simple, neat concept to reinforce social policy.' She argues that it emphasizes repayment in kind as a required duty, which holds none of the optimism of child-rearing. It thus not only re-inforces private obligation, but casts a shadow of hostility and resentment over the caring enterprise, without extending it beyond the child–parent relationship.

What then is known about old age within the private sphere? Is it marked by distance and avoidance, as would be anticipated by obser-vations on public space from Chapter Five and echoed in the social policy deliberations above? Finch's (1989: 242) study of family obligations in the UK concludes that:

> In reality, the 'sense of obligation' which marks the distinctive char-acter of kin relationships is nothing like it's image in the political debate where it appears as a set of ready-made moral rules which all right thinking people accept and put into practice.

There has been little study of intergenerational relations beyond con-cern for care. Minuchin (1974) proposes, from his experience of family therapy, that three-generational families are well adapted to situations of stress and scarcity, but highlights the need for grandparents to respect the authority of parents, particularly with regard to child-rearing:

An extended family may run into problems because of the difficulty of allocating responsibility clearly. Because of the complexity of the family unit, there may be a number of vague boundaries, which create confusion and stress. (Minuchin, 1974: 95)

It is clear from this that the primary unit consists of the two younger generations and leadership should pass to the parental cohort. If there is a general understanding of helping, it would seem, as Finch (1989: 55) herself found, to be in one direction, namely downwards:

In practice support is often one way, and this is regarded as quite proper. Parents give to their children and grandchildren and they continue to give. Whilst certainly they may receive something in return, there does not seem to be a pressure to balance out the gifts.

Schneewind (1990) notes that rules for relations between second and third generations are generally absent from our social repertoire and have to be continually relearned as circumstances change. The transition from carer to cared for might therefore be expected to occasion considerable existential dislocation, both for older people and their children.

Finch and Mason's (1990) study of filial obligation in the North West of England indicates that there are procedural rules, amongst the middle generation, which reduce conflict in working out how caring should emerge rather than precisely what should happen. The aim was to work out what to do and to get others to accept what has been negotiated. Providing care should ideally not fall on relatives, but if this were the only option, then primary responsibility fell on the children. Who provided care depended on the gender of the person needing care, rather than automatically falling on the daughter. This was seen to reflect taboos on intimate physical tending. The main aim seemed to be that roles be shared 'equitably but not equally' between those in an equivalent generational position, bearing in mind the circumstances and other responsibilities of participants. The quality of relations between cared-for and carer was only one factor in coming to a decision, but was thought to be a more legitimate consideration if responsibility fell on an in-law. If there was an obvious carer, such as a spouse, a poor relationship did no exempt them.

Finch (1989) also notes that negotiation has an important role in managing the family reputation in the public world. A family's reaction to transition, the need to be seen as caring, the guilt and conflict that has to be managed, can put a considerable premium on being able to control what happens both within the private sphere and in boundary transactions with the outside world. These priorities may or may not correspond to the projects of elders concerned, depending upon whether they embrace or reject attempts to confirm dependent status.

LOCATING DEPENDENCY

Attempts to locate dependency within the elder, may, if Knight's (1986) discussion of countertransference is correct, be particularly threatening to identity in older age. Both Macdonald and Rich (1984) and Morris (1991) emphasize the pressure on older people to 'pass', to be accepted as 'normal'. This requires a persona that denies an ageing identity lest this disqualifies them from meaningful social interaction. The 'true identity, never acted out, can lose its substance, its meaning, even for ourselves' (Macdonald and Rich, 1984: 55).

The threat to an ageing identity is therefore doubled once limitations associated with age can no longer be ignored. Whilst attempts to maintain an ageless identity require denial of changed priorities associated with ageing, an alternative – acceptance of the projected dependency needs of potential carers – may require a wholesale acceptance of the shadow that had previously been energetically rejected. A similar dynamic might be mirrored in the carer, as location of dependency within the older person, necessary to justify both limitations to her/his own autonomy and control of the elder, might make it difficult to accept external help as this would threaten the psychological status quo.

An elder's transition from relative autonomy to dependency and recognition of this new state of affairs would influence the projects of all family members. Remnet (1987) found that adult children (mean age 44) identified divorce, grandparenthood, retirement and widowhood as significant factors affecting the quality of relationships with their own parents and as provoking curiosity about a number of issues that had previously been ignored. Again, there seemed to have been a lack of norms and accumulated wisdom to draw upon. This provoked a new interest in communication skills across generations, signs of normal and abnormal health in ageing and learning how to negotiate formal resources. In particular, children wished to initiate direct discussion with parents and plan transitions. The older person's ability to cope with change, the author concludes, served as a role model for older age in the self-perceptions of their children. It thus took on personal significance beyond more immediate practical requirements.

This discussion of trends should not underestimate considerable individual differences in informal support. Wenger (1984, 1990) found that the likely demands made on health and welfare services would be influenced by the type of support an elder had access to. Support networks dependent on families provided a high level of practical support, but may occasion isolation from age-peers and outside contacts. Community-based networks contribute to emotional support and high morale, but were less forthcoming in cases of long-term chronic difficulty. Reliance on different forms of support should therefore vary over time as requirements change, if a balanced achievement of potential is to be maintained.

Differences in reactions to change have also been noted. Qureshi (1986: 167), in a study of carer perceptions, points out that elder independence is not always the preferred state as some people '. . . are eager to assume dependency in both practical and emotional terms.' Her Sheffield study found elders who rejected help and elders who actively embraced the dependent role or established an interdependent relationship with their carers. Elders may abandon goals that carers wish them to maintain or take on new ones that are inconvenient. 'It has to be acknowledged that different people will define different goals as desirable and that conflict may arise in a given situation.' (Qureshi, 1986: 168).

Silverstone (1987) in a US book written to assist carers, describes a number of games that can be played between carers and elders depending upon the history of that relationship and relations between siblings in the caring generation. The dynamic of caring can revolve around a number of issues, including manipulation of sibling rivalry, denial or exaggeration of infirmity, self-belittlement or the promise of monetary reward. Qureshi and Silverstone concur in recognizing the way that increased dependency can be used actively to establish power within the family, and it should not be assumed that elders are simply passive recipients. In many cases the aged parent is the most experienced player. The outcome will influence relations within the family and interaction across the public and private boundary even if, as Qureshi (1986) and Finch and Mason (1990) found, it may not reduce an obligation to care.

Differences in the pattern of informal care have also provoked debate on who should be included within the state's definition of carers requiring formal support. An original figure of approximately 6 million carers in the UK (OPCS, 1985), the majority of whom were women between the ages of 45 and 64, provoked considerable unease amongst policy makers in view of increased demand expected on services. A closer analysis of the same data (Parker, 1990), funded by the Department of Health, has revised this figure downward to 1.29 million once a higher threshold of 20 hours caring (excluding 90 per cent of those caring from outside the household) and a focus on personal care, such as dressing, bathing and toileting were used as criteria. The resulting profile identifies a quite different target group, 40 per cent of whom are spouses who are made up equally of women and men. The most vulnerable carers, aged over 75, emerged as men in a ratio of 5:3. Although Evandrou (1991) has claimed that this re-examination emphasizes the heterogeny of the caring population, its policy implications have been to restrict the common sense of care to those in the severest circumstances. An emphasis on intensive spousal care particularly disadvantages women, both as daughters who maintain a level of separation from the caring role and as single elders living alone.

Summary

It would seem, then, that an otherwise tacit 'hierarchy of obligation' can come into play once an elder's autonomy is in doubt, and that this can provoke personal as well as familial realignments. However, this research is marked by an absence of the elder's own voice in these decisions. Although the reason for this is unspecified, it is possible that it reflects the coming together of a rupture of existing expectations of the generational direction of care, a lack of clear roles to take their place, plus a passivity that reflects both the older person's own reaction to changed status and dominant stereotypes of behaviour in old age. If this transition disrupts existing role-reciprocity, for example domestic support whilst the carer works, it is unclear how interdependency between the two generations can be easily re-established. Research in this area is extremely limited. What does seem to emerge, most notably from Parker's (1990) review, is that changes to family structure have not resulted in an abrogation of responsibility, as 'The provision of statutory services has certainly increased since 1948 but this has largely been to support elderly people without families close by rather than to replace or supplement family care.' (Parker, 1990: 38).

FROM PRIVATE TO PUBLIC SPHERES

When a decision is made to seek formal assistance, a number of boundary issues emerge. Care becomes an exchange between public and private worlds. For these purposes, the private sphere and, in particular, families facing decisions about care, have many of the characteristics of a closed system, one with 'sufficient independence to allow most problems to be analysed with reference to their internal structure and without reference to their external environments.' (Bridger, 1980: 5). Closedness and openness refer to the degree that the system interacts with and therefore begins to operate in an external environment. Transactions between the public and private sphere might therefore pose adjustment difficulties for the parties involved.

Although evidence cited earlier indicates a greater wish to involve formal caring, it must be noted that relatively few people call on welfare services for support. Of six million carers, only 6 per cent received regular visits from social workers, 23 per cent from home-helps and 7 per cent meals on wheels (Green, 1988). The private home, whatever its internal problems, is still associated with privacy, a haven against the external environment and defined in contrast to public life. Recognition that existing arrangements cannot cope and that things can no longer go on as they have, would lead to transactions that need to be regulated if perceived safety is to be balanced with continued survival. This is because, as Miller and Rice (1967: 54) point out, 'in the need to take in what is good, the individual also takes in what is bad, and hence threatens to destroy what he wants most to preserve.'

Problems can arise (Singer *et al.*, 1979) if only some of the relevant factors are recognized, participants are not aware of the consequences of letting others manage significant boundaries or their management is not attended to at all.

Discussion of the common sense of caring has already highlighted a number of complicating factors. Members within the caring network may have projects that define acceptable boundaries differently and have expectations that require different forms of exchange. The degree of entry into a public arena may hold different advantages and threats, depending on these priorities as the system moves from relative privacy to openness. Moreover, interdependence that arises between systems 'inevitably brings with it less space for the individual in his or her roles and some threat to that person's independent competence or even identity.' (Bridger, 1980: 16). In other words, participants may find themselves in receipt of new demands, which were not anticipated and may increase uncertainty. The question arises of whether contact between private and public systems requires the export of a more dominant system into another and how the transaction itself is legitimised. The outcome of these issues turns on who becomes the boundary manager, the individual who regulates exchange and the degree of acceptable openness that emerges and it is to this question that we now turn.

COMMUNITY CARE AND CASE MANAGEMENT

The UK welfare system's common-sense definitions of community care took a particular form in the early 1990s (HMSO, 1990) and have implications for the definition of boundaries, the active participants in negotiating care and the tasks that could legitimately be addressed. The background to these developments has been described by a number of writers (Biggs, 1990a; Phillipson, 1990; Jack, 1992) to be part of a long-term project to change the balance of welfare provision from a predominantly public to a mixed welfare economy. Local authorities were to become purchasers of services and adopt a marginal role to provision, which would exist in the private and voluntary sectors. At the same time, the perception of informal care by the community changed, from being a marker of the inability of services to reach community networks to a potential source of alternative care, which could be supported at a reduced cost. The rationale for change was that new schemes, emphasizing monitoring and co-ordination, would increase consumer choice, service flexibility and care quality. In addition it was presented as a response to the perceived wish of service-users to stay in their own homes.

New roles were proposed for welfare workers, consisting of a triangle of quality control, including assessment of need, case management and the inspection of the context of non-domiciliary care. This section will concentrate on the function of case management; inspection will be considered in Chapter Nine.

The US experience

Case management first arose in the US following the Older Americans Act of 1965, which authorized area agencies to support 'services designed to avoid institutionalisation including case management.' (Moxley and Buzas, 1989: 196). It was seen as reducing the inadequacies of caring that resulted from fragmented services and partial funding by insurance companies (Sevick, 1990). By pooling resources and linking them to assessed need, rather than strictly adhering to services covered by payments, the method proved effective in developing a holistic approach, which clearly defines objectives (Pantel, 1990). Once objectives are agreed it is easier for the user to discriminate between options, whilst pooled resources allow chronic problems to be addressed more easily. The method has now been widely adopted as a means of co-ordinating services across health and welfare agencies and payment from 'referral agents' (Moxley, 1989). However, its use has generally been accepted as a response to the twin pressures of increasing numbers of elders in a situation of shrinking public resources (Seltzer *et al.*, 1984; Austin, 1990).

A wide variety of practice can be accommodated within this general framework. Austin and O'Connor (1989), in an extensive review, suggest a continuum of case management activities, whereby any one approach can be placed with respect to its primary orientation toward services or systems. The service pole includes advocacy work with individuals, is integrated with other services and holds a brokerage and co-ordinating function with community organizations. At the system's pole, the focus changes to service organization, whereby a service autonomous from provision functions as a gatekeeper for cost containment, purchasing and terminating services and monitoring providers.

Reviews of the effectiveness of US models have been mixed. Whilst Moxley and Buzas (1989) report some success in disinstitutionalization and maintaining more able elders in community settings, they note that cost containment was rarely achieved, a migration away from more complex cases and a tendency for referring institutions to view their Michigan programme as only appropriate for basic social and practical support followed. Callahan (1989: 181) concludes that 'Fifteen years of research on community based care management fails to support most of the claims of its effectiveness in solving the problems for which it was intended.' He states that much of the early success of the method relied on charismatic leadership pitched against traditional agency ethos and pilot studies that were specially funded. Later studies either showed no effect, actually increased hospitalization (Hendrick and Inui, 1987) or failed to increase quality of life (Capitman *et al.*, 1986; Franklin *et al.*, 1987). Further, in a study for the Robert Wood Johnson Foundation, a grant funding body to 13 service agencies, Callahan found that elders were generally not users of multiple services, and did not see the value of care planning (95 per cent of elders and 85 per cent of carers) or monitoring (95 per cent of elders and 91 per cent of carers), finding that there was 'little interest in case management from either seniors or care-givers. Seniors were particularly adamant that they did not want to be "cases" and that no-one needed to manage their lives.' (Callahan, 1989: 192). These findings are important because of a surprising silence in the literature from the consumer voice, studies focusing instead on referral, purchaser or different professional attitudes to case management.

The UK experience

UK adoption of case management has rested on a number of pilot studies conducted by the Personal Social Services Research Unit in Kent (Challis and Davies, 1986; Knapp *et al.*, 1990), which formed the basis for government policy in this field. Case management became the spearhead of an attempt to engineer a cultural shift in UK welfare toward a market economy. The White Paper *Caring for people* (HMSO, 1989) outlines the proposed shape of case management as follows:

> The Government sees considerable merit in nominating a 'case manager' to take responsibility for ensuring that individual's needs are regularly reviewed, resources managed effectively and that each service user has a single point of contact . . . Case management provides an effective method of targeting resources and planning services to meet specific needs of individual clients.

A reading of these proposals, in the light of the US experience, indicates that the chosen model emphasizes a systems administration model with a prime concern for cost efficiency, service monitoring and a gatekeeping rather than a direct provider role.

What was surprising in this period was the silence of key welfare pressure groups in defending established practice wisdom. Jack (1992: 4) reports that in the rush to meet centrally imposed deadlines 'There was little time for such reflection and busy departments were concerned with the mechanisms of implementation rather than a cool assessment of the value of what it was that was being imposed.' Biggs (1990a: 27) notes that 'The response has been one of anxiety at not knowing what plans were (in practical terms), leading in some cases to attempts to 'second-guess' proposals by changing services in advance of legislation.' These observations tie in with the common sense dynamic of welfare work outlined in Chapter Seven, a mixture that abjures reflection and is haunted by punitive anxiety.

A number of writers have criticized these developments. Phillipson (1990) and Holloway (1991) lament a lack of reference to the difficulties encountered in the US. Biggs (1990a, 1991a,b) notes that pilot studies were concerned primarily with long-term, and therefore relatively predictable, discharge from hospital of chronic cases that may not be generalized to crises, a significant source of referral to private care (Bartlett and Challis, 1985). He also reports a lack of consumer feedback, other than global attitude measures, plus no consideration of cultural and ethnic difference and how that might affect referral and success. Fisher (1991a,b,c) questions the validity of Challis and Davies' (1986) original research in so far as it took place using reduced caseloads, and is insufficiently detailed to shed light on difficulties that might emerge between elders, carers and the use of contracts. Like Biggs (1991b), Fisher (1991a) notes the exclusion of particularly difficult cases from the experimental groups used.

Whilst the pilot studies do show that case management can be effective in institutional rehabilitation and that many carers and elders expressed satisfaction with the extra support achieved, Challis and Davies (1986: 331) note that 'Decisions taken by the client were less of the positive kind, and became more of a veto.' Davies (1990) has noted that 'marginal productivities', or positive attitude change, were not related to the degree of support available. This may indicate a general 'halo' or satisfaction effect, given the well documented difficulty in getting elderly users to complain about services.

Case management and interpersonal relations

It is important to look at the model of interpersonal relations tacit within this conception of community. The very particular view of human relations contained in the 1990 NHS and Community Care Act has been described as a market-place (Biggs, 1991a,b) or consumerist (Fisher, 1991a) model:

That is to say a meeting of two equal individuals coming together to agree a bargain on the exchange of goods and services ... It proposes a vision of single persons, rationally, in possession of relevant information and a cool grasp of their own motivation, finding an agreeable solution to a mutually agreed definition of need. Each then returning to their private activities. (Biggs, 1991a: 73)

Fisher questions the validity of the label of consumer on the grounds that few pay for services and lack this lever of control, may not be able or well enough to shop around and may be captive in the sense of being subject to statutorily mandated intervention.

Biggs goes on to outline a number of omissions. Firstly, case management treats interpersonal relations as unproblematic. There is little concern for conflict or conflict resolution, although, as can be seen from the previous section, the negotiation of caring roles and the entry of a public agency into that system raise a number of potentially conflictual issues. Fisher (1991b) found that a common difficulty was finding out how much the older person knew about a referral and establishing acceptable norms for confidentiality between carer and elder. This might be particularly difficult when the worker knows of differing perceptions of the goals of an intervention, for example the carer might wish to reduce their amount of caring, leaving time for other projects, whilst the elder requires the maintenance of existing relations. This conflict to some degree reflects differences between the first and second stages of life and might occasion considerable stress.

Secondly, the situation is predominantly rational, the motivations underlying transaction being rarely of interest. When they are, common sense concentrates on the quality of the concrete product:

Will it do what he says it will do? What might she do if the goods are faulty? Consideration of unconscious motivation would raise a distinct constellation of alternative questions: Is what he asks for going to fulfil needs of which he is currently unaware? Is she going to use the product that helps solve or add to her expressed problem? The questions are legion and do not lend themselves to products that can be packaged and sold. (Biggs, 1991a: 74)

An example of the role of irrational forces at work has been outlined by Kanter (1988, 1989). He points out that case managers mediate between users and their environment in a distinctive way in so far as they hold resources that users need and attempt to manage their personal strengths. As humans tend to perceive interpersonal situations as a repetition of prior experience, it is important to recognize that management can recreate irrational responses not unlike those of parental authority.

'Conflicts often arise when case manager (parent) and client (child) disagree in their assessment of a client's capabilities' (Kanter, 1988: 18) and 'Attempts to provide clients with some stability and structure are often perceived as attempts to control them.' (Kanter, 1988: 20). Initial positive responses to the dependency and friendship inherent in offers to manage difficult situations are later disappointed and, if case managers rely on a mechanical execution of their package of care, can result in repeated failure unless the unconscious dynamic is recognized. As it has been shown that elders might be sensitized to attempts to erode their personal control in caring situations, such conflicts might be exacerbated.

Finally, the market vision emphasizes the individual without reference to culture, collective allegiances or contexts in which the product will be located and used. As minority groups already experience considerable difficulty in finding acceptable community resources (Patel, 1990), a focus solely on the individual, without reference to the pre-existing common sense of dominant groups, would be expected to exacerbate such problems. Mirza's (1991: 124) analysis of trends in community care services supports this contention:

> Unfortunately, in order to ensure services are cost-effective, departments may develop a standard perception of what services should cost, resulting in an inability to maintain the strides made in catering for black and minority ethnic groups.

Because case management, as promoted in the UK, reinforces trends toward administrative definitions of care, it may be particularly prone to these omissions when the public and private spheres interact.

CO-OPTING THE CARER

A key consideration about how this boundary is regulated in the case of elders and their carers concerns the relatedness of generational projects between them and their case manager. As has been rehearsed previously, Biggs (1989a) proposes that workers are more likely to have current projects and accrued life-experience that make it easier to respond to the needs of peers or younger people. Different existential goals of older age are thereby likely to be defined as in some way deviant or of low priority. Knight's (1986) analysis of the projective mechanisms in operation across generations also indicates that it may be easier for a worker to identify with the often unconscious processes arising from a carer's predicament, or, because of unresolved personal issues fail to remain impartial whilst goals are being negotiated. It is also interesting in this regard to note that care management in both countries has tended to focus on practical tasks, rather than the more intimate areas of counselling around existential limitation in older age. A focus on task performance would itself bias interventions toward the cognitive styles of the first half of life, which might itself contribute to strengthening bonds between carer and worker.

How, then, does case management attempt to resolve the question of boundary regulation? As can be seen from the above review, such questions have rarely been addressed in any detail. What evidence there is suggests that the public–private boundary is redefined by incorporating the carer into the institutional priorities of the worker.

An incorporation of carers into the common sense of welfare is evident from the beginnings of case management in the US. Silverman and Brahce (1979: 79) asserted that 'The family is now considered to be the most important *agency* supporting the elderly' (my italics). Whilst Monk (1981: 63) stated that 'It is the function of social workers to mobilise kin-networks so that they take responsibility for those in the family.' The National Association of Social Workers's (1984: 10) guidelines for case management refer to functions being '. . . shared by the social worker, the client and the client's family, and other professional agencies.' Problems, it assumes, can be addressed by the correct definition of tasks plus adequate information given to the users:

> Family members who have the time, a personal interest in a client and an extensive knowledge of and a trusting relationship with a client can be in an advantageous position to schedule, supervise, monitor, adjust and interpret services. (National Association of Social Workers, 1984: 12)

There is no discussion in that document of situations where the carer and nominated client disagree, have different interests or are working through conflicts arising from their life history together. Rather, emphasis would be on the efficient management of the service system itself, co-opting one party from the informal caring relationship into the rational providing world of the professional co-ordinator. Seltzer *et al.* (1984: 66) give details of how a working relationship might be fostered, which from the current perspective shows a fairly comprehensive socialization:

> The partnership is first formed when the social worker approaches the family member and obtains his/her agreement to participate. The social worker defines the focus and parameters of the partnership – case management activities – and the social worker trains the family member in selected case management tasks. The family member collaborates with the social worker in setting the case managemert agenda and, following training, he/she assumes responsibility for the performance of at least one case management task.

A clear initial contract is seen as essential if both workers and family members are to understand their mutual responsibilities toward the older person. It is not so much that these writers are unaware of conflicts in the carer's life, but that factors such as:

> overwhelming ongoing responsibilities, when the family member is emotionally or cognitively unable to serve as a partner, when the elderly person and the family member are estranged from one another, and when the elderly person is unwilling to allow the family member to assume the role of partner (Seltzer, 1984: 69)

are used to disqualify carers and older people from services rather than to occasion further investigation. This is quite different to a recognition that carers are likely to be expert in what Fisher (1991b) calls arrangements 'finely tuned' to the elder's requirements and their own abilities and patience. Fisher (1991b: 246) does, however, note another twist in the public–private tail:

> Carers and workers can sometimes reach an agreement, unspoken and unwritten, which allows for the issue of personal support for the carer to be legitimately on the agenda without the carer explicitly having to acknowledge and name this as a problem for which service is sought. Although this sort of understanding falls short of an agreement in care management terms, it represents good practice with carers.

This is a very peculiar statement in an otherwise exemplary study of how even older people suffering from dementia can be realistically included in decisions about and monitoring of packages of care. It implies that it is difficult for the carers to acknowledge their own requirements, to be expected if dependency has been submerged in the personal shadow or located in the elder and the method of intervention reinforces a perception of para-professionalism. However, what is interesting from the viewpoint of generational alliance is that workers collude with this definition, even when they are aware of the considerable stress a carer might be under. An attempt to re-examine the status quo would threaten the shared assumptive reality between worker and carer, a reality that coheres case management 'for' rather than with the older person.

Now, when a person moves from within a system, in this case a family, to negotiate or collaborate on behalf of that system with another, for example welfare services, relations with members in the system of origin change. Miller and Rice (1967: 60) state that 'It is not uncommon for representatives to be disowned by the groups represented because they have transferred, or are suspected of having transferred, their allegiances to the groups they visit.'

Depending upon the degree of formalization of the carer role, the nature of the relationship being 'left', an alliance between carer and worker might increase distance from the older person. Unfortunately case management has not been investigated from this viewpoint, and the effects on distance between carer and elder are unknown. What is clear from the above is that a redefinition of boundaries can take place that runs the risk of developing generational alliances to the disservice of the older person, and inhibit carers from receiving help.

The point here is that co-option into a para-professional role does not necessarily help the carer define their own requirements, nor extend existential choice for the elder. It fails to provide alternatives other than assimilation into practitioner common sense through collusive alliance, trends that would need to be avoided if community care were to extend the potential of each party.

NEGOTIATION BETWEEN PRACTITIONERS

A second boundary change occurs on the adoption of case management. Whereas direct caring places workers within the framework of service provision, co-ordination and negotiation moves them to the boundaries of that system. Austin and O'Connor (1989), for example, refer to case managers as 'boundary spanners'. This difference has significant effects on the perceptions and priorities of persons so located (Biggs, 1990a, 1991b, 1992).

Once operating on the boundary between systems, the worker is no longer immersed in everyday care to the same extent as a provider of services. A subtle change comes over the hierarchy of priorities and other actors who influence decision-making. This is particularly the case for the model adopted from Griffiths (1988) and the 1990 NHS and Community Care Act, whereby local authorities are expected to purchase care from the voluntary and private sectors. Using Bridger's (1980) formulation of open and closed systems, it can be seen that case management has qualities most often associated with the former. That is to say, it suggests a system in which roles and solutions are negotiated between multiple interests that increasingly demand the independent exercise of judgement and an outward-looking approach from the organization itself. The degree to which an elder's voice is heard would depend upon whether they can gain access to that negotiating arena. Unfortunately, legislation only refers to complaints procedures once a product had been purchased, even if the product involves significant upheaval and is difficult to reverse. It also sees the local state purchasing, on behalf of ultimate users and through negotiation with other professionals, the providers. For case managers, the problem at hand is simplified in so far that they only need to fit parts of a jigsaw of provision together and subsequently monitor developments. Responsibility for content, what goes on within the package of care, is the job of the provider. Much of the day-to-day anxiety arising from meeting need voiced by consumers themselves, adhering to quality requirements and changing practice as a response to complaint (rather than administering the complaints procedure) can, with little difficulty, be displaced onto these providers of care. Once initial agreement has been made with the user or carer, the manager can take the role of independent arbiter between parties if conflict occurs.

So, key relationships shift toward engagement in contractual agreement and compliance between managers and providers. Comments by Austin (1990) and Austin and O'Connor (1989) that power and authority comes from the manager's gatekeeping role and Moxley and Buzas' (1989) concern for the views of referral agents, must be seen in this light. The criterion for successful negotiation becomes finding an acceptable compromise for those present and the smooth transfer of resources across sector boundaries. These relationships require regular maintenance if the contract is itself to be maintained and the project of developing an enduring service enhanced. Conflict resolution would then focus on compliance, whether the provider had done what they say they would do, whilst the elder's voice would have to be assertained through the filter of participants from another generation. The problems associated with within-generational collusion; that empathy with elders is likely to be less frequent and less accurate than with helpers and clients of a similar age and that priorities from the second half of life are afforded a low or negligible status, would multiply. Empathic compatibility may confirm a bond between harassed provider and case manager, which is reflected in negotiations. The degree to which case managers themselves control relations with providers would vary depending upon the amount of devolved budgeting operating in any one workplace (Peck *et al.*, 1992) and whether block contracts take place with a single provider or with a multiplicity of small provider organizations (Flynn, 1990). However, unless significant space occurs for decisions to be grounded in the first-hand requirements of elders themselves, generational bias should be expected.

ADMINISTRATIVE PRIORITIES

Contracting, negotiation and financial control increase the administrative nature of worker responsibilities. Capitman *et al.* (1986: 399), for example, point out that 'Case management can be considered as an administrative service that directs the client through ... the long term care system.' As a greater part of work requires administration, priorities and definitions of accountability again shift, paradoxically, to reflect a more closed organizational system. Biggs (1990a) outlines three consequences.

Firstly, professional and administrative judgements differ. Whereas the former rely largely on the experience of the practitioner to make a qualitative judgement of need, the latter emphasize quantitative assessment that can be turned into a statistical measure of relative deprivation and cost containment (Etzioni, 1964). This reinforces tendencies to target certain homogenized groups of consumers, which has a doubled effect of reducing the visibility of individualized requirements and allowing the exclusion of certain groups or categories of need. Secondly, the constituency being served shifts from contact with the expressed needs of users to decisions that err on the side of responsibility to funders, in this case the tax-payer as represented by the public body in question (Scott, 1967). Decisions, then, move away from user-defined problems to be influenced by general attitudes at large in the non-user population, which are then interpreted by the service system. Again the extra dimension of difference across generations and prejudices arising from global attitudes to old age would be likely to increase. Finally, administrative systems focus on the internal efficiency of an organization, whether, as an organization, it is running smoothly, rather than the effectiveness of actions approved (Butt and Palmer, 1985; Garner, 1989). A danger lies in the possibility that procedure, itself valuable in the interests of equity, becomes the only criterion by which satisfactory outcomes are judged. Caputo (1988: 131) says such circumstances 'Exacerbate the all too common bureaucratic tendency to convert political and ethical issues to administrative and technical problems, to translate values into tasks' and 'Since these systems cancel the human factor, the concept of the person as a responsible agent of decision vanishes and capitulation to the blueprint follows.' (Caputo, 1988: 135).

Athough professional judgement can easily obscure user requirements, as seen in Chapter Seven, a change to administrative values moves decision-making even further away from the user. Defining practitioner tasks as simply the technical execution of skill or procedure, would also reinforce those tendencies noted in professional common sense (see Chapter Seven) to dehumanize relations between user and practitioner.

Summary

Using the case management model to consider boundaries between users and practitioners has pinpointed difficulties additional to those arising from the professional common sense of practitioners engaged in community care. Paradoxically, community care, as defined, evidences a migration away from direct contact between elders and practitioners. Firstly, it leads to the incorporation of carers into the common sense of services with unforeseen implications for dynamics within the private sphere. Secondly, a shift of location from direct provision to the boundaries between caring systems refocuses priorities onto negotiation with other professionals rather than enhancing the user's voice. Finally, the increased administration entailed can emphasize internal efficiency to the detriment of effectiveness in line with user requirements. At each point, the possibility of collusive alliances between generational peers, particularly with regard to priorities from the 'first half of life', may marginalize the existential needs of older people themselves. A trend, noted at various points in the caring system, works toward homogenization of elders as a group, denies the role of difference and conflict between perspectives, and thereby obscures the reality of these user's perspectives with results that closely follow commonly held prejudices against elders. The practice of community care, it would seem, produces a new form of institutional ageism.

CONCLUSIONS

When practice seems to exhibit trends that move in the opposite direction to espoused aims, that community contributes to the marginalization of older people, it is not unreasonable to speculate on irrational influences at work within such systems.

Hoggart (1989) refers to a 'culture of uncertainty' that is emblematic of everyday life in Western communities. This uncertainty has its roots in an experience of failed dependency, whereby attempts to rely on existing cultural images are repeatedly disappointed as they are found to be insubstantial. Richards (1989a: 47) proposes that the complexity and speed of modern life, and the many roles that it offers, can lead to 'A fragmentation of the subject, the superficiality of affect, the break up of stylistic norms.' In these circumstances it is increasingly difficult to sustain meaning, resulting in a rigid clinging to areas of supposed certainty as part of an attempt to simplify experience and make it manageable. Elsewhere, Richards (1989b) proposes that the dominant model of interpersonal behaviour – market relations – serves a number of psychological functions. The amorality and freedom associated with the market mark a protest against restrictions and dependency that inevitably emerge as limits to one's own power through contact with other people:

> We can understand the demand for freedom in the market as a narcissistic refusal to accept the boundaries of the self and to be prepared to negotiate ones needs with those of others. While critics of the market lament the isolated individual bereft of community, pro-marketeers celebrate the omnipotently free individual unfettered by binding forms of relatedness to others. (Richards, 1989b: 16)

It is perhaps here that some understanding can be gained of why case management has emerged as a preferred form of managing the boundaries of community care for older people. It is quite possible, given this context, for the need to humanize images of ageing simply to be abolished in favour of a strategy to cope with chaos. This is at the same time an indication of despair that social problems cannot be resolved and an attempt to maintain hope that they can at least be managed. The particular twist given by the common sense of the market would allow dominant parties to indulge in fantasies of untrammelled omnipotence, which fail to place a check on psychological inflation. The older person could easily become enmeshed in a series of relations that enforce passivity in order to sustain the activity of the practitioner or co-opted carer. A focus on negotiation with service providers and increased bureaucratic administration reinforce distance from service users' actual experience.

This is not to ignore advantages arising from case management. Setting clear objectives has within it the seeds of a more realistic appraisal of what is being offered and required, which might counteract unreasonable demands for dependency and omnipotence. However, participants would need to construct their requirements separately for this to happen, and priority would need to be given to those defined by the older person. Space would also need to be created in which users and workers could identify their common interests. That this is notoriously difficult reflects not only ageist values internalized by all participants, but that community care and case management have already been defined as enhancing user choice whilst conspicuously avoiding so doing.

The question arises whether community care can provide the environment necessary to enhance the projects of the second half of life. How far does it allow space for consideration of the limitations that age sets on time left, the body and images of the self? How far can dialogue move away from forms that emphasize task and work-related anxieties toward those of consolidation, maintenance and life review? At present, community has been successively distilled down to family, and then to responsible individuals within it. The development of a collective identity and within that the exploration of personal existential need that can be named would face many hurdles, not least being whether the now maladaptive exigencies of the first half of life can be shed with dignity by both helpers and helped.

9

Older people and residential care

INTRODUCTION

Thus far, relations between older service users and practitioners have been reviewed and special attention given to the growth of community care. Residential care has become associated with an opposite, often negative pole, partly as a result of its enclosed and protective nature and partly because of the positive value given to community living. Both points intensify the psychological and commonsensual meaning that residence has come to contain. Any consideration of it is therefore fraught with difficulty in disentangling image from reality.

Residential care is closely linked in many people's minds to old age, both for younger people considering their own ageing and as a concrete option for elders who encounter increasing difficulty in daily living. It has taken a symbolic significance, marking a life-transition, and has come to contain many of the negative attributes of ageing. The mental act of distancing oneself from a potential negative future finds a place to locate unwanted potential, whatever the actual circumstances existing in such institutions might be.

When compared to community living, residential care provides a smaller, more manageable environment. The boundaries between it and other situations are relatively clear, so that what is inside and what is outside become easier to distinguish. It can contain a world that is relatively autonomous, a life of its own. Whilst this helps those inside to manage, it can also intensify feelings and relationships. That it is easily located and defined contributes to its attractiveness as a repository for uncomfortable associations, leaving other forms of existence relatively free from consideration. People who are not in an institution no longer have to think about the issues it comes to contain. In this sense the very existence of institutional provision is a threat to many older people in the same way as Bassaglia (in Schepper and Lovell, 1988) describes mental hospitals as oppressive to sufferers from mental illness. The potential for incarceration, of exclusion from everyday life and the identity that it conveys, hangs above the heads of any who fail to pass as normal. When normality is defined in age-specific terms, this takes on a particular importance for old age. The reason for admission becomes that of failure to cope with difficulty rather than finding an arena in which further potential can be achieved.

Institutional provision has variously been described as a 'social death sentence' (Miller and Gwynne, 1972), or as 'playpens for the old' (Kuhn, 1977), in other words as lacking projects which can be meaningfully engaged.

SIMULTANEOUS PUBLIC AND PRIVATE SPACE

The argument above has identified a number of factors that might influence perceptions of transition and residence and has attempted to locate institutional care within the broader dynamic of attitudes to ageing. A difficulty arises when, as Willcocks *et al.* (1987) have pointed out, elders are paradoxically expected to live their private lives in a public space. It becomes a private space in so far as residents are expected to live the majority of their lives within it and therefore require a degree of privacy and autonomy; it becomes a public space in so far as it is staffed and regulated as a working environment, which wider society has charged to manage the difficulties circumscribed therein. Because it holds importance, not simply for residents, but for the way disability in old age is managed socially and psychologically, institutional care comes to inhabit both the private and the public sphere simultaneously. In addition to a quality of hiddenness from the wider consciousness, this space has itself to be regulated. It is perhaps not accidental that behaviour in this setting is often inhibited and stereotyped (Townsend, 1962; Wilkin and Hughes, 1987), allowing little opportunity for self-expression excepting when the integrity of the Self is itself under threat of disintegration, as in the case of dementia. Communication thus becomes either superficial or chaotic, in both cases conforming to the stereotype that requires suppression in the consciousness of those outside it. It is in this way that residence comes to both reflect and contain aspects of behaviour that are unacceptable elsewhere.

This is not to say that the idea of a more manageable, contained space is in itself hostile to a fulfilling older lifestyle. Nussbaum (1991) identifies the potential held by residential care in so far as it occasions closeness, increased control and reduces anxiety. He points out that within this new social world, age is far less variable, giving the opportunity for common projects to emerge. Homogeneity and close proximity can, he argues, overcome class, ethnicity and gender as predictors of friendship. Voluntary association can lead to egalitarianism, consensus and the sharing of good times, which is markedly free from the dead hand of family obligation. A positive use of residence would need to balance the value of the protection it affords with the requirements of autonomy to define one's own goals and creative and interdependent social interaction.

This discussion has pointed to a number of factors that require further examination if residence is to become the positive choice for elders envisaged by social policy initiatives such as the Wagner Report (1988). Firstly, how far transition to residence marks a significant boundary change that effects how future ageing will be perceived. Secondly, how far conditions within residence will limit or enhance the development of potential in older age and contribute to the humanization of its social image. Finally, how far different forms of care in a mixed welfare economy influence choice and provide opportunities for elder participation.

CHOICE, RESIDENCE AND COMMUNITY

The perceptions that elders and carers have of residential provision will colour practical matters such as evaluating an institutional option and preparations that are made. This might effect potential projects that are seen as realistic and the degree to which a passive persona is adopted as a consequence of accepting the projections located in residential care.

One way of accessing anticipations is to look at how potential residents use information about care. A British study by Roberts *et al.* (1991) discovered that, taking into account the low quality of information available at the time, elders were resistant to using such sources unless an active choice had been made to seek residence. The overriding response of older people living in the community was to hope the need would not arise. Seeking information was itself associated with a loss of independence and privacy. If the option was considered at all, then personal contact with people found helpful in the past, GPs, home-helps, bank managers, were named as potential contacts, even when previous contact was not necesssarily on the same issue:

> One of the most prominent themes to emerge from the survey was the extent of people's psychological and emotional resistance to the idea of residential care. Residential care is seen as something unpleasant – considering it is tantamount to accepting a dramatically reduced standard of life, to the point that it is viewed as 'a place to die'. For carers, considering residential care is equivalent to

admitting defeat, and will often generate feelings of guilt at having failed to live up to one's responsibilities. (Roberts *et al.*, 1991: 119)

Loss of independence and being required to mix with uncongenial others were seen as major disadvantages by elders in the community (Campbell, 1971; Salvage *et al.*, 1986). Campbell found that only 5 per cent of his sample of London elders, aged 75 and over, were interested in residential care, a subgroup who were themselves quite fit; whilst 16 per cent of Salvage's Glamorgan sample were prepared to consider a residential option. Zarb (1992) notes that residential care may represent a particular problem for those who had previously spent their early adult life in institutions. Disabled people who have worked hard to achieve independence might find the prospect of further residence unacceptable.

In an extensive review, Sinclair (1988) cites poverty, inadequate housing, increasing disability and lack of appropriate community services as being primary factors in provoking actual admission. He notes (Sinclair, 1988: 263–4) that in two-thirds of cases, elders were either hospitalized or living in someone else's home at the time of admission and in many cases there was considerable pressure on them to move elsewhere:

> In these circumstances, it is hard to assess how far applicants chose to go into care, and how far any regrets about this are more properly seen as regrets about the circumstances that made it necessary.

This combination of disadvantages illuminate the reality faced by many older people, which Wilkin and Hughes (1987: 175) describe as a 'Choice between an unpleasant battle to survive in their own homes and an equally unpleasant enforced dependence in the institution.'

Tobin's (1989: 139) sample of elderly Americans anticipating admission, would reinforce the view that transition provokes profound dissonance that has to be resolved: 'Psychological effects of this anticipatory period are a result of feelings of abandonment and, also, of a redefinition of self as a person who can only survive if provided with institutional care.' As he found no differences in adverse physical and social changes experienced between waiting list respondents and elders planning to remain in the community, he concludes that this self-redefinition was part and parcel of the process of psychological preparation for residence itself.

ELDERS AND CARERS

Roberts *et al.* (1991) found that where elders were frail or confused, transition was often straight from hospital. There was usually one key relative involved in arranging the move and the older person was little involved in making the decision or seeking information. However, regardless of the elder's location '... very few of the carers talked about discussing the matter with the person being cared for, or presenting them with the information' (Roberts *et al.*, 1991: 85).

Once a decision had been made, the pressure for carers to take responsibility for admission came from professionals and elders alike, and it would seem from this study that they were expected to bear not only their own ambivalence, but also that of other parties. Because the final decision is often made in a climate of urgency, closely following an event such as a fall or other evidence of declining powers, anxieties often centre on whether a place is available and the mechanics of admission. Both elder and carer may therefore fail to consider other options, as it is painful and disorienting enough to consider an event that in itself is taken to mark a radical change in potential futures. Roberts *et al.* found that applicants rarely asked questions reflecting the implications of a move, being concerned instead with quality of life within the home, cleanliness, type of room, financial and procedural matters. These factors foreclosed on existing situations in favour of concrete arrangements associated with the narrowed horizon of transition itself. Consideration of the implications of care on future potential and autonomy seem to have been eclipsed, by needs for reassurance that the new identity could be maintained with the maximum comfort.

Whether elders and carers agree on the appropriatenes of residence is a matter of debate. Sinclair (1988) notes that 'problems associated with informal carers' account for approximately two-thirds of applications to local authority care, and initiate about one-half of admissions to voluntary or private care. Although there is some evidence that carers encourage applications either straightforwardly, or by sowing doubt in an elders mind about their ability to cope (Neill *et al.*, 1989), Sinclair cautions against the conclusion that carers push elders into permanent care on flimsy contexts. For example, Allen (1983) found that although 39 per cent of relatives wanted elders on short stay to take up full residence, they recognized that few elders (18 per cent) would want that to happen.

What does seem to emerge from a number of studies is that both carers and users hold a differing set of priorities from those arising from professional wisdom. Rather than requiring information about different alternatives (Roberts *et al.*, 1991) both groups wanted to know about quality of life within homes. This is in contrast to trends noted by Phillipson (1982) and Biggs (1990a) that increasingly emphasize professional concern with transfer across caring boundaries and inspection of physical conditions that can be easily measured (Challis, 1985; Biggs, 1987a; Davis, 1987). Perring (1991) interprets user concern with care quality as a refusal to reject residential care *per se* and an interest in increased choice of lifestyle and activities within homes. Users from a variety of age groups, including older people, wanted small scale, ordinary housing that enabled a choice of lifestyle. Older people were particularly concerned that residence should not be seen as permanent, rather than a means to rehabilitation as it was assumed by service providers that frailty and dependency would inevitably increase with age. A crucial factor here was the reduced security that entry into care brought when it entailed the loss of one's own home, thus severely diminishing other options. If users wanted to see choice in where and how they live, carers required choice over whether and how far to provide care. Whilst they wanted the status of both formal and informal care to be raised, this did not necessarily imply becoming paraprofessional themselves.

Most researchers agree that an active choice of residential care by elders has a positive affect on the process of admission (Tobin, 1989, Roberts *et al.*, 1991) and well-being in residence itself (Weaver *et al.*, 1985; Tobin, 1989; Nussbaum, 1991). Although previous knowledge was often accidentally acquired, Roberts *et al.* found that residents who were most independent had clearly made the decision to move on their own. Time to plan and control the decision were crucial to subsequent adaptation to residential life, the most commonly reported advantages being comfort, physical care and reduced loneliness. Tobin (1989: 148) reports that:

> Those who transformed the situation so as to make the move totally voluntary and also to perceive their relocation environment as ideal were those most likely to survive intact through one year following admission.

Failure to 'magically master' the situation in this way increased vulnerability amongst residents, particularly if they had been passive during the move and continued that way once in care. Residents who responded aggressively to what Tobin calls the 'one month syndrome'; disorientation, depression, deterioration and bizarre behaviour following relocation; managed to achieve transition with little enduring change to their core sense of self. They had adopted an active strategy to cope with underlying painful feelings. A determining factor in such personal adjustment was the degree of fit between the new and the preceding environment, thus allowing existing coping strategies to be used. Tobin's accent on the one month syndrome indicates caution on assuming that changes evidence a different and henceforth unchanging personality. Neither dependency nor disability, as Booth (1985) and Zarb (1992) remind us, should be thought of as static conditions, they are, rather, statements about the nature of a relationship between users and providers. Left to themselves they are often temporary difficulties arising from particular circumstances. Unfortunately, dislocation, into a new culture, with new people and new expectations can fossilize both the roles residents are allowed and others' perceptions of their global capabilities.

Unfortunately, help with transition as psychologically threatening in itself seems sadly lacking:

It is assumed that new residents will discover the personal resources neccesary to instigate major adjustments to a lifetime's conception of home as intimate, personal and private in favour of a model whose physical and social dimensions are daunting and where the lifestyle is communal and public. (Willcocks *et al.*, 1987: 140)

Entry into residence means that the older person has to accommodate to an institutional culture that previous experience may or may not have prepared them for.

RESIDENCE AS FAMILY

A positive attribute of residence is commonly thought to be the degree to which environment and relations approximate those of a family (Phillips *et al.*, 1986). A report by Counsel and Care (1991) notes that the association of family and residential care arose from an attempt to reject the 'harsh, bleak and institutional' legacy of the poor law and workhouse, which many elders would associate with residence. Associations with family leads to a number of contradictions between this ideal and the reality of relations within institutions. Firstly, it has led to practices that take little account of the essentially public nature of institutional life, and the coping strategies that this requires. Whereas sharing living regimes, toileting and even bedrooms with family members may be moderately acceptable, shared use with strangers is not. In fact many of the factors that maintain dignity in the public sphere, such as lockable space, clearly defined private refuge, appropriate use of formal address, would run against the familist ideal. Secondly, it leads to the conclusion, as residence is in reality very different from family life, that 'real caring' can only happen elsewhere. Residence comes to contain a counterfeit version, which may actually inhibit new and contextually appropriate forms of collective living from emerging. As Counsel and Care (1991) notes, a consequence is to associate residential work with amateur status. Finally, it may actually increase tension between actual family members, who often experience guilt and stress following admission, and workers who seem to be aspiring to occupy the same psychological space for the older person. Nussbaum (1991: 154) reports that whilst natural families generally visit frequently, it is difficult to find satisfactory ways to negotiate the new situation. This often serves to increase feelings of dependency in the elder and obligation by family members:

With each visit to the nursing home the elderly resident is reminded of his or her dependence. Feelings of guilt and resentment emerge with both the family and resident to the extent that each visit becomes a chore.

Nussbaum and others (Wilkin and Hughes, 1987; Tobin, 1989) note that these feelings can then become displaced onto staff. There is some evidence that family members become idealized when they are not actually present, which Nussbaum describes as the 'common coin' of discussion between residents. Such responses would be expected once staff become associated with substitute families, as parties react to an image which bears little relation to experience.

ELDERS AND STAFF

Communality in residence centres on two sets of relations. First, many people with similar requirements inhabit the same physical and social space. These are generally defined as clients, patients or users. Second, the buildings are a workplace for nurses, care and social workers, whose job it is to maintain that environment. The quality of relations within the institution will depend upon how these groupings interrelate both within and between themselves. Together they act to maintain a common sense, which locates actors within that social space and determines which parts of the Self can be owned and which are rejected. It is perhaps an indicator of the degree to which residence has come to contain negative attributions of ageing and disability as failure, that the potentially transforming strength of communal life (Greenwell, 1989; Nussbaum, 1991), a pivotal defining feature of the residential experience, is so often associated with lack.

Relations between staff and older residents are perhaps one of the most studied of areas of applied gerontology, and it is both distressing and a sign of the resilience of the patterns that institutions create, that so little seems to have changed over years of study and report. For a detailed review of the UK context, the reader is referred to Townsend (1962), Booth (1985), Sinclair (1988) and Brearley (1990). Although Lawton (1989: 21) claims that 'There is no level of competence so low that an increment in wellbeing cannot be maintained by self-directed alteration of the environment', residential care consistently reproduces patterns reinforcing resident–staff relationships that turn on dependency and distance. There is some evidence that this is not what elders require, but may be what they have come to expect. Giles and Coupland (1991a) report that elders wish for communication that is both affiliative and respectful, but often end up with professional behaviour that reproduces the least attractive features of intergenerational discourse – superficiality, a focus on limited problem-based issues and a tendency to infantilize. Nussbaum (1991), whilst emphasizing the positive potential of cross-generational communication, found the content of conversation 'quite controlled and unidirectional', whilst the best that Wilkin and Hughes (1987: 183) can describe is 'Formal politeness and an avoidance of personal contact which might invade the individual's right to privacy' and 'The relationship was thus one of gratitude for services rendered, it was an instrumental relationship.' (Wilkin and Hughes, 1987: 192).

In an unremittingly public arena it is, of course, quite an effective strategy to protect one's self-integrity by keeping others at a distance, thereby protecting what little privacy is left. Rejection of others, especially if what can be expected is superficial and demeaning, may be one of the few avenues left to express autonomy. The maintenance of rigid and superficial communication by staff would also serve to protect them from recognizing hidden parts of the Self that have been projected on to residents. Attributes of dependency and associations with personal old age can then be more easily displaced in order to maintain the professional persona of the helper. Boundaries are thus maintained on both sides, which unfortunately replace common humanity with homogenized and stereotyped perceptions of the other.

In such environments, elders also distance themselves from other residents. Wilkin and Hughes (1987) report that although only a minority of older people in the homes studied could be thought of as dementing; many who were interviewed perceived other residents to be disturbed and not responsible for their own actions.

Certainly, there seems little scope for the age-related project of passing on accrued experience or for developing a collective understanding of the existential projects of older age.

However, criticism of relations between staff and residents is not universal. Sinclair (1988) points out that researchers' criticisms of institutions as unnatural and unstimulating environments are not necessarily shared by elders in care. He notes that lack of choice, attempts by regimes to enhance functional abilities and experiments in group living, aimed to reduce loneliness, have not been related to self-reported satisfaction and attempts to improve residential environments may actually lead to increased dissatisfaction amongst residents. Staff, he reports often receive higher praise than other residents, being mentioned for their 'kindness and willingness to oblige'. In summary, Sinclair isolates five requirements voiced by residents: (i) an appreciation of comfort; (ii) physical security and freedom from worry that residence can provide; (iii) the ability to be private when one chooses and have companions by choice; (iv) control over the immediate physical environment, such as opening windows, security and tenure; and (v) interesting and varied activities.

It is difficult to judge how far reports of satisfaction with the status-quo reflect the candid thoughts of elders in residence. Older residents have been found to be singularly uncritical of the care they receive. Chiriboga (1990) noted that elders showed a predisposition to respond favourably to questions about satisfaction. Wilkin and Hughes (1987) explain this as an 'unwillingness to bite the hand that feeds' and suggest that it works to maintain established routines and attitudes among staff. Tobin (1989: 151) notes that 'in many facilities . . . even the most minor of deviations from ideal compliance and gratefulness are not tolerated.' Similar observations have led Kuypers (1969) to develop a measure of both the manifest and latent attitudes toward residential care. These considerations have also led to considerable concern about the effectiveness of formal complaints procedures in homes. Willcocks (1991: 11) notes that 'A culture of not "letting-on" or not being critical develops and is extremely difficult to penetrate.'

She itemizes a number of reasons why both care staff and residents are reluctant to blow the whistle on malpractice, which include; power politics within homes, denial and unwillingness to accept the validity of consumer critiques both within and outside residential homes and a fear of reprisal, which could lead to 'being bullied or victimized, either with the slow answering of a bell or being left until last to be served tea' (Willcocks, 1991: 11). Staff may fear dismissal or disciplinary proceedings. The pressure on staff to comply with existing practice was emphasized by the Royal College of Nursing's (1992) attempt to remove 'gagging clauses' in health worker's contracts and to highlight the case of Graham Pink, a nurse sacked for campaigning against poor conditions on a ward for elderly patients. The right of employers to silence staff concern was eventually supported at ministerial level.

Reports of the superficiality of staff–resident relations must be set against a context in which limited numbers of staff are often obliged to concentrate on practical and domestic tasks (Willcocks *et al.*, 1987; Sinclair, 1988; Counsel and Care, 1991; Nussbaum, 1991). Little time is allowed for care assistants and auxiliary nurses to engage residents in social interaction, which might actually be defined as outside their supervised responsibilities. The difference in priorities that then emerge have been summarized by Willcocks *et al.* (1987: 155):

Residents look for an environment designed to offer maximum flexibility, continuity and real friendship from their carers . . . Residential staff, in contrast, generally require a routine bounded by a set of rules together with a predetermined set of responsibilities that is strictly timetabled to allow them to complete their busy daily round.

In such circumstances, Counsel and Care (1991) report that the increased frailty of some residents often means that all older people lose further control over privacy and are subject to blanket rules.

It has been reported earlier that Robertson (1991) found working conditions and relations with management to be important indicators of staff morale and quality of life for residents. Archer and Whitaker (1991: 8) found that if care staff were allowed time and spare energy for participation in thinking and planning the residential environment, both staff and resident well-being increased. The involvement of staff in democratic decision-making:

> ... does not mean neglecting residents in favour of staff. On the contrary, it may be the most direct route toward releasing time and energy on the part of staff for work with residents. All of the staff we have studied, had the welfare of residents in mind as their primary task. When they set a goal which was primarily directed toward their own needs, this was never done frivolously, but always in response to a sense that there was something unsatisfactory in their own working situation which blocked best service to residents. We found no exceptions to this.

The study noted that participation reduced blaming between institutions and increased resident participation, who became more 'critical and alive'.

Greenwell (1989) indicates that a clear distinction between homes as residence and as workplaces was necessary in order to reduce confusion over whose home it actually was. Staff were discouraged from calling an establishment their home, which reduced a sense of possessiveness and complemented a distinction between resident's private space and communal living. Greenwell found that once elders were appraised of the reasons for meeting, they took an active role in planning the development of a new residential complex, achieving a continued dialogue with architects and social workers. Elders contributed an eye for detail that increased ability to exercise choice and maintained an approximation of normality in the final development. This report also found training that actively challenged ageist attitudes to be a valuable tool in establishing respect for residents' personal and civil rights. Willcocks (1991) found that resident self-expression was similarly enhanced in homes engaged in active debate about equal opportunities and anti-discrimination, where 'equal opportunities is a tangible force in everyday activities and experiences'. Willcocks *et al.* (1987) and Greenwell (1989) recommend a clear distinction between areas of public and private space, elders can then choose to interact with peers or others whilst also having a protected 'power-base'.

These studies would lead to conclusions that if mutual expectations

are clarified between residents and staff and the institutional environment is facilitative for both to find self-expression, certain work-styles
may help to humanize relations. However, these reports are exceptional
and must be seen against a background in which institutional care
reproduces and then contains the most negative attributes and fears
about older age. Although manifestly dysfunctional for both those who
are contained and those charged with their containment, the location
and maintenance of such environments serves a wider societal project
of excluding, physically, socially and psychologically, attributes of ageing that no longer fit within the limits of defined adult behaviour. To
survive in this residual space, elders are often either encouraged to
adopt personae that reproduce the role allotted to them or, in preserv-
ing their core integrity, reject both peers and helpers by condemning
themselves to a superficial loneliness. The potential of an environment
where peers are in the majority and younger people share time and
space with elders has for the most part been wasted.

CHOICE AND THE MIXED WELFARE ECONOMY

The 1980s saw a significant structural change in the welfare economy
with the growth of private residential homes from a figure that was
insignificant to approximately half of all places by the mid-1980s (Bartlett
and Challis, 1985). By 1991, the proportion of state-funded older residents in private and voluntary care homes had increased to 69 per cent
(Laing and Buisson, 1992). This trend was in part encouraged by Government ambition to extend market forces into the welfare sector. Concern
over the cost of funding places from the exchequer and a number of
scandals provoked increased interest in forms of regulation. The Registered Homes Act (1984) and The NHS and Community Care Act (1990)
extended the powers of Local Authority inspectors, the latter opening
state provision to inspection at 'arm's length'. The local state thus moved
toward quality control, whereby inspection of the context of care complemented care management and assessment of need.

Biggs (1987a,b) catalogued a number of implications of these changes.
Firstly, choice concerning nursing and residential care came to be
defined as existing between sectors of the welfare economy, that is to
say choices made at the point of sale, when an elder or their relative
decided which place to purchase. Secondly, Government guidelines
emphasized an enabling rather than a policing role for inspection of the
private and voluntary sectors, and made no requirement that resident's
views be taken into account (although this was recommended by informal
guidelines issued by the Centre for Policy on Ageing (Avebury, 1984)
entitled *Home life*). Workable standards were achieved in collaboration

with home owners, whilst elders themselves were essentially excluded from the negotiating space. Finally, the nature of inspection, located at the boundary between sectors, left inspection officers relatively isolated without professional identity and bureaucratic power at a crucial period in the creation of this new role.

These factors raise two interesting questions for the current discussion. Whether there are significant differences between care provided by different sectors of a mixed welfare economy, and how boundary negotiation has shaped the common sense of monitoring care.

PUBLIC, PRIVATE AND VOLUNTARY SECTORS

The project of engineering welfare structures in this way owes much to developments in the US. Gilbert (1984) has reviewed different sectors there and concludes that there is a lack of comparative evidence suggesting that forms of ownership influences care quality, as there is as much variation within sectors as there is between them. He does, however, note that non-profit-making institutions tend toward user participation and an atmsophere that promotes the moral value of social welfare, whilst profit-making ones centre on protecting the financial interests of ownership groups and accountability upward to those groups. On this basis the private sector '... engenders little compassion for the economic circumstances of others and hardly cultivates the idea of individual sacrifice for the common good.' (Gilbert, 1984: 73). He concludes by favouring non-profit-based organizations in cases where the vulnerability of residents precludes the sampling of alternatives. Other writers indicate that marketplace relations also affect voluntary and non-profit-making agencies. Powell and Friedkin (1987: 191) point out that:

As the activities and programs of a non-profit become more complex and require sophisticated technical, legal and financial knowledge in order to execute them ... non-profit is most vulnerable or susceptible to change, both in its mission and methods of operation.

Perlmutter and Adams (1990) note that uncertainty engendered by market forces provokes a change in emphasis from fulfilling the mission, the primary task of an agency, to fiscal concerns. This has been described by Garner (1989) as a search for 'cash-cows', parts of an institution that are profitable and can be enhanced, and the dropping of previous commitments or processes that do not conform to financial priorities. McMurty *et al.* (1990) note that variation in the financial climate may require speedy changes in strategic decision-making, which militate against lengthy consultation. Whilst Hardena (1990) noted that, during the 1980s – a period of reduced welfare spending under President Reagan – many agencies responded by restricting client eligibility and reducing access strategies, client participation and employment. Methods such as case management were used to '. . . increase professionals' ability to control both resource distribution and dissemination of information about organisational rules and processes' (Hardena, 1990: 35), even when they had been devised originally to enhance user advocacy. As financial control begins to override equity 'Grass-roots funded organisations in poorer communities have a limited capacity to raise funds and are less able to sustain formal access mechanisms.' (Hardena, 1990: 44).

Kettner and Martin (1990) indicate that an important factor in determining the profile of the mixed welfare system would be the model of funding and monitoring adopted. Partnership models involving joint ventures between purchasers and providers tend toward continuity of provision. Market models that encourage competition between providers might drive down costs and specify contractual requirements, but can lead to instability of provision.

It would seem from this brief review that, at least in the US context, market forces might or might not increase choice between options, if the product is such that users can sample different options; however, within options opportunities for participation might be reduced.

Comparative evidence from the UK is less systematic, perhaps reflecting the recency of the cultural shift toward market welfare and that the issue is politically charged to a greater degree. Weaver *et al.* (1985) have compared the staffing profiles of private and state residential homes. The most distinctive feature of private homes was the relative absence of supervisory staff and delegated authority from proprietors. Care staff were more likely to be younger (52 per cent under 34 years) and domestic staff older (51 per cent over 55) than public sector workers (59 per cent between 35 and 54 years). Work in the private sector was more likely to be part-time and involve split shifts and unscheduled overtime. Staff turnover also varied considerably between sectors. In the private sector 24 per cent had been appointed 6 months prior to the study, with some homes indicating a turnover of 40 per cent, as compared to 8 per cent in state homes. Biggs (1986) found that although numbers of trained staff were low in the state sector, applications to courses were significantly higher here, and from voluntary homes, than for private care staff.

Sinclair (1988), comparing Weaver's findings on choice at the point of admission with findings from the public sector, found that private residents were marginally more likely to have had a choice of home (at 26 per cent). However, he echos Weaver's sentiment that the proportion of residents exercizing choice was so small as to provide no regulatory function. Sinclair also notes differences in what might best be described as the quality of under-stimulation between sectors. State residents were more likely to be inactive in communal areas, whereas private residents were more likely to be 'marooned in their rooms', partly because of a lack of public space to be in. Counsel and Care (1991) noted differences in accommodation between private and voluntary care. Whereas 41 per cent of the latter had their own room, this was true for only 14 per cent of private residents. Whilst the reason for allocation was more likely to reflect the relative disability experienced by the older person in voluntary care, a private single room depended on ability to pay, occasionally requiring residents to move into shared roomspace if their financial circumstances deteriorated. Other factors affecting well-being, such as privacy when using a commode and lockable space for possessions, were also more likely to be present in voluntary homes.

A significant structural difference between sectors is the likelihood of bankruptcy affecting continuity of care in the private sector, either by occasioning a change of proprietor or of residence if a home is forced to close completely. Figures on bankruptcy are difficult to obtain, however, in 1986 the average life of a private care home was estimated to be three years, with bankruptcies running at 10 per cent (Royal Institute of Public Accountancy, 1986). The implications of these figures are reflected in residents' concerns. Power *et al.* (1983) report that whereas private residents were more likely to be worried about money and security of tenure, local authority residents were more concerned by health as a factor, as this might result in transfer to a long-stay hospital. Laing and Buisson (1992: 2), report that:

> With the decline in interest rates and the uprating of income support, pressure on care home operators' margins has now eased, though the sector is still feeling the effects of high levels of borrowing taken on in the late eighties and the property price slump of the last two years.

This emphasizes the private market's continued vulnerability to a number of economic factors. One casualty of these changes would be the advantage of small-sized establishments run by 'husband and wife' teams. Economy of scale would inevitably favour larger establishments and businesses run corporately.

In conclusion, what little evidence there is from the UK scene would tend to bear out the concerns expressed by some US commentators. A combination of poor staffing arrangements, proprietor control driven by concerns of financial viability and uncertainty of tenure would make it less likely that conditions within private residences would allow the time or space for user participation beyond the initial decision to enter a home.

QUALITY AND INSPECTION

Attempts to ensure quality in residential care have focused on registration and inspection (HMSO, 1984). Inspection, in particular, constitutes a means of regulating the context in which care takes place and is therefore less concerned with the individual requirements of older residents, which according to this model is left to care management. However, it would be wrong to see the mixed welfare economy as a pure market, as policy has also attempted to use care planning as a means of engineering the profile of care in any one geographical area. Both within health (Harrison and Wistow, 1992) and social care (Biggs, 1990a) funds available have been determined centrally, whilst being administered locally in order to target 'those most in need'. This bureaucratic allocation of resources has been labelled a 'quasi-market' by Le Grand (1990) and has a number of implications for the nature of transactions across care boundaries.

First, as Klein (1983: 140) points out, it reflects an attempt by central government to use local purchasers and providers as a buffer between it and the implications of its policies 'The stress now is on diffusing blame for the inevitable shortcomings in an era of economic crisis: to decentralise responsibility is also to disclaim blame', a function that inspectors, as boundary managers between sectors, are particularly liable to, given their distance or quasi-independence from the local state (Biggs, 1987a,b). This tends to leave them without a secure professional base in the purchasing authority, whilst having to absorb much of the tension between sectors as disputes arise through, for example, tribunals that adjudicate deregistrations.

Second, once operations move to the boundaries of the caring system, negotiation between interested parties takes on a central significance for the regulators if contracts are to be agreed and honoured. The system focuses on transactions between purchasers and providers, which has implications for the degree of influence that the eventual users can exert. In health (Hudson, 1992: 132) one finds 'A scenario in which potential users of goods and services . . . have no power to engage directly in market transactions based upon their personal preferences.'

In social welfare (Biggs, 1987a: 242):

Competing interests include the proprietors and their pressure groups, the statutory obligations of the authority and, to a far lesser extent, a general climate of influence from voluntary agencies concerned with the welfare of the elderly. Elderly people themselves are rarely a focus or have a voice on decisions made in a direct sense. This set-up emphasises 'doing-for' or 'doing-to' old people.

The emphasis on negotiation and exchange across the boundary, rather than what goes on either side of it, also means that the task of the regulating official becomes that of finding an acceptable compromise between the most vocal interests and those that are actually present in the negotiating arena. One is no longer concerned so much with what happens once the boundary transaction has been made, but rather that competing interests are satisfied. Both of these trends would strengthen the priorities of purchasers and providers over users, first, because they are the parties present, and second, because of differences in what the two groups see as being important. For example, Perring's (1991) finding that whilst professionals saw their role as co-ordinators between options, carers and users were most concerned with quality of life within homes, shows a clear difference in emphasis between transaction and content.

There is even some evidence that the logic of the negotiating arena affects who is seen as the client, with care providers replacing recipients as the main focus of support. Phillips *et al.* (1986) note that proprietors' financial vulnerability and the stressful nature of caring for frail and confused older people, when added to the officer's obligation to facilitate the growth of the private sector, place the proprietor in a client-like role, both in terms of being the subject of investigation and the recipient of certain forms of advice. Both Archer and Whitaker (1991) and Perring note the anxiety that inspection and negotiation can provoke in providers, placing them in a dependent position. Regulators and providers are also likely to be of similar age and have similar work experience, which the elder would not share, but could form a common empathic basic for collaboration.

When disputes between purchasers and providers arise, the often adversarial climate requires that clearly defined breaches of contract can be identified. A number of commentators (Challis, 1985; Biggs, 1987a; Brooke-Ross, 1987; Davis, 1987) note that quantifiable factors, such as room size and drug registers, are most likely to be used as criteria. Dispute over quality has had to demonstrate gross misconduct such as persistent physical and verbal abuse before tribunals will act. If content of care has to be so defined, it is unlikely to address the questions of quality that its recipients require and is no substitute for exclusion from the negotiating arena.

The change of emphasis from within to across boundaries means then that the older user's voice, is at best heard second-hand, or perhaps more likely, not at all.

A final consequence of the move to boundary transaction within a market context is a tendency to assume that the thing, or person, being moved is relatively passive and unaffected by the change. The older person, dehumanized by exclusion, becomes the commodity in which others are dealing. Again a number of factors come into play. Trends favouring block contracts (Flynn, 1990), where large numbers of places are agreed with a limited number of providers, would refocus concern in the arena on to the quantity and location of resources, rather than how individuals cope with relocation. Pressure of work means that inspectors rarely have time to visit homes more than once a year, reducing monitoring to a minimum, and in any case they are required to assess the overall context of care of which user views might be but are generally not a requirement. This is not to say that officers are not concerned about the welfare of older people in homes, but that the dynamic of the system places less stress on this than on other factors. Change as experienced by service users and to the quality of a service over time becomes minimalized as a consideration. It is unlikely that contract compliance will pick these changes up partly because decisions based on monitoring are originally defined within the negotiating arena and return to it for validation, and partly because it is simply not designed to assess them. Given Tobin's (1989) evidence on the psychological effects of transition, it would be wrong to assume that transition itself does not significantly influence one's state of mind immediately prior to relocation and changes in requirements once a move has been completed.

There may thus be a number of trends in the move to quality control through contract compliance and inspection that marginalize the voice and requirements of older people in or about to enter residence. They reflect a particular consequence of boundary management within the context of a market model of relations based on a 'quasi-market' structure.

TOWARDS BOTH OPEN AND CLOSED SYSTEMS

A striking feature in this and the adoption of case management is that in systems terms they both appear to be pulling in different directions at the same time. On the one hand, there has been a move to boundary negotiation and the adoption of what Bridger (1980) would describe as the qualities associated with an open system. These would include a climate in which roles and solutions are negotiated between multiple interests, which increasingly become interdependent and outward-looking. On the other, there is evidence of centralization and bureaucratization of power, reinforcing adherence to procedure, the high value of administration and reduced risk-taking, in other words a closed system. Older people may therefore find themselves confronted with the rhetoric of consent and involvement, and the practice of marginalization.

However, both trends have a common thread, as both are effective means of obscuring conflict. The former by moving from context to boundary, redefines tasks from the problems of delivering services to that of negotiating mutually agreeable solutions with providers. They are more likely to inhabit the same common-sense world as the purchaser by way of age-related projects, if not by content and relation to the service, thus removing difficulties of communication and objective that might be present with disadvantaged elders. The latter replaces the 'solution' of disadvantage with its efficient administration. The use of administrative checks and monitoring also generates large amounts of information that increases decision load (Caputo, 1988) about an organization's internal processes without necessarily addressing questions of effectiveness in the outside world. As such there is a tendency in both to redirect attention toward the means by which policies are carried out, rather than to the effects that such policies might have for the user population. The worker ends up trying to manage the chaos caused by poverty and infirmity by at least being able to order the internal mechanisms of welfare and negotiate between incorporated interests.

An irony of this tendency to task avoidance, if the primary task of caring agencies is accepted as being the direct amelioration of medical and social problems, is that it generates its own forms of pressure. An 'open system' can not only leave the boundary manager feeling exposed and vulnerable (because it is not clear where professional expertise now lies) it can generate strong feelings of envy and rivalry (Bridger, 1980). Procedures and contracts go some way to reduce this uneasiness, but when added to the tendency for each negotiation to demand accommodation to other views and changing priorities, leaves less room for individual discretion.

Rather than operating freely within predefined limits the worker engages in a constant balancing act between policy and competing priorities, coupled with the nagging feeling that one has been inadequately briefed. Resentment at these pressures can become displaced on to colleagues who continue to engage in direct work or users themselves, who are now perceived as protected from and out of touch with the 'real world' of the negotiating space.

CONCLUSIONS

Whether it be negotiation within or about residence, it would seem that elders end up holding a marginalized and passive role in contexts that more often than not make it difficult or dangerous to express existential concerns. By contrast, the mirror image, being central and active in roles that are both simplified and powerful are reserved for others. Others, who by degree can play out age-appropriate behaviour through work-roles without interference, although these rarely seem to provide the time or flexibility necessary to engage with the important process of intergenerational regeneration. The flip side can thereby be submerged in the psyche on both sides, reinforcing by projection the position of the other. In spite of the considerable promise that collective and protected space can provide, institutional care rarely allows self-expression becoming a restricted or purposeless domain in which conformity to stereotype is maintained. Possibilities for humanizing the image become significantly reduced if relations across generations, within the institution and between it and the wider social world, are diminished by distance.

Conclusion

The social and psychological worlds that younger and older adults inhabit and the confusion that can arise when they overlap, has led to a number of issues for health and welfare. These arise, in part, from differences between existential priorities at those times of life, that younger adults' projects are more greatly valued in the public sphere than elders' projects and particular circumstances that surround care provision for older people. Important questions follow, such as how to utilize specialized skills without transferring professional preoccupations on to the service-user. How to operationalize social policy without obscuring social deprivation. How to support the eye for detail and loving concern of many carers without co-option. How to enhance opportunities for collective living without losing the essential humanity of each individual. How to enhance alliances between workers and service-users in the pursuit of shared objectives. This list is neither exhaustive nor particularly original. However, it has been argued that the particular construction of older age in Western society gives each a characteristic slant. Further, an attempt has been made to explain why they take place in the way they do.

I am not saying that elders should lead their lives in a specified manner, excepting that there are universal facts about later life, limits to body and time, that become increasingly apparent and are obscured by social images. If such existential questions are not allowed expression, this can lead to a distorted conception of Self, which fails to allow the whole personality to develop in both younger and older people. Services that are intended to meet elders' requirements should therefore contribute to circumstances that allow age-related, self-directed need to be given voice.

When dominant definitions of ageing value the projects of relative youth at the expense of older age, both parties risk responding simply on the basis of stereotypes. This process at once atomizes and homogenizes. Elders are often left lonely in experience whilst being perceived as having common requirements that have been defined by others. The

fundamental questions for older age can be both threatening and perceived as unrelated to the everyday concerns of working life, whilst later
life itself is often trapped in a discourse on middle-age whereby changes
in existential development are almost always viewed negatively. Workers
are left imprisoned in the limited self-definitions that work roles allow
and eschew the challenge to self transformation that collaborative ventures beyond stereotyping would promise.

Faced with this, the first step for practitioners is to recognize age-
related contradictions within the helping situation. Their own priorities,
associations and the tacit logic of work-discourse will reinforce a limited
perspective arising from the first half of life and therefore need to be
understood. Second, it is important to allow space for reflection on how
these contradictions are constellated in their own working environment.
Third, space must be allowed for elders themselves to define and rede-
fine requirements. The working relationship that emerges might then
capitalize on the essential interdependence of the helping endeavour.
Elders' experience lends subtlety to specialist expertise, tension between
continuity and difference enhances the personal development of both
parties, whilst the self-activity of both increases engagement with the
world.

It is clear from such a rereading that age-related practice implies more
than the efficient delivery of services and extends to the personal and
political development of those engaged in it. Elders have 'been there' in
a most universal sense and can offer practitioners a deeper understanding of life than flight from a supposedly negative personal future. Equally,
older people cannot exist independently from younger people, whether
this reflects a need to pass on experience, or to make the necessities of life
easier to obtain, itself a prerequisite for continued revitalization. As rigidly
split distinctions attributed to age begin to break down, a new personal
and social synthesis can emerge. Both parties have the opportunity to
shed the self-stereotyping that categorizes the other as someone, or
something to be used without reference to the future developments of
either.

Beyond the interaction with professionals, it emerges that elders might
have much to gain from entering communities of interest, both with
age-peers and other marginalized groups. Collective situations, themselves often arising from homogenous perceptions of ageing, provide
an opportunity to discover that many hidden concerns are widely shared.
A collective experience of old age, once given voice, would allow pro-
tagonists to act for themselves, define requirements and create alternatives to the dominant stereotype rather than simply making limited choices
within it. Similarly, conditions for many older people, exclusion from the
workforce, reliance on services, marginalization from the concerns of
wider society, point to collaboration with other groups on a number of

shared objectives. If the climate engineered by social policy continues to deteriorate, health and welfare workers will also find that their interests increasingly coincide with those of older people and eclipse other priorities. As both workers and users implicitly share the same political space, interdependence would become a strategy for survival as well as a route to mutual understanding.

Currently such collaborations are rare in the UK, and might appear to some readers as simply utopian. The understanding of older age proposed in this book also has relevance for those concerned with developing services as they currently exist. A shopping list of new services is therefore proposed. First, an evident lack of shared projects between age-groups obviates the need for intergenerational mediation at this stage of life, formal services that can be called into play as conflicts of perception and interest arise. The service would facilitate the understanding of common misconceptions, identify shared and diverging requirements and, where possible, lead toward mutually agreeable solutions. The pay-off in terms of finding solutions that last, maintaining emotional and practical bonds and gaining psychological ownership by each party, would promise long-term fiscal as well as psychological benefit. Second, older age has emerged as a period of significant transition, whether this be in terms of location, lifestyle or existential meaning. As subsequent positive prognosis has been linked to how transitions are negotiated, this would be a key area in which to make information available, assist in its understanding and facilitate the consideration of alternative futures. As such this second point already exists in professional common sense. The problem is that defining the helping task as concerning transition alone, the adoption of administrative case management and an exclusion of elder's voices from decision-making arenas, can easily obscure the fact that transition is essentially a means to a changed, but continuing existence. The quality of that continuing existence would depend upon whether life-goals can be addressed legitimately within the new context, leading any third proposal to return to questions of voice and choice. A continuing theme that has emerged from this book is that elders are active players in the intergenerational game, although the circumstances in which they find themselves rarely recognize it. If participation is not addressed, both younger and older people will be the losers.

Finally, education and training should encourage awareness of how professional practice itself limits perception as well as equipping practitioners with specialized understanding. If differences between age priorities are not addressed, the most perceptive practitioner might fall back on tacit and highly personal conceptions of family, community and age-typical behaviour, which lead to a misreading of what an elder is trying to convey and leave them incapable of being open to alternative possibilities. A task for gerontology would be to explore distinctions between the content of what elders say and the processes that lead to the saying, thereby giving greater emphasis to tension between continuity and change in later life. Such a priority would lend greater critical understanding of middle-age as an image of successful ageing and the role of impression management between generations. Ageing, as constructed and lived, emerges on the cusp of a number of contradictions, not the least being expanded existential priorities and reduced social opportunity. If choice is to become a reality in all our futures, the interaction between the two needs to be understood.

None of the above exist in a vacuum. Power relations within and between institutions and groups to which parties belong, inevitably give rise to collusive alliances, which more often than not disenfranchize the excolluded. Deepened understanding of old age and intergenerational relations requires that the links be made between these different levels of discourse, a task to which this book has, hopefully, made a contribution.

References

Adelman, R.D., Greene, M.G. and Charon, R. (1991) Issues in physician-elderly interaction. *Ageing & Society*, 11, 127–47.

Age Concern (1985) *Information Factsheet*. Age Concern, London.

Age Concern (1990) *Information Factsheet*. Age Concern, London.

Age Concern (1992) *Information Factsheet*. Age Concern, London.

Ahmad-Aziz, A., Froggatt, A., Richardson, I. *et al*. (1992) *Anti-Racist Social Work Education: Improving Practice with Elders*. CCETSW, London.

Aleszewski, A. and Manthorpe, J. (1990) The new right and the professions. *British Journal Social Work*, 20, 237–51.

Alexander, B.B., Rubenstein, R.L., Goodman, M. and Luborsky, M. (1992) Generativity in cultural context. *Ageing & Society*, 11, 417–42.

Allen, I. (1983) *Short Stay Residential Care for the Elderly*. Policy Studies Institute, London.

Archer, L. and Whitaker, D. (1991) *Improving and Maintaining Quality of Life in Homes for Elderly People*. SWRRU, University of York.

Association of Directors of Social Services (1975) *Who Goes Where?* Association of Directors of Social Services, London.

Austin, C. (1990) Case management: myth or reality? *Families in Society*, September, 398–405.

Austin, C. and O'Connor, K. (1989) Case management: components and program contexts. In Peterson, M.E. and White, D., *Health Care for the Elderly*. Saga, New York.

Avebury, K. (1984) *Home Life*. Centre for Policy on Ageing, London.

Baker, P.M. (1985) The status of age. *Journal of Gerontology*, 40, 506–8.

Bandura, A. (1965) *Aggression: A Social Learning Theory Analysis*. Prentice-Hall, New Jersey.

Barbato, C. and Feezel, J. (1987) Language and aging in different age groups. *The Gerontologist*, 27, 4, 527–31.

Barr, H. (1988) *Training for Residential Care*. CCETSW, London.

Barry, N.P. (1985) The state, pensions and the philosophy of welfare. *Journal of Social Policy*, 15, 467–90.

Bartlet, H. and Challis, L. (1985) Time to act on what we know. *Health and Social Services Journal*, 96, 40–1.

Bassili, J.N. and Reil, J.E. (1981) The dominance of the old age stereotype. *Journal of Gerontology*, 36(6), 682–8.

Bender, M.P. (1984) The neglect of the elderly by British psychologists. *Bulletin of the British Psychological Society*, 39, 414–16.

Berger, P.L. and Luckman, T. (1971) *The Social Construction of Reality*. Allen Lane, London.

Bernstein, D. (1979) Female identity synthesis. In Roland, A. and Harris, B., *Career and Motherhood*. Human Sciences, New York.

Bhalla, A. and Blakemore, K. (1981) *Elders of the Minority Ethnic Groups*. (Birmingham Survey). AFFOR, Birmingham.

Biggs, S.J. (1980) The me I see. *Human Relations*, 33(8), 575–88.

Biggs, S.J. (1983) Choosing to change in video-feedback. In Dowrick, P.W. and Biggs, S.J., *Using Video*. Wiley, Chichester.

Biggs, S.J. (1986) *The Registered Homes Act 1984, Staff Training Issues*. CCETSW, London.

Biggs, S.J. (1987a) Local authority registration staff and the boundary between public and private care. *Policy & Politics*, 15, 4, 235–44.

Biggs, S.J. (1987b) Quality of care and the growth of private welfare for old people. *Critical Social Policy*, 20, 74–82.

Biggs, S.J. (1989a) Professional helpers and resistances to work with older people. *Ageing & Society*, 9, 43–60.

Biggs, S.J. (1989b) *Confronting Ageing*. CCETSW, London.

Biggs, S.J. (1990a) Consumers case management and inspection obscuring social deprivation and need? *Critical Social Policy*, 30, 23–38.

Biggs, S.J. (1990b) Ageism and confronting ageing. *Journal of Social Work Practice*, 4(2), 49–65.

Biggs, S.J. (1991a) Community care, case management and the psychodynamic perspective. *Journal of Social Work Practice*, 5(1), 71–82.

Biggs, S.J. (1991b) Case management: advantages and disadvantages. In Thompson, T. and Mathias, P., *Standards and Mental Handicap*. Balliere Tindall, London.

Biggs, S.J. (1992) Groupwork and professional attitudes to older age. In Morgan, K., *Gerontology Responding to an Ageing Society*. Jessica Kingsley, London.

Biggs, S.J. and Phillipson, C. (1992) *Understanding Elder Abuse*. Longman, London.

Bleise, N. (ed.) (1982) Media in the rocking chair. In *Intermedia*. New York, Oxford University Press.

Booth, T. (1985) *Home Truths*. Gower, London.

Bornat, J., Phillipson, C. and Ward, S. (1985) *A Manifesto for Old Age*. Pluto, London.

Breadline (1985) *Greenwich's Afro-Carribean and South Asian Elderly People*. Greenwich Social Services Department, London.

Brearley, C.P. (1990) *Working in Residential Homes for Elderly People*. Routledge, London.

Bridger, H. (1980) *Consultative work with communities and organisations*, Monograph, Aberdeen University Press, pp. 1–31.

British Gas (1991) *The British Gas Report on Attitudes to Ageing*. British Gas, London.

Bromley, D.B. (1988) *Human Ageing*. Penguin, London.

Bromley, D.B. (1991) The idea of ageing: a historical and psychological analysis. *Comprehensive Gerontology*, 2, 30–41.

Brooke, R. (1991) *Jung and Phenomenology*. Routledge, London.

Brooke-Ross, R. (1987) *Registered Homes Tribunal Decisions*. Social Care Association, London.

Buber, M. (1958) *I and Thou*. Scribner, New York.

Butler, R.N. (1963) The life review: an interpretation of reminiscence in the aged. *Psychiatry*, 26(1), 895–900.

Butler, R.N. (1975) *Why Survive? Being Old in America*. Harper and Row. San Francisco.

Butler, R.N. (1987) Ageism. In *Encyclopedia of Ageing*. Springer, New York.

Butler, R. and Lewis, M.I. (1977) *Ageing and Mental Health*. Mosby, St Louis.

Butt, H. and Palmer, B. (1985) *Value for Money in the Public Sector*. Blackwell, London.

Bytheway, B. and Johnson, J. (1990) On defining ageism. *Critical Social Policy*, 29, 12–18.

Callahan, J.J. (1989) Case management for the elderly: a panacea? *Journal of Aging and Social Policy*, 1(1/2), 181–97.

Campbell, M.E. (1971) Study of attitudes of nursing personnel toward the geriatric patient. *Nursing Research*, 20, 147–51.

Capitman, J., Haskins, B. and Bernstein, J. (1986) Case management approaches in coordinated care demonstration. *The Gerontologist*, 26(4), 120–9.

Caputo, R.K. (1988) *Management and Information Systems in Human Services*. Haworth, New York.

Carpy, D.V. (1989) Tolerating the countertransference. *International Journal of Psychoanalysis*, 70, 287–94.

Challis, L. (1985) Controlling for care. *British Journal of Social Work*, 17, 43–56.

Challis, L. (1990) *Organising Public Social Services*. Longman, Harlow.

Challis, D. and Davies, B. (1986) *Case Management and Community Care*. Gower, London.

Chapman, N.J. and Neal, M.B. (1990) Intergenerational experiences between adolescents and older adults. *The Gerontologist*, 30, 825–32.

Chappell, N.L. (1983) Informal support networks amongst the elderly. *Research on Ageing*, 5.1, 77–99.

Chiriboga, D.A. (1990) The measurement of stress exposure in later life. In Markides, K.S. and Cooper, C.L., *Aging Stress and Health*. Wiley, New York.

Chudacoff, H.P. (1989) *How Old are You?* Princetown, New Jersey.

Coleman, P.G. (1986a) Issues in the therapeutic use of reminiscence with elderly people. In Handley, and I. Gilhooly, M., *Psychological Therapies for the Elderly*. Croom-Helm, Beckenham.

Coleman, P.G. (1986b) *Ageing and Reminiscence Processes: Social and Clinical Implications*. Wiley, Chichester.

Coleman, P.G. (1988) Mental health in old age. In Gearing, B., Johnson, M. and Heller, T., *Mental Health Problems in Old Age*. Wiley, Chichester.

Comfort, A. (1977) *A Good Age*. Mitchell Beasley, London.

Conway, M.A. (1990) *Autobiographical Memory*. Open University Press, Milton Keynes.

Conway, M.A. (1991) Cognitive psychology in search of meaning: autobiographical memory, *The Psychologist*, 4, 301–5.

Corrigan, P. and Leonard, P. (1978) *Social Work Practice under Capitalism*. Macmillan, London.

Counsel and Care (1991) *Not Such Private Places*. Counsel and Care, London.

Coupland, N., Giles, H. Henwood, K. and Wiemann, J. (1988) Elderly self-disclosure: interactional and intergroup issues. *Language & Communication*, 8, 109–33.

Coupland, J., Coupland, N. and Grainger, K. (1991) Intergenerational discourse: contextual versions of ageing and elderliness. *Ageing & Society*, 11, 189–208.

Cox, H. (1965) *The Secular City*. Springer, New York, pp. 44–5.

Croake, J., Myers, K. and Singh, A. (1988) Fears expressed by elderly men and women. *International Journal of Aging & Human Development*, 26(2), 139–46.

Crockett, W.H. (1979) The effect of deviations from stereotyped expectations on attitudes to older persons. *Journal of Gerontology*, 34(3), 368–74.

Cummings, E. and Henry, W.E. (1961). *Growing Old*. Basic Books, New York.

Daatland, S. (1990) What are families for? On family solidarity and preference for help. *Ageing & Society*, 10, 1–17.

Dalley, G. (1988) *Ideologies of Caring*. Macmillan, London.

Davids, M.F. and Davison, S.C. (1988) Two accounts of the management of difference in psychotherapy. *Journal of Social Work Practice*, 3(3), 30–56.

Davies, B. (1990) *Resources, Needs and Outcomes in Community Services*. PSSRU, Canterbury.

Davis, A. (1987) *Managing to Care*. Patten Press, Hayle, Cornwall.

Davis, R. (1988) TV's boycott of old age. *Ageing*, March, 346.

de Beauvoir, S. (1970) *Old Age*. Penguin, Middlesex.

de Beauvoir, S. (1972) *The Second Sex*. Penguin, Middlesex.

Deikmann, H. (1985) Some aspects of the development of authority. In Samuels, A., *The Father*. Free Association Books, London.

Department of Health (1988) *Family Expenditure Survey*. HMSO, London.

Department of Health (1989) *Terms of Service for Doctors in General Practice*. HMSO, London.

Descartes, R. (1968) *Discourse on Method and Other Writings*. Penguin, Middlesex. (Originally published 1637.)

Disch, R. (1988) Whom the gods would destroy they first make popular. *Journal of Gerontological Social Work*, 12(3/4), 1–6.

Dittman-Kohli, F. (1990) The construction of meaning in old age. *Ageing & Society*, 10, 279–94.

Dowd, J.J. and Bengston, V.L. (1978) Ageing in minority populations: an examination of the double jeopardy hypothesis. *Journal of Gerontology*, 33, 14–31.

Dreher, B.B. (1987) *Communication Skills for Working with Elders*. Springer, New York.

Eichenbaum, L. and Orbach, S. (1982) *Outside In Inside Out*. Penguin, Middlesex.

Eisdorfer, C. and Wilkie, F. (1977) Stress, disease, aging and behavior. In Birren, J. and Schaie, K. *Handbook of the Psychology of Ageing*. Van Nostrand, New York.

Elmhurst, S.I. (1990) The value of grandparents. *Psychoanalytic Psychotherapy*, 5(1), 11–19.

Equal Opportunities Commission (1980) *The Experience of Caring for Elderly and Handicapped Dependants*. Equal Opportunities Commission, Manchester.

Erikson, E.H. (1963) *Childhood and Society*. Norton, New York.

Erikson, E.H. (1982) *The Life Cycle Completed*. Norton, New York.

Erikson, E.H., Erikson, J.M. and Kivnick, H.Q. (1986) *Vital Involvement in Old Age*. Norton, New York.

Ernst, S. (1989) Gender and the phantasy of omnipotence. In Richards, B., *Crises of the Self*. Free Association Books, London.

Estes, C. (1979) *The Ageing Enterprise*. Jossey-Bass, San Francisco.

Etzioni, A. (1964) *A Comparative Analysis of Organisations*. Free Press, New York.

Evandrou, M. (1991) *Challenging the Invisibility of Carers*. London School of Economics, London.

Ezquerro, A. (1989) Group psychotherapy with the pre-elderly. *Group Analysis*, 22, 299–308.

Faraquer, M. and Bowling, A. (1991) Older people and their GPs. *Generations Review*, 1(1), 7–10.

Farrah, M. (1986) *Black Elders in Leicester*. Leicester Social Services Department.

Featherstone, M. and Hepworth, M. (1989) Ageing and old age. In Bytheway, B., Kiel, T., Allat, P. and Bryman, A., *Becoming and Being Old*. Sage, London.

Fennell, G., Phillipson, C. and Evers, H. (1988) *The Sociology of Old Age*. Open University Press, Milton Keynes.

Fenton, S. (1987) *Ageing Minorities: Black People as they Grow Old in Britain*. CRE, London.

Ferraro, K. (1990) Widowhood and health. In Markides, K.S. and Cooper, C.L., *Aging, Health and Stress*. Wiley, New York.

Finch, J. (1984) Community care: developing non-sexist alternatives. *Critical Social Policy*, 9, 6–18.

Finch, J. (1987) Family ties. *New Society*, March, 16–18.

Finch, J. (1989) *Family Obligations and Social Change*. Polity Press, Oxford.

Finch, J. and Groves, D. (1985) Old boy–old girl. In Brook, E. and Davis, A., *Women, the Family and Social Work*. Tavistock, London.

Finch, J. and Mason, J. (1990) Filial obligations and kin support for the elderly. *Ageing & Society*, 10(2), 151–78.

Fisher, M. (1991a) Defining the practice content of care management. *Social Work & Social Sciences Review*, 2(3), 204–30.

Fisher, M. (1991b) Care management and social work: clients with dementia. *Practice*, 4(4), 229–41.

Fisher, M. (1991c) Care management and social work: working with carers. *Practice*, 4(4), 242–52.

Fitzgerald, J.M. (1988) Vivid memories and the reminiscence phenonenon. *Human Development*, 31, 261–73.

Flynn, N. (1989) The new right and social policy. *Policy & Politics*, 17(2), 97–109.

Flynn, N. (1990) *Contracts for Community Care*. HMSO, London.

Fordham, F. (1956) *An Introduction to Jung's Psychology*. Penguin, Middlesex.

Foucault, M. (1979) *The Archeology of Knowledge*. Routledge, London.

Foucault, M. (1982) The subject and power. In Dreyfus, H. and Rainbow, P.,

Michel Foucault: Beyond Structuralism and Hermeneutics. University of Chicago Press, Chicago.

Fraisse, P. (1984) Perception and evaluation of time. *American Review of Psychology*, 35, 1–36.

Frankel, V. (1969) *The Doctor and the Soul*. Penguin, Middlesex.

Franklin, J., Solovitz, B. and Miller, S. (1987) An evaluation of case management. *American Journal of Public Health*, 77, 674–8.

Freire, P. (1970) *Pedagogy of the Oppressed*. Penguin, Middlesex.

Freire, P. (1972) *Cultural Action for Freedom*. Penguin, Middlesex.

Freud, S. (1900) *The Interpretation of Dreams*. Hogarth, London.

Freud, S. (1910) *Problems of Psychoanalytic Technique and Therapy*. Hogarth, London.

Freud, S. (1919) The uncanny. In Strachey, J. (ed.), *Standard edition of the Collected Works*, vol. 17. Hogarth, London, pp. 218–56.

Frosh, S. (1989) Melting into air: psychoanalysis and social experience. *Free Associations*, 16, 7–30.

Gallup (1988) *Living Longer*. Gallup, London.

Game, A. (1991) *Undoing the Social*. Open University Press, Milton Keynes.

Garner, L.H. (1989) *Leadership in Human Services*. Jossey-Bass, San Francisco.

Genevay, B. and Katz, R.S. (1990) *Countertransference and Older Clients*. Sage, Newbury Park, California.

Gerbner, G., Gross, L., Morgan, M. and Signorelli, N. (1980) Aging with television. *Journal of Communication*, 30, 34–47.

Giddens, A. (1984) *The Constitution of Society: Outline of the Theory of Structuration*. University of California Press, Berkeley.

Gilbert, N. (1984) Welfare for profit. *Journal of Social Policy*, 13, 63–73.

Giles, H. (1991) Gosh you don't look it: a sociolinguistic construction of ageing. *The Psychologist*, 3, 99–106.

Giles, H. and Coupland, N. (1991a) *Language: Contexts and Consequences*. Open University Press, Milton Keynes.

Giles, H. and Coupland, N. (1991b) Language attitudes: discursive, contextual and gerontological considerations. In Reynolds, A.G., *Bilingualism, Multiculturalism and Second Language Learning*. Lawrence Erlbaum Inc., Hillsdale, New Jersey.

Giles, H., Coupland, N., Henwood, K. and Coupland, J. (1989) The social meaning of R P: an intergenerational perspective. In Ramsaran, S., *Studies in the Pronunciation of English*. Routledge, London.

Giles, H., Coupland, N. and Weimann, J. (1991) Talk is cheap. In Bolton, K. and Kwok, H., *Sociolinguistics Today*. Routledge, London.

Glendenning, F. and Pearson, M. (1988) *The Black and Ethnic Minority Elders in Britain*, Keele University Press, Keele.

Goffman, E. (1959) *Asylums*. Penguin, Middlesex.

Goffman, E. (1963) *Stigma*. Penguin, Middlesex.

Goffman, E. (1969) *The Presentation of Self in Everyday Life*. Penguin, Middlesex.

Goffman, E. (1971) *Relations in Public*. Penguin, Middlesex.

Goldfarb, A.I. (1956) The rationale for psychotherapy with older persons. *American Journal of Medical Sciences*, 232, 181–5.

Goldfarb, A.I. and Turner, H. (1953) Psychotherapy for aged persons. *American Journal of Psychiatry*. 229, 19–27.

Gramsci, A. (1971) *Selections from Prison Notebooks.* Lawrence and Wishart, London.

Green, H. (1988) *Informal Carers.* OCPS Series GHS No. 15, Supplement A. HMSO, London.

Greene, M., Adelman, R., Charon, R. and Hoffman, S. (1986) Ageism in the medical encounter. *Language and Communication*, 6, 113–124.

Greenwell, S. (1989) *Whose Home is it Anyway?* Bath University Press, Bath.

Greer, G. (1991) The dodging time. *The Independent on Sunday Magazine*, 29 September, 8–11.

Griffiths, R. (1988) *Community Care: An Agenda for Action.* HMSO, London.

Group for the Advancement of Psychiatry, Committee on Aging (1971) *The Aged and Community Mental Health.* GAP, New York.

Grundy, E. (1992) Paper to the Royal Society of Physicians, London.

Gubrium, J.F. and Wallace, J.B. (1990) Who theorises age? *Ageing and Society*, 10, 131–49.

Guggenbuhl-Craig, A. (1971) *Power in the Helping Professions.* Spring, Dallas.

Gunter, B. (1987) The psychological influences of television. In Bellof, H. and Colman, A.M. *Psychological Survey 6.* British Psychological Society, Leicester.

Guttman, D. (1988) *Reclaimed Powers.* Heinemann, New York.

Hadley, R. (1982) Origins of dissent. In Philpot, T. (ed.), *A New Direction for Social Work.* Community Care Press, London, pp. 63–7.

Haffenden, S. (1991) *Getting It Right for Carers.* HMSO, London.

Hall, S. (1991) Paper to Psycho-Analysis and the Public Sphere Conference, London.

Hamner, J. and Statham, D. (1988) *Women and Social Work.* BASW/Macmillan, London.

Hardena, D. (1990) The effects of funding sources on client access to services. *Administration in Social Work*, 14(3), 33–46.

Harel, Z. (1987) Older Americans act related homebound aged: what difference does racial background make? *Journal of Gerontological Social Work*, 9(4), 133–147.

Harris, L. (1975) *The Myth and Reality of Ageing in America.* National Council On the Aging, Washington.

Harrison, S. and Wistow, G. (1992) The purchaser/provider split in English health care: towards explicit rationing? *Policy and Politics*, 20(2), 123–30.

Hassard, J. (1991) Aspects of time in organisation. *Human Relations*, 44(2), 105–26.

Havinghurst, R. (1963) Successful ageing. In Williams, R.H., Tibbits, C. and Donahue, W. (eds), *Processes of Ageing* vol. 1. University of Chicago Press, pp. 311–15.

Heidigger, M. (1962) *Being and Time.* Harper and Row, New York.

Heimann, P. (1950) On countertransference. *International Journal of Psychoanalysis*, 31, 9–15.

Henderson, J.L. (1990) *Shadow and Self.* Chiron, Wilmete, Illinois.

Hendrick, S.C. and Inui, T.S. (1987) The effectiveness and cost of home care. *Health Services Research*, 20(6), 851–80.

Henwood, M. (1990) Age discrimination in health care. In *Age the Unrecognised Discrimination.* Age Concern, London.

Hess, N. (1987) King Lear and psychotherapy with older patients. *British Journal of Medical Psychology*, 60(3), 209–16.

Heycox, K. (1989) Self-imposed limitations: social work with the elderly. *Australian Social Work*, 42(3), 17–24.

Hildebrand, P. (1982) Psychotherapy with older patients. *British Journal of Medical Psychology*, 55, 19–28.

Hildebrand, P. (1986) Dynamic psychotherapy with the elderly. In Hanley, I. and Gilhooley, M., *Psychological Therapies for the Elderly*. Croom-Helm, London.

Hillman, J. (1983) *Archetypal Psychology: A Brief Account*. Spring, Dallas.

Hinshelwood, R.D. (1986) A dual materialism. *Free Associations*, 4, 36–50.

HMSO (1984) *The Registered Homes Act*. HMSO, London.

HMSO (1988) *Social Trends*. HMSO, London.

HMSO (1989) *Caring for People*. HMSO, London.

HMSO (1990) *The NHS and Community Care Act*. HMSO, London.

Hobman, D. (1990) A bad business. In *Age the Unrecognised Discrimination*. Age Concern, London.

Hoggart, P. (1989) The culture of uncertainty. In Richards, B., *Crises of the Self*. Free Association Press, London.

Holloway, F. (1991) Case management for the mentally ill. *International Journal of Social Psychiatry*, 37(1), 2–13.

Hopkins, T. (1980) A conceptual framework for understanding the three isms. *Journal of Education for Social Work*, 16(2), 63–70.

Hudson, B. (1992) Quasi markets in health and social care in Britain. *Policy and Politics*, 20(2), 131–42.

Ingesol, B. and Antonucci, T. (1988) Reciprocal and non reciprocal support. *Journal of Gerontology*, 43(3), 565–73.

Ingham, R. and Fielding, P. (1985) Review on the nursing literature on attitudes towards old people. *International Journal of Nursing Studies*, 22(3), 171–81.

Itzin, C. (1986) Ageism awareness training. In Phillipson, C., Strang, P. and Bernard, M., *Dependency and Interdependency in Old Age*. Gower, London.

Jack, R. (1992) Case management and social services. *Generations Review*, 2(1), 4–7.

Jacobi, J. (1971) *C.G. Jung, Psychological Reflections*. Routledge and Kegan Paul, London.

Jacoby, M. (1984) *The Analytic Encounter*. Inner City Books, Toronto.

Jameson, F. (1984) Post modernism or the cultural logic of late capitalism. *New Left Review*, 146, 53–93.

Jaques, E. (1965) Death and the mid-life crisis. *International Journal of Psycho-Analysis*, 46(4), 507–14.

Johnson, P., Conrad, C. and Thompson, D. (1989) *Workers vs Pensioners*. Manchester University Press, Manchester.

Jones, G. (1986) Training social workers to work with older people. In Glendenning, F., *Social Work with Older People*. Beth Johnson Faudatia, Keele.

Jung, C.G. (1933) *Modern Man in Search of a Soul*. Routledge and Kegan Paul, London.

Jung, C.G. (1967) *Collected Works*. Routledge and Kegan Paul, London.

Jung, C.G. (1972) *Four Archetypes*. Routledge and Kegan Paul, London.

Kanter, J. (1988) Clinical issues in the case management relationship. In Harris, M.E. and Bacharach, L., *Clinical Case Management*. Jossey-Bass, San Francisco.

Kanter, J. (1989) Clinical case management: definition, principles and components. *Hospital and Community Psychiatry*, 40, 361–8.

Kaufmann, S.R. (1986) *The Ageless Self*. University of Wyoming, Wisconsin.

Kearl, M.L. (1982) An inquiry into the positive personal and social effects of old age. *International Journal of Ageing and Human Development*, 14(4), 277–90.

Keith, L. (1991) Unpublished discussion paper, PSI Seminars.

Keller, M.L., Leventhal, E.A. and Larson, B. (1989) Ageing: the lived experience. *International Journal of Ageing and Human Development*, 29, 67–82.

Kettner, P.M. and Martin, L.L. (1990) Purchase of service contracting. *Administration in Social Work*, 14(1), 15–30.

Kinnon, U. (1988) Racism awareness: who helps the client? *Journal of Social Work Practice*, 3(3), 80–91.

Kivnick, H.Q. (1988) Grandparenthood, life-review and psychosocial development. *Journal of Gerontological Social Work*, 12(3/4), 63–82.

Klein, R.E. (1983) *The Politics of the National Health Service*. Longman, London.

Knapp, M. Cambridge, P., Thompson, C. *et al.* (1990) *Care in the Community: Lessons from a Demonstration Programme*, PSSRU, Canterbury.

Knight, B. (1986) *Psychotherapy with Older Adults*. Sage, Beverly Hills.

Knox, J., Gekooski, W. and Johnson, E. (1986) Contact and perception in cross-generational contact. *The Gerontologist*, 26(3), 17–24.

Kogan, N. (1979) A study of age categorisation, *Journal of Gerontology*, 34(5), 358–67.

Kotre, J. (1984) *Outliving the Self: Generativity and the Interpretation of Lives*. Johns Hopkins, Baltimore.

Kubey, R. (1980) TV and ageing. *The Gerontologist*, 20, 16–35.

Kuhn, M. (1977) *Maggie Kuhn on Ageing*. Westminster, Philadelphia.

Kuypers, J. (1969) 'Elderly person en route to institution.' Unpublished doctoral dissertation, University of Chicago.

Lacan, J. (1977) *Ecrits*. Norton, New York.

Laczko, F. and Phillipson, C. (1991) *Changing Work and Retirement*. Open University Press, Milton Keynes.

Lagergren, M. (1991) Paper to the 4th International Conference on Systems Science in Health and Social Services for the Elderly and Disabled, Barcelona.

Laing, R.D. (1961) *Self and Others*. Penguin, Middlesex.

Laing and Buisson (1992) *Laing's Review of Private Health Care*. Laing and Buisson, London.

Lalive d'Epinay, C. (1986) Time, space and socio-cultural identity. *International Social Services Journal*, 107, 89–104.

Lambert, J., Laslett, P. and Clay, H. (1984) *The Image of the Elderly on TV*. University of the Third Age, Cambridge.

Lawton, M.P. (1989) Environmental proactivity in older people. In Bengtson, V. and Schaie, K.W., *The Course of Later Life*. Springer, New York.

Lee, G. (1985) Kinship and social support. *Ageing and Society*, 5(1), 19–38.

Lee, G. and Shehan, C. (1989) Social relations and the self esteem of older persons. *Research on Ageing*, 11(4), 427–42.

LeGrand, J. (1990) *Quasi Markets and Social Policy*. Studies in Decentralisation and Quasi Markets, No. 1. School of Advanced Urban Studies, Bristol.

Lemon, B.W., Bretigan, V.L. and Peterson, J.A. (1972) Activity types and life satisfaction in a retirement community. *Journal of Gerontology*, 27(4), 511–23.

Leonard, P. (1984) *Personality and Ideology*. Macmillan, London.

LeRiche, P. and Rowlings, C. (1990) Feminist groupwork with older women. *International Social Work*, 33, 121–36.

Leslie, A. and Fowell, I. (1988) A view of home help service: the decisions of home help organisers. *Social Services Research*, 6, 18–26.

Levin, J. and Levin, J.C. (1980) *Ageism: Prejudice and Discrimination Against the Elderly*. Wadsworth, Belmont, California.

Leyotard, J. (1984) *The Postmodern Condition*. University of Minneapolis Press, Minneapolis.

Long, P. (1979) Speaking out on age. *Spare Rib*, 92, 14–17.

Lynn, M. and Hunter, K. (1983) Perception of age in the elderly. *Journal of Gerontology*, 8, 483–488.

Macdonald, B. and Rich, C. (1984) *Look Me in the Eye*. The Women's Press, London.

Main, T. (1990) Knowlegde, learning and freedom from thought. *Psychoanalytic Psychotherapy*, 5(1), 59–78.

Malan, D.H. (1978) *Towards the Validation of Dynamic Psychotherapy*. Plenum, New York.

Maquarrie, J. (1973) *Existentialism*. Penguin, Middlesex.

Markides, K.S. (1988) Minority status, aging and mental health. *International Journal of Ageing and Human Development*, 23(4), 285–300.

Marks, L. (1991) Paper to the Psycho-analysis and the Public Sphere Conference, London.

Marshall, M. (1990) Attitudes to age and ageing. In *Age the Unrecognised Discrimination*. Age Concern, London.

Marx, K. (1884) *The German Ideology*. Lawrence & Wishart, London.

Matthews, S.H. (1979) *The Social World of Old Women*. Sage, Beverly Hills.

Mattinson, H. and Sinclair, I. (1979) *Mate and Stalemate*. Blackwell, Oxford.

McGarty, C. and Penny, R.E.C. (1988) Categorisation, accentuation and Social judgement. *British Journal of Social Psychology*, 34, 762–73.

McGoldrick, A.E. (1990) Stress, retirement and health. In Markides, K.S. and Cooper, C.L., *Aging, Stress and Health*. Wiley, New York.

McIntosh, M. (1981) Feminism and social policy. *Critical Social Policy*, 1, 1–22.

McKenzie, S.C. (1980) *Aging and Old Age*. Scott Foresman and Co., Glenview, Illinois.

McMahon, A. and Rhudick, P. (1964) Reminiscence: adaptational significance in the aged. *Archive of General Psychiatry*, 10, 292–8.

McMurty, S.L., Netting, F.E. and Kettner, P.N. (1990) Critical inputs and strategic choice in non-profit human service organisations. *Administration in Social Work*, 14(3), 67–82.

Menzies, I. (1970) *Functioning of Social Systems as a Defence Against Anxiety*. Tavistock, London.

Migliano, L.R. and Misceraca, P. (1982) The theory of modern bureaucracy. In Showstack-Sassoon, A., *Approaches to Gramsci*. Writers and Readers, London.

Miller, L. (1987) The professional construction of old age. *Journal of Gerontological Social Work*, 11, 141–54.

Miller, E. and Gwynne, G. (1972) *A Life Apart*. Tavistock, London.

Miller, E.J. and Rice, A.K. (1967) *Systems of Organisation*. Tavistock, London.

Minkler, M. and Robertson, A. (1991) The ideology of age/race wars. *Ageing and Society*, 11, 1–22.

Minuchin, S. (1974) *Families and Family Therapy*. Tavistock, London.

Mirza, K. (1991) Community care for the black community. In *One Small Step Toward Racial Justice*. CCETSW, London.

Mitchell, J., MacKenzie, D., Holloway, J., *et al.* (1980) *In and Against the State*. Pluto, London.

Moody, H.R. (1988) Twenty five years of life-review. *Journal of Gerontological Social Work*, 12(3/4), 7–24.

Monk, A. (1981) Social work with the aged. *Social Work*, 26(1), 61–8.

Morris, J. (1991) *Pride Against Prejudice*. The Women's Press, London.

Morris, J. (1992) Us and them? Feminist research, community care and disability. *Critical Social Policy*, 33, 22–39.

Moxley, D.P. (1989) *The Practice of Case Management*. Sage, Beverly Hills.

Moxley, D.P. and Buzas, L. (1989) Perceptions of case management services for elderly people. *Health and Social Work*, August, 197–203.

Mullen, C. and Von Zwanenberg, E. (1988) *Study of Television Viewing*. BBC Books, London.

National Association of Social Workers (1984) *Standards and Guidelines for Social Work Case Management for the Functionally Impaired*. Standards, No. 12. NASW, New York.

Neill, J.E., Sinclair, I., Gorbach, P. and Williams, J. (1989) *The Need For Care*. Gower, London.

Neugarten, B. (1977) Personality and ageing. In Birren, J.E. and Schaie, K.W., *Handbook of the Psychology of Ageing*. Van Nostrand, New York.

Nielsen, A.C. (1975) *National Audience Demographic Report*. Nielsen Estimates, Chicago.

Norman, A. (1985) *Triple Jeopardy*, CPA, London.

Nussbaum, J.F. (1991) Communication, language and the institutionalised elderly. *Ageing and Society*, 11, 149–65.

Nussbaum, J.F., Thompson, T. and Robinson, J.D. (1989) *Communication and Ageing*. Harper and Row, New York.

Oliver, M. (1990) *The Politics of Disablement*. Macmillan, London.

OPCS (1985) *General Household Survey*. HMSO, London.

OPCS (1988) *General Household Survey*. HMSO, London.

Opportunities for Women (1991) *From Care to Work*. Opportunities for Women, London.

Palmer, I. (1985) State theory and statutory authorities. *Sociology*, 20, 223–40.

Palmore, E. (1970) *Normal Ageing*. Duke University Press, Durham, North Carolina.

Palmore, E. (1977) Facts on aging. *The Gerontologist*, 17, 315–20.

Pantel, E. (1990) *Systems Designed for People*. SYSTED'90 Conference, Bologna.

Pardeck, J.T., Murphy, J.W. and Jung Min Choi (forthcoming) Postmodernism and social work practice. *Journal of Social Work Practice*, in press.

Parker, G. (1990) *A Typology of Caring*. SPRU, University of York.

Patel, N. (1990) *A Race Against Time*. Runnymede, London.

Peck, E., Richie, P. and Smith, H. (1992) *Contracting and Case Management in Community Care*. CCETSW, London.

Perlmutter, F.D. and Adams, C.T. (1990) The voluntary sector and for-profit ventures. *Administration in Social Work*, 14(1), 1–13.

Perring, C.A. (1991) *Residential Care and Community Care*. Caring in homes initiative working paper, Brunel University, Reading.

Peterson, C.C., Hall, L.C. and Peterson, J.L. (1988) Age, sex and contact with elderly adults as predictors of knowledge about psychological aging. *International Journal of Aging and Human Development*, 26(2), 129–37.

Pezeshgi, L. (1989) Paper to the 2nd European Conference on Child Sexual Abuse, Brussels.

Pfeiffer, E. (1971) Psychotheraphy with elderly patients. *Postgraduate Medicine*, November, 254–8.

Phillips, D., Vincent, J. and Blackwell, S. (1986) Petit-bourgeois care. *Policy and Politics*, 14(2), 189–208.

Phillipson, C. (1982) *Capitalism and the Construction of Old Age*. Macmillan, London.

Phillipson, C. (1990) *Delivering Community Care Services for Older People*. Working paper No. 3. Keele University Press, Keele.

Phillipson, C. (1991a) Intergenerational relations: conflict or consensus in the twenty-first century? *Policy and Politics*, 19, 27–36.

Phillipson, C. (1991b) The social construction of old age: perspectives from political economy. *Reviews in Clinical Gerontology*, 1, 403–10.

Phillipson, C. (1992) Family care in Great Britain: social and policy perspectives. In Kosburg, J.I. (ed.), *Family Care of the Elderly in a Changing World*. Sage, New York.

Phillipson, C. and Strang, P. (1986) *Training and Education for an Ageing Society*. Keele University Press, Keele.

Pietroni, P. (1990) *The Greening of Medicine*. Gollancz, London.

Pietroni, P. (1991) Stereotypes or archetypes? *Journal of Social Work Practice*, 5(1), 61–70.

Pincus, L. (1974) *Death in the Family*. Faber, London.

Pincus, L. (1981) *The Challenge of a Long Life*. Faber, London.

Powell, W. and Friedkin, R. (1987) Organisational change in non-profit organisations. In Powell, W., *The Nonprofit Sector: A Research Handbook*. Yale, New Haven.

Pratek, P., Sander, E., Maloney, W. and Jackson, C. (1966) Phonatory and related changes with advanced age. *Journal of Speech and Hearing Research*, 9, 353–60.

Prunchno, R. and Symer, M.A. (1983) Mental health and aging. *International Journal of Aging and Human Development*, 17, 123–39.

Quereshi, H. (1986) Responses to dependency. In Phillipson, C. and Walker, A., *Dependency and Interdependency in Old Age*. Gower, Aldershot.

Quereshi, H. (1990) A research note on the hierarchy of obligations among informal carers. *Ageing and Society*, 10(4), 455–8.

Rautman, A. (1962) Role reversal. *Geriatric Medical Hygiene*, 64, 116–20.

Remnet, V.L. (1987) How adult children respond to role transitions in the lives of their aging parents. *Educational Gerontology*, 13, 341–55.

Richards, B. (1989a) *Crises of the Self*. Free Association Books, London.

Richards, B. (1989b) Visions of freedom: the subject in market relations. *Free Associations*, 16, 31–42.

Richardson, A. (1991) *A New Deal for Carers*. HMSO, London.

Roberts, S., Steele, J. and Moore, N. (1991) *Finding Out About Residential Care.* Working Paper 3. Policy Studies Institute, London.

Robertson, A. (1991) Nurse morale and quality of care of the demented elderly. In Proceedings of the Systed 1991 Conference, Systed Press, Barcelona.

Rodwell, G., Davis, S., Dennison, T. *et al.* (1992) Images of old age on British television. *Generations Review,* 2(3), 6–8.

Rogers, W.L. and Herzog, A.R. (1987) Interviewing older adults: the accuracy of factual information. *Journal of Gerontology,* 42(4), 387–94.

Rosenmayr, L. and Kockeis, E. (1963) Propositions for a sociological theory of ageing and the family. *International Science Journal,* 15, 410–26.

Rott, C. and Thomae, H. (1991) Bonn longitudinal study. *Journal of Cross-cultural Gerontology,* 6(1), 23–40.

Rowlings, C. (1986) Social work and older people. In Glendenning, F., *Social Work with Older People,* Beth Johnson Foundation, Keele.

Royal College of Nursing (1992) *Nurses Speak Out.* RCN, London.

Royal Institute of Public Accountancy (1986) Big business in private care, Seminar Report. *Health Services Journal,* 19, June, 817.

Ruszczynski, S. (1991) Unemployment and marriage. *Journal of Social Work Practice,* 5(1), 19–30.

Ryan, W.J. and Burk, K. (1974) Perceptual and accoustic correlates of aging. *Journal of Communication Disorders,* 7, 181–92.

Salvage, A.V., Vetter, N.J. and Jones, D.A. (1989) Opinions concerning residential care. *Age and Ageing,* 18, 380–6.

Salvage, A.V., Vetter, N.J. and Jones, D.A. (1986) Attitudes to hospital care among a community sample aged 75 and over. *Age and Ageing,* 17, 270–4.

Samuels, A. (1985a) *The Father.* Free Association Books, London.

Samuels, A. (1985b) *Jung and the Post-Jungians.* Routledge and Kegan Paul, London.

Samuels, A., Shorter, B. and Plaut, F. (1986) *A Critical Dictionary of Jungian Analysis.* Routledge and Kegan Paul, London.

Sartre, J.P. (1943) *Being and Nothingness.* Methuen, London.

Sartre, J.P. (1958) Existentialism is a humanism. In Kaufmann, W. *Existentialism from Dovstoyevsky to Sartre.* Meridian, New York.

Sartre, J.P. (1976) *The Psychology of the Imagination.* Heinemann Education, London.

Schepper, H.N. and Lovell, A.M. (1988) *Psychiatry Inside Out: Selected Writings of Franco Bassaglia.* Columbia University Press, New York.

Schlossberg, N.K. (1984) *Counselling Adults in Transition.* Springer, New York.

Schneewind, E.H. (1990) Reaction of the family to the institutionalisation of an elderly member. *Journal of Gerontological Social Work,* 15(1/2), 121–36.

Schonfield, D. (1982) Who is stereotyping whom and why. *The Gerontologist,* 22(3), 267–72.

Schroots, J. and Birren, J.E. (1990) The nature of time. *Comprehensive Gerontology,* 2, 1–30.

Schutz, A. (1945) *Collected works.* Nijhoff, The Hague.

Schutz, A. (1967) *The phenomenology of the social world.* Heinemann Education, London.

Scott, R.W. (1967) Organisational evaluation and authority. *Administrative Science Quarterly,* 12, 93–117.

Seltzer, M.M. (1990) Role reversal: you don't go home again. *Journal of Gerontological Social Work*, 15(1/2), 5–14.

Seltzer, M.M., Simmons, K. and Litchfield, L. (1984) Agency-family partnerships. *Journal of Gerontological Social Work*, 8(1/2), 57–112.

Seve, L. (1977) *Marxism and the theory of human personality*. Lawrence and Wishart, London.

Sevick, M. (1990) 'Case Management in Pittsburgh.' Unpublished PhD Dissertation, University of Pittsburgh.

Shelburne, W.A. (1988) *Mythos and Logos in the Thought of Carl Jung*. State University of New York, New York.

Shipp, T. and Hollien, H. (1969) Perception of the aging male voice. *Journal of Speech and Hearing Research*, 12, 30–6.

Silverman, A.G. and Brahce, C.I. (1979) As parents grow older: an intervention model. *Journal of Gerontological Social Work*, 2(1), 77–85.

Silverstone, B. (1987) *You and Your Aging Parent*. Jossey-Bass, San Francisco.

Sinclair, I. (1988) Elderly. In Sinclair, I., *Residential Care: the Research Reviewed*. NISW, London.

Singer, D.L., Astrachan, B.M., Gould, J. and Klein, E.B. (1979) Boundary management in psychological work with groups. In Lawrence, G., *Exploring Individual and Organisational Boundaries*. Wiley, Chichester.

Sivanandan, A. (1991) Black struggles against racism. In *Setting the Context for Change*. CCETSW, London.

Sontag, S. (1977) The double standard of aging. In Allman, L.R. and Jaffe, D.T., *Readings in Adult Psychology*. Harper and Row, New York.

Sontag, S. (1979) *On Photography*. Penguin, Middlesex.

Sprung, G.M. (1989) Transferential issues in working with older adults. *Social Casework*, 70(10), 597–602.

Stokes, J. (1991) 'Work with multidisciplinary teams'. Unpublished discussion paper, Association of Child Psychotherapists.

Stokols, D. (1975) Toward a psychological theory of alienation. *Psychological Review*, 82(1), 26–44.

Storr, A. (1983) *Jung: Selected Writings*. Fontana, London.

Tajfel, H. (1969) Cognitive aspects of prejudice. *Journal of Social Issues*, 25, 79–97.

Thompson, D. (1989) The welfare state and generational conflict. In Johnson, P., *Workers vs Pensioners*. Manchester University Press, Manchester.

Thompson, P. (1992) I don't feel old: subjective ageing and the search for meaning in later life. *Ageing and Society*, 12, 23–48.

Thompson, P., Itzin, C. and Abendstern, M. (1991) *I Don't Feel Old*. Oxford University Press, Oxford.

Tobin, S.S. (1989) The effects of institutionalisation. In Markides, K.S. and Cooper, C.L., *Aging, Stress and Health*. Wiley, New York.

Townsend, P. (1962) *The Last Refuge*. Routledge and Kegan Paul, London.

Townsend, P. (1986) *Ageism and social policy*. In Phillipson, C. and Walker, A., *Ageing and Social Policy*. Gower, Aldershot.

Trades Union Congress. (1983) *TUC Workbook on Sexism*. TUC, London.

Turner, J.C. (1991) *Social Influence*. Open University Press, Milton Keynes.

Unruh, D.R. (1983) *Invisible Lives: Social Worlds of the Aged*. Sage, Beverly Hills.

Victor, C. (1987) *Old Age in Modern Society*. Croom-Helm, London.

Victor, C. (1991) Continuity or change: inequities in health in later life. *Ageing and Society*, 11, 23–39.

Victor, C. and Evandrou, M. (1986) Does social class matter in later life? In Gregorio, S., *Social Gerontology New Directions*. Croom-Helm, London.

Vischer, A.L. (1978) On growing older. In Carver, A. and Liddiard, P., *An Ageing Population*. Hodder and Stoughton, Sevenoaks.

Waddell, M. (1989) Living in two worlds: psychodynamic theory and social work practice. *Free Associations*, 15, 11–35.

Wagner, G. (1988) *A Positive Choice*. NISW, London.

Walker, A. (1986) Pensions and the production of poverty in old age. In Phillipson, C. and Walker, A. *Ageing and Social Policy*. Gower, Aldershot.

Walsh, G. and Lehnert, F. (1967) In Schutz, A., *The Phenomenology of the Social World*. Heinemann Education, London.

Ward, R.A. (1984) *The Ageing Experience*. Harper and Row, New York.

Warner, R.E. (1989) The most negative life experiences of the elderly. *Canadian Social Work Review*, 6(2), 176–85.

Weaver, T., Willcocks, D. and Kellaher, L. (1985) *The Business of Care*. CESSA, Polytechnic of North London, London.

Weimann, J.M., Gravell, R. and Weimann, M.C. (1990) Communication with elders: implications for healthcare and social support. In Giles, H., Coupland, N. and Weimann, J., *Communication, Health and the Elderly*. Fullbright Papers 8. Manchester University Press, Manchester.

Wenger, C. (1984) *The Supportive Network: Coping with Old Age*. Allen & Unwin, London.

Wenger, C. (1990) Elderly carers: the need for appropriate intervention. *Ageing and Society*, 10, 197–220.

West, P., Illsley, R. and Kelman, K. (1984) Public preference for the care of dependency groups. *Social Science and Medicine*, 18(4), 287–95.

Wicks, M. (1982) Community care and elderly people. In Walker, A., Blackwell, B. and Robertson, M., *The Family, The State and Social Policy*. Gower, Aldershot.

Willcocks, D. (1991) Criticism Welcome. *Care Weekly*, 25 October, 10–11.

Willcocks, D., Peace, S. and Kellaher, L. (1987) *Private Lives in Public Places*. Tavistock, London.

Wilkin, D. and Hughes, B. (1987) Residential care of elderly people: the consumer's views. *Ageing and Society*, 7, 175–201.

Williams, E.I. (1988) Social decline and vulnerability in old age. *Geriatric Medicine*, 15(1), 33–5.

Williamson, J. (1978) *Decoding Advertisements*. Marion Boyars, London.

Wilson, G. (1991) Models of ageing and their relation to policy formation and service provision. *Policy and Politics*, 19(1), 37–47.

Wober, M. and Gunter, B. (1982) Television and personal threat? *British Journal of Social Psychology*, 21, 239–47.

Woodhouse, P. and Pengelly, P. (1991) *Anxiety and the Dynamics of Collaboration*. Aberdeen University Press, Aberdeen.

Woodward, K. (1988) Reminiscence, identity, sentimentality: Simone de Beauvoir and the life review. *Journal of Gerontological Social Work*, 12(3/4), 25–47.

Woodward, K. (1991) *Ageing and it's Discontents*. Bloomington, Indiana.

Wright, M. (1984) Using the past to help the present. *Community Care*, 11 October, 20–22.

Zarb, G. (1992) Creating a supportive environment. In Oliver, M., *Disabled People and Disabling Environments*. Macmillan, London.

Name index

Subject index

THE SOCIOLOGY OF OLD AGE

Graham Fennell, Chris Phillipson and Helen Evers

The sociology of old age is a vital but relatively neglected field. This book provides a clear, incisive and comprehensive introduction to the social aspects of ageing in an advanced industrial society. It is suitable for students of sociology, social administration, social policy and social work and will also be important both as an introduction for those professionals who regularly have dealings with old people (such as nurses, day centre and residential care staff, health visitors) and as a critical text for researchers and lecturers in this field of study.

Contents

Part I – Towards a sociology of old age – The history of old age – Social theory and old age – Researching old age – Part II – Men and retirement – Women and old age – Race, ethnicity and old age – Part III – Old age in special settings – Death and dying – Conclusion – Bibliography – Index.

208pp   0 335 15860 9 (Paperback)   0 335 15861 7 (Hardback)

CHANGING WORK AND RETIREMENT
SOCIAL POLICY AND THE OLDER WORKER

Frank Laczko and Chris Phillipson

The fall in the proportion of older workers in paid employment has been a major social trend over the past two decades in most industrialized countries. The trend has been especially marked among men and in Britain, for example, half the men aged 60–64 and a third aged 55–59 are no longer in paid work.

Frank Laczko and Chris Phillipson examine how this situation has developed and consider the social policy and sociological implications of the growth both of early exit from the labour force and of retirement as a social and economic institution. They analyse how the transition between work and retirement has become more complex, how the pathways include sickness and unemployment as well as early retirement, and how the transition is influenced by gender and social class. They also set out an agenda for policy change towards older workers and retirement; this takes full account of demographic changes which will mean a scarcity of youngsters entering the labour market and a greater demand for older workers.

Contents
Introduction: between work and retirement – Retirement and early exit – Ageing and discrimination in the labour market – Social policy and early exit – The social consequences of early exit – The implications of early exit for the labour market – The politics of early exit – The future of retirement – Reconstructing later life – References – Index.

160pp   0 335 09930 0 (Paperback)   0 335 09931 9 (Hardback)

HEALTH AND HEALTH CARE IN LATER LIFE
Christina R. Victor

One of the most potent images of later life is the general association between age and ill health. The stereotype of later life is that it is characterized by universal and inevitable ill health. The ageing of the population is, therefore, regarded as problematic because of the high consumption of health and social care by older people. These two issues, the health status of older people and the provision of health and social care, are addressed in this volume. The first section of the book presents an overview of physical and mental health in later life. It also addresses the health beliefs and behaviour of older people. The second section of the book describes current patterns of health and social care utilization by older people and concludes with a discussion of how these may be affected by recent policy changes in Britain.

Contents
Introduction – The demographic context – Physical health: patterns of mortality – Physical health: patterns of morbidity – Mental health in later life – Health beliefs and behaviour – Health care provision and use – Provision and use of social care – Some issues in health and social care provision – References – Index.

192pp   0 335 09283 7 (Paperback)   0 335 09284 5 (Hardback)

JOHN RYLANDS
UNIVERSITY
LIBRARY

UNDERSTANDING AGEING
IMAGES, ATTITUDES AND PROFESSIONAL PRACTICE

What are the possibilities for understanding older age? A question with profound implications for communication between generations and for professional practice. Simon Biggs explores these possibilities by integrating psychodynamic and social perspectives to provide new insights into how older age is imagined, defined and experienced.

Old age is, more often than not, hidden from the not-yet-old, by belief in a potentially negative personal future and by a commonsense world that allows little opportunity for active collaboration between age groups. This book examines the conscious and unconscious attitudes and feelings of practitioners towards their older clients and looks at the way in which these feelings affect their ability to function as professionals should. By studying self-perception, communication and power relations, and applying his conclusions to the helping professions, institutions and community care, Simon Biggs unsettles easy assumptions, offers a new framework for constructive social gerontology and gives priorities for improved practice. *Understanding Ageing* will be of interest to a broad range of students and professionals alike.

Simon Biggs, PhD, CQSW, worked as a community psychologist before going to the Central Council for Education and Training in Social Work where he heads a national programme on community care. He has a wide experience of working with service users, students and professional workers and has published in the fields of training, social policy and attitudes to old age, including *Confronting Ageing* (1989) and, with Chris Phillipson, *Understanding Elder Abuse* (1992). He is a fellow of the Centre for Social Gerontology at Keele University.

 **Open University Press**

ISBN 0-335-15724-6

9 780335 157242